THE WORKS OF SHAKESPEARE

EDITED FOR THE SYNDICS OF THE
CAMBRIDGE UNIVERSITY PRESS
BY
JOHN DOVER WILSON

TIMON OF ATHENS

EDITED BY
J. C. MAXWELL

THE LIFE OF
TIMON OF ATHENS

CAMBRIDGE

AT THE UNIVERSITY PRESS

1968

PUBLISHED BY
THE SYNDICS OF THE CAMBRIDGE UNIVERSITY PRESS

Bentley House, 200 Euston Road, London, N.W. 1
American Branch: 32 East 57th Street, New York, N.Y. 10022

©

CAMBRIDGE UNIVERSITY PRESS

1957

First published 1957
First paperback edition 1968

First printed in Great Britain at the University Press, Cambridge
Reprinted in Great Britain by Hazell Watson & Viney, Ltd.,
Aylesbury, Bucks

CONTENTS

PREFATORY NOTE

In *Pericles* Mr Maxwell tackled the insoluble problems of a thoroughly bad text. In *Timon of Athens* he was confronted with something texually better but dramatically scarcely less baffling. An unfinished Shakespearian play offers of course an almost unlimited field for speculation. Who for example was to bury Timon, and presumably rear his gravestone? And if the faithful Flavius be suggested as a not improbable candidate, that only provokes further questions. Would he not then have been given a funeral oration in soliloquy? And if so might he not have furnished us with a clue, perhaps the master clue, to the enigma of the misanthrope's character? Mr Maxwell wisely leaves such questions to the type of amateur novelist who finishes *Edwin Drood* to his own satisfaction but no one else's. Yet I think many readers of pages xxii–xlii below will agree with me that he has come nearer to fathoming Shakespeare's intentions than any previous critic and probably as near as will ever be possible.

J.D.W.

INTRODUCTION

AUTHENTICITY AND DATE

The Life of Tymon of Athens was first printed in the
1623 Folio, in the space in the Tragedies left by the
temporary withdrawal of *Troilus and Cressida*.[1] It is
at least possible that it was not originally intended to
print it at all,[2] and the rough condition of the text has
given rise to many speculations. In the eighteenth and
early nineteenth centuries, the blame was generally laid
on actors, transcribers and printers,[3] and Charles Knight
in the *Pictorial Shakespeare* (1838) seems to have been
the first to suggest the presence of a second hand other
than that of a mere garbler. His view was that our text
represents Shakespeare's partial rewriting of an earlier
play, and since his time all possible variations have been
devised on the disintegration theme. Some have agreed
with Knight; others, following Verplanck's edition of
1847, have thought that an unfinished or mutilated
play by Shakespeare was botched up by a later hand.
The two views can even be combined. Thus G. Kullmann solemnly argued that Shakespeare began to
rewrite an earlier play, that the manuscripts of both

[1] See Note on the Copy, p. 87.

[2] W. W. Greg, *The Shakespeare First Folio* (1955), p. 411;
this suggestion is also made in the edition by W. A.
Neilson and C. J. Hill (1942).

[3] Thus Steevens, on 5. 2. 8, talks of many passages which
'have been irretrievably corrupted by transcribers or
printers', and Coleridge, if J. P. Collier's report is to be
trusted, held that 'the players...had done the poet much
injustice' and that 'only a corrupt and imperfect copy had
come to the hands of the player-editors of the Folio of
1623' (Collier's 1842–4 ed., VI, 501–2; T. M. Raysor,
Coleridge's Shakespearean Criticism (1930), I, 85).

versions were somehow preserved together, and that a
'redactor', the real villain of the piece, conflated them
and added further confusions of his own.[1] Almost all
dramatists active in the first decade of the seventeenth
century have at one time or another been called in to
take a hand in the making or marring of *Timon*. In
general, the belief that Shakespeare's was at any rate
the first hand at work on the play gained ground, and
received its best formulation in 1910 in E. H. Wright's
monograph, *The Authorship of 'Timon of Athens'*,
which gave Shakespeare more of the play than had
most earlier disintegrators. But by the very thorough-
ness of his analysis, Wright demonstrated the weakness
of his theory. A second writer had been called in to
remove irregularities and inconsistencies in the play as
Shakespeare left it, but all the irregularities and inconsistencies which Wright detected arose, according to
him, precisely from the process of addition and revision.

Meanwhile another theory about the play had been
put forward from time to time. In a sense, it was the
natural successor of the older view which attributed the
whole play to Shakespeare, chastened by greater scepticism about the ravages likely to be caused by actors,
transcribers and printers. *Timon*, it was suggested, was
a Shakespearian rough draft that had never been completed. Sir Edmund Chambers[2] credits this view to
Ulrici, but he expressed himself fairly vaguely, and the
first writer[3] I have found who clearly states that the

[1] *Archiv für Litteraturgeschichte*, XI (1882).
[2] *William Shakespeare* (1930), I, 482.
[3] The view that it is an unrevised and 'imperfectly
thought-out' play is stated in the brief remarks in *Cassell's
Illustrated Shakespeare* [1864–8] by C. and M. Cowden
Clarke, who show no signs of believing in the presence of
a second hand. A. Müller, *Über die Quellen, aus denen
Shakespeare den Timon von Athen entnommen hat* (1873),

play is, in substance, faithfully printed from a draft left unfinished by Shakespeare is W. Wendlandt.[1] His long-winded but often acute essay at first attracted little attention—E. H. Wright described him as 'arguing as feebly' as the egregious Kullmann—but the tide soon began to turn. F. S. Boas in 1896 was very chary about admitting the presence of non-Shakespearian matter,[2] and K. Deighton in the Arden edition of 1905 gave more of the play to Shakespeare than any previous separatist, including (in agreement with Boas) Act 3, scene 5. Finally E. K. Chambers in the *Red Letter* edition[3] (1908) came out explicitly for Wendlandt's view, and his opinion, restated in *William Shakespeare* (1930), has been generally accepted, and has been further elaborated by U. M. Ellis-Fermor in *The Review of English Studies*, XVIII (1942). The one notable dissentient since 1930 has been T. M. Parrott, whose account of *Timon* in *Shakespearean Comedy* (1949) merely summarizes his own Shakespeare Association Paper of 1923.

The date of *Timon* is uncertain. Little help can be drawn from metrical tests with a text in such a rough state, and the student of the play is left very largely to his personal sense of the fitness of things. The most obvious affinities of *Timon* are with *King Lear*, as a

---

p. 5, regarded it as possible that the play was unfinished, but also thought that the Folio had to print from an imperfect copy.

[1] *Shakespeare Jahrbuch*, XXIII (1888).

[2] He held that though the Folio text 'cannot represent a complete, genuine Shaksperean work', yet 'all attempts to rigidly separate the genuine from the spurious parts of the work must be viewed with suspicion' (*Shakspere and his Predecessors* (1896), p. 495).

[3] The introductions to this edition (1904–8) are reprinted as *Shakespeare: a Survey* (1925).

number of scholars, most notably A. C. Bradley,[1] have
pointed out. Bradley noted that metrical tests, for what
they were worth, suggested a place 'between *King
Lear* and *Macbeth*', and added that 'this result corre-
sponds, I believe, with the general impression which
we derive from the three dramas in regard to versifica-
tion'. Sir Walter Raleigh, in my opinion more
plausibly, thought *Timon* 'a first sketch of *King Lear*,
set aside unfinished because the story proved intractable
and no full measure of sympathy could be demanded
for its hero'.[2] A radically different view of its place in
Shakespeare's career was taken by Sir Edmund Chambers, both in his introduction to the *Red Letter* edition,
and in *William Shakespeare*. For him, it comes between *Coriolanus* and the Last Plays, and he even
suggests, with a flight of fancy which is unusual in his
work, and which he admits may be judged 'sub-
jective', that Shakespeare 'dealt with it under conditions of mental and perhaps physical stress, which led
to a breakdown'.[3] Among more recent scholars, there
is perhaps a slight preponderance of opinion, with
which I am in sympathy, in favour of the earlier dating.
Dover Wilson writes that 'unless [*Timon*] be the still-
born twin of *Lear* then we may give up talking about
Shakespearian moods altogether'.[4] Alexander thinks
that the two plays 'cannot be far apart in date',[5] and in
his most recent account seems to agree with Raleigh in
particular, describing Timon as 'a tentative treatment

[1] *Shakespearean Tragedy* (1904), note S.

[2] *Shakespeare* (1907), p. 115.

[3] *William Shakespeare* (1930), 1, 483; cf. C. J. Sisson,
'The Mythical Sorrows of Shakespeare', *Proceedings of
the British Academy*, xx (1934), 49–50, with quotation from
Henry Hallam (1837).

[4] *The Essential Shakespeare* (1932), p. 131.

[5] *Shakespeare's Life and Art* (1939), p. 187.

of the theme so majestically handled in *Lear*'.[1] Willard
Farnham,[2] like Bradley, placès it between *Lear* and
Macbeth, *c.* 1605, and the most recent general study of
Shakespearian chronology, by K. Wentersdorf,[3] accepts
a date close to that of *Lear*. Chambers's chronology is
favoured by Clifford Leech, who sees *Timon* as 'con-
taining the germ of the romances',[4] and as representing
'a stage in Shakespeare's development that is logically
if not chronologically subsequent to'[5] that of *Antony
and Cleopatra* and *Coriolanus*. He suggests that here,
as in the romances, 'characters are good or bad simply
because they are constituted that way',[6] and less influenced by their environment than in the major
tragedies. Sisson also prefers a date 'during the years
of his close study of Plutarch for dramatic purposes and
near to the years of *Coriolanus* and *Antony and Cleopatra*. Alcibiades is a first sketch for Coriolanus'.[7] The
use of Plutarch is, indeed, the only thing that seems to
me to make such a late date at all plausible. It would
give a neat pattern to believe that Shakespeare got the
first idea of *Timon* while reading the life of Antony for
Antony and Cleopatra, and that a reading of the life of
Alcibiades stimulated by work on *Timon* was in its turn
responsible for taking him to the parallel life of
Coriolanus. But there is no obligation to believe that
Shakespeare read the life of Antony carefully only when
he had *Antony and Cleopatra* in immediate prospect,

---

[1] *A Shakespeare Primer* (1951), p. 115.
[2] *Shakespeare's Tragic Frontier* (1950), p. 7.
[3] *Shakespeare-Studien: Festschrift für Heinrich Mutsch-
mann* (1951), p. 180.
[4] *Shakespeare's Tragedies and Other Studies in Seventeenth Century Drama* (1950), p. 113.
[5] *Ibid.* p. 114.
[6] *Ibid.* p. 117.
[7] P. 910 of his edition [1954].

and he had certainly already consulted it for *Julius Caesar* (especially 4. 1). Topical allusions seem to be almost entirely absent, but it is only fair to mention one which may tell against the view I prefer, as favouring a date not earlier than 1606. In my note on 3. 3. 32–3, I have suggested that an allusion to the Jesuits may be intended, and this would perhaps be more apt after than before the Gunpowder Plot.

The Sources

The story of Timon was widely familiar during the Renaissance in England and elsewhere. It has been admirably sketched by Willard Farnham,[1] whose account I follow.[2] The earliest substantial account of Timon occurs in a digression in Plutarch's *Life of Antony* (ch. 70). As this is the only existing version which Shakespeare quite certainly used, I quote it in full:

Antonius followeth the life and example of Timon Misanthropus the Athenian.	Antonius, he forsook the city and company of his friends, and built him a house in the sea, by the Isle of Pharos, upon certain forced mounts which he caused to be cast into the sea, and dwelt there, as a man that banished himself from all men's company: saying that he would lead Timon's life, because he had the like wrong offered him, that was before offered unto Timon: and that for the unthankfulness of those he had done good unto, and whom he took to be his friends, he was angry with all men, and would trust no man. This Timon was a citizen of Athens,

---

[1] *Shakespeare's Tragic Frontier* (1950), pp. 50–67.
[2] In *Notes and Queries*, n.s. 1 (1954), 16, I have added a few minor details relating to William Paynter.

Plato and Aristo- phanes' testimony of Timon Misan- thropus, what he was.

that lived about the war of Peloponnesus, as appeareth by Plato[1] and Aristophanes' comedies: in the which they mocked him, calling him a viper and malicious man unto mankind, to shun all other men's companies but the company of young Alcibiades, a bold and insolent youth, whom he would greatly feast and make much of, and kissed him very gladly. Apemantus, wondering at it, asked him the cause what he meant to make so much of that young man alone, and to hate all others: Timon answered him, 'I do it', said he, 'because I know that one day he shall do great mischief unto the Athenians'. This Timon sometimes would have Apemantus in his company, because he was much like of his nature and conditions, and also followed him in manner of life. On a time when they solemnly celebrated the feasts called Choae at Athens (to wit, the feasts of the dead, where they make sprink- lings and sacrifices for the dead), and that they two then feasted together by themselves, Apemantus said unto the other: 'Oh, here is a trim banquet, Timon'. Timon answered again, 'Yea,' said he, 'so thou wert not here'. It is reported of him also, that this Timon on a time (the people being as- sembled in the market-place about dispatch of some affairs) got up into the pulpit for orations, where the orators commonly use to speak unto the people: and silence being made, every man listening to hear what he would say, because it was a wonder to see him in that place: at length he began to speak in this manner. 'My Lords of Athens, I have a little yard in my house where there groweth a fig tree, on the which many citizens have

[1] The comic dramatist, not the philosopher.

hanged themselves: and, because I mean to make some building on the place, I thought good to let you all understand it, that, before the fig tree be cut down, if any of you be desperate, you may there in time go hang yourselves.' He died in the city of Hales, and was buried upon the seaside. Now it chanced so, that, the sea getting in, it compassed his tomb round about, that no man could come to it: and upon the same was written this epitaph:

The epitaph of Timon Misanthropus

> Here lies a wretched corse, of wretched soul
> bereft,
> Seek not my name: a plague consume
> you wicked wretches left.

It is reported that Timon himself when he lived made this epitaph: for that which is commonly rehearsed was not his, but made by the poet Callimachus:

> Here lie I, Timon, who alive all living men
> did hate,
> Pass by, and curse thy fill: but pass, and
> stay not here thy gate.

Many other things could we tell you of this Timon, but this little shall suffice at this present.[1]

It will be seen that this version, though it refers in passing to the 'unthankfulness...of those whom he took to be his friends', contains no suggestion that he had fallen from great wealth; and far from living in the wilderness, he practises his misanthropy in Athens itself. Plutarch's other reference, in the *Life of Alcibiades*, adds nothing of moment. It is Lucian's dia-

---

[1] *Plutarch's Lives of Coriolanus, Caesar, Brutus, and Antonius in North's Translation*, ed. R. H. Carr (1906), pp. 229-31 (a modern-spelling reprint of the 1595 edition, which I have corrected from the original).

logue, *Timon, or the Misanthrope*, that introduces us to Timon as a prodigal reduced to poverty by flatterers who now neglect him, but who flock back to him when he digs up a treasure of gold. He drives them off, and announces his intention of continuing to live a solitary life in a tower built upon the place where he has found the treasure. Farnham notes the references to Timon's false friends as beasts and birds of prey—a theme prominent in Shakespeare's play.

The earliest Renaissance treatment is Matteo Boiardo's play *Timone* (*c.* 1487), which is based on Lucian. The picture of the solitary life Timon proposes to lead on the mountains or in the forest carries us nearer to Shakespeare's version. The next important account is that of Pedro Mexía in *La Silva de varia lección* (1540). Mexía's Timon lives alone in the neighbourhood of Athens, and never visits the city unless he has to. The cutting-off of his tomb by the sea, an accident in Plutarch, now becomes something deliberately planned by Timon himself. Mexía's version came to England, through the French translation by Gruget (1552), in William Paynter's *Palace of Pleasure* (1566), Novel 28, with the heading 'Of the strange & beastlie nature of Timon of Athenes enemie to mankinde, with his death, buriall, and Epitaphe'. The other French and English versions, stemming ultimately from Mexía, need not detain us. It is enough to note with Farnham the constant emphasis on the beast-like nature of Timon. None of these versions introduce the Lucianic theme of Timon's lost wealth, and discovery of gold. This, however, is again the basis of the anonymous academic play of *Timon*, which must be discussed in connection with the question of Shakespeare's immediate sources.

It is clear from this brief sketch that, besides having read the account in Plutarch's *Life of Antony*, from which the two epitaphs are taken with the alteration of only one word, Shakespeare had a general familiarity with the Lucianic version, on which, indeed, his plot is based. No English translation of the dialogue is known to have existed in the early seventeenth century, but it was accessible in Latin, French and Italian, and there was nothing to prevent Shakespeare from consulting some more learned friend if he found it necessary. Close parallels to Lucian's text are few, and none of those noted, for instance, by Deighton in his Arden introduction is verbally striking. But the mention in chapter 47 of the toady Philiades who received two talents as dowry for his daughter as a reward for praising Timon, and in chapter 49 of Demeas who was freed from a debtor's prison, make it, on the whole, rather more likely that Shakespeare read Lucian for himself than that he merely knew of his version at second hand.

The secondary authorities can be divided into the Plutarchan (by way of Mexía) and the Lucianic. Of the former, Shakespeare had probably read Paynter's version in the *Palace of Pleasure*, which he had used for *All's Well* and probably for *Romeo and Juliet*: see the note on 5. 1. 214–18 for a fairly close verbal parallel. The Lucianic derivatives are more of a problem. Richard Garnett's *obiter dictum*[1] that Shakespeare had read Boiardo has been defended by R. Warwick Bond,[2] but the evidence is not strong. Some of Shakespeare's references to life in the wilderness and to man's defencelessness have fairly close parallels in Boiardo, who also has the ideas '(1) that beasts have more feeling for their kind than man for his, (2) the wish that earth would pervert her nature to man's destruction'.[3] But the resemblances are by no means

[1] *Italian Literature* (1898), p. 230.
[2] *Modern Language Review*, XXVI (1931), 52–68.
[3] *Ibid.* p. 63.

beyond the range of coincidence—the first is a commonplace and the second is found in Shakespeare as
early as *Richard II*, 3. 2. 12 ff.—and Bond's claims for
an influence exercised by Boiardo on the plot of *Timon*
are much less plausible. An additional reason for
scepticism is that no edition of Boiardo's play later than
1518 is recorded, and none at all published outside
Italy.

The most puzzling relationship is that between
Shakespeare's play and the anonymous *Timon* preserved
in manuscript in the Victoria and Albert Museum
(Dyce MS. 52) and first published by Alexander Dyce
for the Shakespeare Society in 1842. Like Shakespeare's play, this shows Timon both in his prosperity
and after his fall, the ending keeping very close to
Lucian. There are minor resemblances between the
plays; in both, Timon immediately decides to bury
again the newly discovered gold, which he does not do
in Lucian. But the two most notable links are the
banquet to the false friends, at which, in the anonymous
play, Timon pelts his guests with stones painted as
artichokes, and the presence of a faithful steward,
Laches, who is insulted and dismissed by Timon (1. 5),
but returns to serve him in disguise (2. 2), and remains
with him after his ruin. This is beyond coincidence;
one play must be indebted to the other, or both to a
common source. It is unlikely that Shakespeare's play
was accessible before it was printed in the Folio, so that
the choice lies between the other two alternatives. The
date of the anonymous play is uncertain. G. C. Moore
Smith,[1] pointing out a borrowing from the Cambridge
Latin drama *Pedantius* (*c.* 1581)—a play on words
that might in fact have an earlier source—suggested
that it also was of Cambridge origin, and dated it

---

[1] *Modern Language Review*, III (1907–8), 143.

1581–90. J. Q. Adams[1] linked it with such school plays as *Roister Doister*, and, also favouring an early date, thought that it was written for presentation in London rather than in a university town. Certainly a passage such as he quotes from 2. 4 has, as he says, 'the ring of the metropolis'; and the final lines of the epilogue, 'Let louing hands, loude sounding in the ayre, | Cause Timon to the citty to repaire', are apter for London, as a parallel to Athens, than for Cambridge. Dyce had suggested a later date, *c*. 1600, and Malone[2] had written that the play 'appears to have been written after Ben Jonson's *Every Man out of his Humour* (1599), to which it contains a reference'. The relation of the play to this and other plays of Jonson has recently been discussed in the Herford and Simpson edition of Jonson,[3] but the passages cited do not clearly prove indebtedness either way. The faithful steward Laches, returning to serve his master in disguise, reminds us also, as Steevens noted, of Kent in *King Lear*. Kent derives substantially from the Perillus of the old *Leir*, but, unlike Perillus and like Kent, Laches has actually been driven away by his master. This gives some colour to the hypothesis that Shakespeare had already read the anonymous *Timon* when he wrote *King Lear*.

The chief objection to supposing that Shakespeare knew the anonymous play is that it is clearly an academic work and was not available in print. Adams tentatively suggested that it is 'not impossible that the play—reworked perhaps—was presented to a London audience'.[4] The other hypothesis about the relationship, that of a common source, has recently been pre-

---

[1] *Journal of English and Germanic Philology*, IX (1910), 511–12.

[2] 1821 Variorum, II, 455.   [3] IX, 482–5.

[4] *Journal of English and Germanic Philology*, IX (1910), 522.

sented, with some new arguments, by G. A. Bonnard,[1] who even goes so far as to suggest that this source was also accessible to Shadwell, the love-intrigue in whose adaptation Bonnard regards as the 'exact replica' of that in the anonymous play. Apart from the fact that Shadwell's Melissa fawns on Timon in his prosperity, abandons him at his fall, and returns to him when she hears he has found gold—all inevitable results of introducing a false and mercenary mistress in the first instance—I can see no resemblance. The claim that the anonymous author echoes other Shakespeare plays is less far-fetched, but not irresistible. His is the only version of the story in which Timon's ruin is immediately precipitated by the loss of ships at sea (3. 5), although his steward has, as in Shakespeare, prophesied disaster from sheer prodigality (3. 2). But this is scarcely sufficient ground for attributing the wreck to the influence of *The Merchant of Venice*. Nor is the scene (5. 3) where Timon offers to accompany Gelasimus to a cliff on the sea-shore and help him 'at a push' necessarily indebted to *King Lear*. It is very much a matter of personal impression, but the pedantic author of the anonymous *Timon*, his Lucian open before him and tags of Plautus in his head, does not strike me as very likely to conflate these sources with reminiscences of the popular drama. With some reluctance, I am inclined to suppose, then, that Shakespeare somehow came across the anonymous play. If it was a London school play, as Adams thinks, he could have been dragged to see it by some fond father of his acquaintance.

Plutarch, Lucian and the anonymous *Timon* seem, then, to be the only sources of any moment. The figure of Apemantus (roughly corresponding to Lucian's Thrasicles as well as to the more shadowy Apemantus

[1] *Études Anglaises*, VII (1954), 63–9.

of Plutarch) owes something to the traditional accounts
of Diogenes the cynic, many of which were accessible
to Shakespeare,[1] notably Lyly's *Campaspe*.[2] Two sug-
gestions made by Kittredge in his edition (1936) seem
to me to have little substance: that the behaviour of
Apemantus in 1. 1 and 1. 2 owes something to the
cynic Alcidamas as described in Lucian's *Symposium*,
§ 12, and that the crime of the unknown soldier in
3. 5 recalls the murder of Phrynichus, which is mentioned briefly in Plutarch's *Life of Alcibiades*,
chapter 25.

THE PLAY[3]

Timon has not been a popular play on the stage,
though, as the Stage History shows, adaptations by
Shadwell and others, not more drastic than those to
which some of the major plays were subjected, were
performed oftener than might have been expected. The
play certainly lacks many of the qualities which make
for theatrical success, and it is natural that it should
have had more interest for readers than for theatre-
goers.

Some of the judgments it has evoked are remarkably
enthusiastic. Even apart from the opinion of G. Wilson
Knight that it 'includes and transcends' *Hamlet*, *Troilus
and Cressida*, *Othello* and *King Lear*,[4] we have Hazlitt's
statement that it 'always appeared to us to be written
with as intense a feeling of his subject as any one play

---

[1] P. Reyher, *Essai sur les Idées dans l'Oeuvre de Shakespeare* (1947), pp. 566–7, cites two typical references from
Nashe, *Works*, ed. R. B. McKerrow, II, 109, 237.

[2] G. Gervinus, *Shakespeare* (3rd German ed. 1862), II,
388, mentioned this, and also Lucian's *Vitarum Auctio*.

[3] Part of this section was first published in *Scrutiny*, XV
(1947–8), 195–208.

[4] *The Wheel of Fire*, 4th ed. (1949), p. 236.

of Shakespear. It is one of the few in which he seems
to be in earnest throughout, never to trifle nor go out
of his way',[1] and George Saintsbury's characterization
of it as 'that in some ways most Shakespearian of all the
plays *not* greatest'.[2] But none, except Wilson Knight
(and possibly A. S. Collins), have been entirely satisfied
by it. His challenging account cannot be ignored, but
I find it difficult to bring into relation with the play
itself. He has had the advantage, since his essay was
first published, of producing *Timon* and acting in the
title-role, and he writes that these and other experiences
have increased his respect for it.[3] The essay, however,
is an example of the difficulties of 'interpretation',
conceived by Wilson Knight as a process distinct from,
and in various ways opposed to, 'criticism'.[4] Much of
it strikes me as an account rather of a play that Shakespeare might have written on this theme than of *Timon*
as we have it, and the particular qualities of the play
tend to disappear behind vast cosmic rhythms depicted
as running through Shakespeare's work as a whole.
This unwillingness to grant artistic autonomy to the
individual work comes out perhaps most clearly in the
claim that 'in *Timon of Athens* we have a logical ex-
position of the significance of earlier plays'.[5] Those
who do not see the working of Shakespeare's imagination in such terms are likely to remain unconvinced.
Again, the relative absence of the concrete and specific
is too readily treated as evidence of 'universal tragic

[1] *Characters of Shakespear's Plays*, in *Works*, ed. P. P.
Howe (1930–34), IV, 210.
[2] 'Shakespeare and the Grand Style', *Essays and
Studies*, I (1910), 129. Saintsbury is less enthusiastic in
Cambridge History of English Literature, V (1910), 196.
[3] *The Wheel of Fire*, 4th ed. p. 239.
[4] *Ibid.* ch. 1.
[5] *Ibid.* p. 223.

significance',[1] or 'universal philosophical meaning',[2] while in a later discussion, *Timon* 'is found to express the central essence of tragic drama'.[3] Wilson Knight certainly records with powerful eloquence an intense imaginative response to the play, and I have begun by referring to his essay because I regret not having been able to incorporate as much from him into my own reading of it as I have into my reading of, for example, *Lear* and *Othello*.

The most obvious structural peculiarity of the play is its division into two sharply contrasting halves. It could not exist at all except in terms of these two pictures of Timon before and after his fall, and it is a superficial criticism—or else a deliberate rejection of all that Shakespeare is trying to do—to talk of it as 'two plays, casually joined at the middle'.[4] But to recognize what Shakespeare has aimed at is not necessarily to find the result satisfactory, and the working-out of the main theme must be examined. The rather simple, schematic nature of the outline means that we are more than usually dependent on achieving the appropriate response to the central figure. Because he is in most ways so much less individualized than Hamlet or Lear or Othello, such a response is, more than in the other plays, a matter of grasping the moral category to which he belongs, and seeing him as an example of that category. This does not involve turning the play into a moral treatise, but it does involve an attention to the abstract and general of a kind that Shakespearian tragedy does not usually demand from us, or that is, at least, usually no more than a subordinate element in our response to something richly unique.

[1] *Ibid.* p. 207.   [2] *Ibid.* p. 220.
[3] *Principles of Shakespearian Production*, Pelican ed. (1949), p. 177.
[4] Mark Van Doren, *Shakespeare* (1939), p. 288.

Whatever other judgments may be made on Timon, he is certainly the prodigal. Even his true friends and admirers confess it; he himself glories in it after his fall (4. 3. 278–80). Much of the disagreement about the play and the hero has been on the question of just what prodigality involves. It is clear that no simple moral or prudential condemnation is conveyed. Though Shakespeare has not gone as far as he sometimes does in presenting us with firmly placed subordinate characters from whom we can take our bearings with regard to the hero,[1] he makes up for this by at least one undiluted piece of choric comment, the dialogue between the 'three strangers' at the end of 3. 2. Timon's 'right noble mind, illustrious virtue and honourable carriage' elicit disinterested admiration, and the ingratitude with which he is treated appears as monstrous. This in itself is enough to refute the view, developed in its most extreme form by O. J. Campbell,[2] that Timon is set before us merely for derision, and that the play is Shakespeare's attempt at a 'tragical satire' in the manner of Jonson's *Sejanus*. It is true that the sycophants and false friends also call Timon noble; but that is perhaps one reason why Shakespeare goes out of his way to give us also the impartial judgment of the strangers. We are surely meant to assent when Timon exclaims, 'Unwisely, not ignobly, have I given' (2. 2. 180). Campbell's interpretation of the play depends on strictly selective reading. It is perhaps only natural that, approaching it with such prepossessions, he should assume without argument that Timon commits suicide,

[1] Cf. U. M. Ellis-Fermor: 'Unlike *Hamlet*, unlike *Lear*, the play of *Timon* does not endow its minor characters with the function of focusing, by their nature and actions, our thought and attention on its central figure' (*Review of English Studies*, XVIII (1942), 282).
[2] *Shakespeare's Satire* (1943).

a view for which there is no good warrant in the text.[1]
But even so, it argues a curiously blinkered response to
poetry to write, 'even his choice of a grave is food for
scorn',[2] and immediately go on to quote the reference to

> his everlasting mansion
> Upon the beachéd verge of the salt flood,
> Who once a day with his embosséd froth
> The turbulent surge shall cover.　(5. 1. 214–17)

One may distrust such biographical conjectures as that
'in Timon's tomb Shakespeare buried his own bitter-
ness',[3] but it is clear that something that never happens
to Sejanus has happened to the Timon who speaks these
words, and who a few lines earlier has said

> My long sickness
> Of health and living now begins to mend,
> And nothing brings me all things.　(5. 1. 185–7)

What this makes us think of is nothing in Jonson, but
rather the Cleopatra whose

> desolation does begin to make
> A better life.

Such passages are perhaps fragmentary, and Shakespeare
may not have developed them organically out of his
theme—perhaps the recognition that he had failed to

---

[1] A number of critics, the earliest I have come across
being Gervinus, have thought that Timon committed
suicide, while some have thought that Shakespeare leaves
the question open. But no earlier version makes him die
in this way, and the onus of proof is on those who think
that Shakespeare made the innovation. It must be admitted that the text as we have it leaves some details
uncertain—notably, who buried Timon.

[2] *Shakespeare's Satire*, p. 192.

[3] Mark Van Doren, *Shakespeare* (1939), p. 292 (tentatively).

do so led him to leave the play unfinished—but they are there, and they disrupt Campbell's neat scheme.

Shakespeare's treatment of the 'prodigal', then, is not that of the pure Jonsonian satirist. Yet Timon, if he has not given 'ignobly', certainly has given 'unwisely', and it has often been thought that this unwisdom robs him of more of the audience's sympathy than a tragic hero can afford to lose. For Ellis-Fermor, one of the unsolved questions that make the play unsatisfactory is, 'if he is of mature age, why is he such a fool?',[1] and Farnham comments that 'he is so completely lacking in wisdom that one wonders how he could ever have been useful to Athens in a responsible position'.[2] Such comments may point to weaknesses in the play, but Shakespeare does not encourage us to identify ourselves with the cold prudential verdict. The comment by the 'three strangers' has already been cited, and cold calculation in the world of the play is represented by the 'usuring senate'. As Alexander writes, 'the criticism that finds in his untimely death a judgment on his "kindly self-indulgence" or "easy generosity" is exactly in the senatorial vein'.[3] Yet just as it is true that Lear 'hath ever but slenderly known himself', however repellent it is to hear such a piece of cold analysis from the daughter who has just been

[1] *Review of English Studies*, XVIII (1942), 281.
[2] *Shakespeare's Tragic Frontier* (1950), pp. 46–7. An interesting recent discussion of the differences between Shakespeare's sympathetic heroes and the unsympathetic ones (including Timon) is Huntington Brown's 'Enter the Shakespearean Tragic Hero', *Essays in Criticism*, III (1953), 285–302. In *Unity in Shakespearian Tragedy* (1956), Brents Stirling briefly refers to *Timon* as one of the plays which present 'the problem...of a deliberately minimized hero' (p. 188).
[3] *Shakespeare's Life and Art* (1939), p. 184.

loading him with adulation, so Shakespeare has provided some (if not all) of the material for a balanced
and complex response to Timon. To achieve this, we
must do justice to the form of the play. So I revert to
some questions raised in passing at an earlier stage.

The abstract and schematic nature of the play has
evoked comment of two contrasting kinds. Neither is
entirely satisfactory by itself, but taken together they
help to define its special quality. On the one side it has
been suggested by A. S. Collins that *Timon* is Shakespeare's 'true morality play in the straight sense';[1] the
minor characters scarcely even pretend to be individuals;
'Apemantus is a fairly simple "humour" of Railing
Envy, Timon is Ideal Bounty and Friendship, Alcibiades alone is a man, a soldier, practical, sensual, yet
a true friend, but still barely individualized'.[2] There
is truth in this, but it scarcely answers all the questions
the play raises for us. When, for instance, Mark Van
Doren in a similar vein writes, 'Timon is not so much
a man as a figure representing Munificence, an ab-
straction in whom madness may not matter',[3] we are
entitled to ask why it should not matter. If the Morality
convention were as one-sided as this, it would be
incapable of presenting real moral situations. Even a
relatively crude work like Skelton's *Magnificence* does
not absolve its central figure from criticism simply by
giving him a name that is predominantly laudatory.
There is, in fact, no need for such subterfuges in order
to make sense of *Timon*. Timon is, if you like, a sim-
plified, schematized figure; but Shakespeare makes it
quite clear that his madness does 'matter', that his

[1] *Review of English Studies*, XXII (1946), 98. This essay,
though I think it has some faults of emphasis, is a fine
piece of criticism.
[2] *Ibid.* p. 99.
[3] *Shakespeare* (1939), pp. 289–90.

prodigality is to be judged by ordinary moral standards.
Equally unacceptable is Collins's account in which 'the
abstract Virtue' of Bounty is transformed 'to a similarly
abstract Vice'.[1] Collins does not really, as the better
parts of his valuable essay show, read the play as any
such unearthly ballet of bloodless categories, but he is
betrayed into talking like this by taking as the moral of
the early acts that 'such Ideal Bounty should have
infinity of riches to draw on, for it is Noble Bounty'.[2]
That, complete to the capital letters, is no doubt how
Timon sees himself in the distorting mirror provided
by his flatterers, but it is not how the audience sees
him, and it does not make sense of the play. The two
halves of it are contrasting studies in excess, and both
excesses quite intelligibly belong to the same character.
This element of the play is summed up in Timon's
reply to Apemantus's statement that he is proud 'that
I was no prodigal'—'I, that I am one now' (4. 3.
279–80). It is the same nature that, according to circumstances and the twist they have given it, can turn
to love or hate, but to each with prodigality, and the
gold that embodies the corrupted and corrupting spirit
of Athens affords an equally fit instrument for the
expression of each.

It is this corrupting spirit that is stressed in the rival
accounts, which insist on the contemporary social
relevance of the play. J. W. Draper, discussing 'The
Theme of "Timon of Athens"', claims that theme to
be usury: we are shown in the hero 'a sort of liberal
young Bassanio, who, without the moneyed backing of
Antonio and Portia, experienced to his sorrow the hard
economic facts of the Jacobean age'.[3] In this form, the
claim cannot be accepted. Timon is too much of a
special case, and the relation of usury to the society that

[1] *Op. cit.* p. 104.   [2] *Ibid.* p. 99.
[3] *Modern Language Review,* XXIX (1934), 31.

tolerates it is no longer treated in the light-heartedly
'black *versus* white' spirit that in the main characterizes
The Merchant of Venice. The social approach to the
play is more judiciously represented by E. C. Pettet,
who sees the difference between it and *The Merchant
of Venice*. But his description of *Timon* as 'a straightforward tract for the times'[1] also over-simplifies. Perhaps one of the things that ultimately dissatisfy us about
Timon is that neither the Morality pattern nor the
stylized, but basically realistic, presentation of the
erosion of old-fashioned 'feudal' values in a commercial
society is whole-heartedly worked out. But that Shakespeare means to show us an Athens corroded by com-
mercialism is clear enough.[2]

How does Shakespeare set about presenting us with
a play that shall combine some of the qualities of a
moral apologue with an adequate degree of realism?
The opening scene is effective from this point of view
in that it plunges us into the bright but unstable world
of Timon's bounty, and at the same time isolates the
'morality' aspect of the situation in the poet's account
of his 'rough work' (I. I. 46 ff.). Already we are being
brought to realize how precarious Timon's prosperity
is. It is customary to contrast Timon in his prosperity
with Timon after his fall, and I do not think sufficient
stress has been laid on the fact that when the play opens
he is already ruined.[3] It is true that we do not know
this for certain at the very start, but there is an ominous
atmosphere about even the first scene that makes it only
the fulfilment of what we have expected when Timon's

---

[1] *Review of English Studies*, XXIII (1947), 321.

[2] The fullest survey from this point of view is that of
J. E. Phillips, *The State in Shakespeare's Greek and Roman
Plays* (1940).

[3] It is partly recognized by W. Farnham, *Shakespeare's
Tragic Frontier* (1950), p. 43.

ruin is first announced by Flavius in 1. 2. We have had
the well-worn apologue of the hill of Fortune, and the
hope, after a vivid description of Timon's prodigality,
'Long may he live in fortunes!' (1. 1. 285). No
audience could doubt what that foreshadowed. The
insubstantiality of the glittering pageant is suggested in
the opening lines, 'Magic of bounty, all these spirits
thy power | Hath conjured to attend' (1. 1. 6–7). The
picture of Fortune which the Poet presents is almost
like a challenge on Shakespeare's part—he announces
that he is going to deal with one of the most familiar of
commonplaces, and prompts our interest in the question
how he is going to give an individual turn to it; as the
painter says:

> 'Tis common:
> A thousand moral paintings I can show,
> That shall demonstrate these quick blows of Fortune's
> More pregnantly than words.   (1. 1. 92–5)

This crucial opening scene holds the balance deli-
cately between the two extremes to be avoided in our
attitude towards Timon. It is the one scene in which
there is clear indication of genuine personal feeling in
his generosity, and it is shown in contrast with a typical
representative of the spirit of Athens, the 'old Athenian'.
Timon as shown here is not adequately described by
the more rigorous critics, such as Warwick Bond, 'the
great spendthrift, avoiding all that is unpleasant,
allowing himself to expand in a foolish glow of lazy
benevolence, and prompted as much by love of admiration and flattery as by a real charity',[1] and O. J.
Campbell, 'The similarity of his response to each one
of these adulators in turn makes his generosity seem
automatic and therefore ridiculous'.[2] This episode is

---

[1] *Modern Language Review*, XXVI (1931), 53.
[2] *Shakespeare's Satire* (1943), p. 187.

an exception to that 'similarity', but at the same time it does show the subtle corruption exercised by the materialistic spirit of Athens. Timon cannot really overcome it; he can only outbid it in its own currency of gold—and it is a further irony that he cannot, by now, even do that: the audience is already conscious that his 'to build his fortune I will strain a little' is a grim understatement of his financial embarrassments. This theme of the impossibility of genuinely defeating the ethos of Athens is perhaps most clearly expressed in a passage of detached comment at the end of the scene, where one of the Lords remarks, 'no gift to him | But breeds the giver a return exceeding | All use of quittance' (1. 1. 281–3). We are soon to learn that Timon has been having recourse to usurers in the literal sense, but the implications of these lines are more profound: by his habit of lavish recompense, Timon is turning even those who ostensibly give him free gifts into usurers, more successful usurers than the real ones: the word "breeds" recalls the traditional doctrine about 'barren metal'.[1] In this sense of the guilt shared both by lender and borrower, and infecting all trans-actions in a usurious society, lies the advance in com-plexity in Shakespeare's treatment of usury since *The Merchant of Venice*.

This first scene has foreshadowed the approaching fall, and has shown us in some measure how even the more genuinely fine sides of Timon's nature are cor-rupted by the spirit of his society, but on the whole we have so far seen him at his best. In the second scene the conceptions of 'bounty' and 'goodness' begin to receive penetrating criticism. Already in 1. 1, the

---

[1] Cf. 2. 1. 7–10, where the unnaturalness of this 'breeding' is stressed by the grotesque picture of the horse that foals twenty when given to Timon.

merchant's obviously interested reference to Timon's 'untirable and continuate goodness' has caught our attention. Perhaps we are already meant to have a sense of its being too much 'on tap'—'automatic' in Campbell's phrase already quoted—and when Lucilius says

> never may
> That state or fortune fall into my keeping
> Which is not owed to you!   (1. 1. 152–4)

it is clear that Timon is in danger of complacently accepting superhuman honours. In 1. 2, Timon in the opening exchange with Ventidius brushes aside all idea of return of favours, but he later (ll. 88–107) expresses his ideal of friendship—'so many like brothers commanding one another's fortunes!'. By doing so, he makes us realize how his whole mode of life has cut him off from the possibility of really entering into the relationship of reciprocity which he here describes so feelingly, if with a touch of sentimentality.

It will be best at this point to interrupt the chronological order and to trace this theme through the subsequent acts. For some time the spotlight is upon the baseness of Timon's beneficiaries rather than on his own feelings, and this part of the play culminates in the choric comment of the Stranger in 3. 2. 77–88. It makes an appearance in Flavius's speech in 2. 2, where there is the usual reference to bounty (l. 170), and the flatterers are quoted as saying, 'Great Timon, noble, worthy, royal Timon'. We accept the claim, 'Unwisely, not ignobly, have I given' (l. 180), but the whole context forbids us to forget that wisdom, prudence, is a considerable part of human virtue in its widest sense, and it is at his own risk that a private citizen displays 'royal' qualities.

The critical attitude towards this sort of 'goodness'

is firmly established by the time we come, after the fall,
to Flavius's paradoxical summing-up of Timon's fate:

> Undone by goodness:[1] strange, unusual blood,
> When man's worst sin is, he does too much good.
> Who then dares to be half so kind again?
> For bounty, that makes gods, does still mar men.
>
> (4. 2. 38–41)

Shakespeare is here using his gnomic technique with a
good deal of subtlety. We are meant to accept what
Flavius says, but not to regard him as having adequate
insight into Timon's nature, and the special connota-
tions that the play has given to 'goodness' and 'bounty'
enable us to achieve both these ends at once. For
Flavius, his old master is in a straightforward sense 'too
good for this world', but the audience is meant to take
his comments, which for the speaker are really a con-
fession of inability to understand the ways of the
universe, as literal truth. The audience can see, if
Flavius—his heart stronger than his head—cannot, that
an attempt on the part of man to ape divine bounty,
ever spontaneously giving without receiving anything
in return, is presumptuous and must inevitably be
frustrated. Timon cannot grasp the notion of the
necessary reciprocity of creation. This is the point of
the curious lines, 4. 3. 438–44. Since for Timon giving
must be only giving, receiving only receiving, even if
he has in his adversity expected a reversal of the roles,
the normal processes of give-and-take in nature[2] appear
as thievery, on the analogy of the corrupted society of

[1] Ruth L. Anderson in her article, 'Excessive Goodness
a Tragic Flaw' (*Shakespeare Association Bulletin*, XIX (1944),
85–96), traces the theme through the plays to its culmina-
tion in *Timon*, but without any very penetrating insight
into the specific way in which it occurs in each play.

[2] Recognized in 4. 3. 68–9, 'But then renew I could not
like the moon; | There were no suns to borrow of'.

Athens, which has also lost the notion of reciprocity;
which has, indeed, destroyed it in Timon's mind.
Flavius's own goodness, in contrast, is the genuine,
human thing: his determination to seek out Timon and
serve him is immediately and ironically followed by
Timon's soliloquy, 'O blessed breeding sun'. And
human, *costing* generosity has already been presented
in 3. 5, a scene introducing a motif which I suspect
Shakespeare would have exploited more fully if he had
completed the play. Alcibiades, who pleads for his
friend's life, and has kept back the state's foes, is 'rich
only in large hurts' (l. 111), and it is he who most
explicitly denounces the 'usuring senate' (l. 112).

Like 'bounty' and 'goodness', 'free' is a word which
meets with keen criticism in the course of the play. The
words are linked directly in Flavius's gnomic lines
which close Act 2:

> I would I could not think it.
> That thought is bounty's foe;
> Being free itself, it thinks all others so.
>
> (2. 2. 238–40)

And 'free' occurs with a subtle gradation of senses in
various passages. The very first time it occurs is at
1. 1. 48, where there is something ominous about the
'free drift' that 'moves itself | In a wide sea of wax'.
The next two occurrences have a sense of paradox
about them: the 'slaves and servants' of the Poet's
representation of Timon 'through him | Drink the
free air' (ll. 85–6); and the implication that Timon's
'freeness' is oppressive to its recipients is even more
directly expressed when to his 'I'll pay the debt and
free him', the messenger rejoins 'your lordship ever
binds him' (ll. 106–7). It adds to the irony that Ventidius does not in fact consider himself bound when
Timon really needs him, but Timon's bounty is of the
kind that offers a temptation to throw off the rather

stifling burden it imposes. We are ready by this time
to let any passing allusions have their effect. Ventidius
makes an attempt to restore Timon's gift to his 'free
heart' (1. 2. 6), but it is refused—Timon 'gave it
freely ever', and it turns out that this time Ventidius
takes him at his word for good. Another, more hum-
drum sense of the word is introduced when Apemantus
prays never to trust 'a keeper with my freedom' (l. 67).
The 'five best senses...come freely | To gratulate thy
plenteous bosom' (ll. 124–6); and an interested donor
claims to be making his gift 'out of his free love'
(l. 186). The theme naturally becomes less prominent
as the play advances. Lucullus, in his greedy expectation of further gifts, refers to 'that honourable, complete, free-hearted gentleman of Athens, thy very
bountiful good lord and master' (3. 1. 9–11), com-
bining all the words I have been discussing; and in the
last reference before his ruin, Timon ironically com-
bines the play's primary sense for the word, 'generous',
with the more prosaic, Apemantean sense of mere
freedom from restraint:

> Have I been ever free, and must my house
> Be my retentive enemy, my gaol?   (3. 4. 81–2)

In the last two acts we have one concentrated use,
where Timon looks back on the past, and talks of

> The sweet degrees that this brief world affords
> To such as may the passive drugs of it
> Freely command.   (4. 3. 254–6)

Whether 'drugs' or 'drudges', or a pun on both, is
intended,[1] the notion is conveyed that Timon's
liberality has been something that involves subservience
on the part of its instruments, human or material.
Act 4, like Act 2, ends with a gnomic couplet in which

[1] See note.

the word 'free' occurs, though in a less pregnant sense, 'fly, whilst thou art blest and free', and Act 5 has only one unremarkable instance of the word (5. 1. 44). Although the dangers of reading profound significance into recurrent words is obvious, I think that 'free' does run through this play in such a way as to constitute a comment on what Timon's situation and behaviour involve in terms of human relationships.

The other topics I should like to discuss are the relation between Timon and Lear, and the parts played by Alcibiades and Apemantus.

Timon's invective has often been compared with that of Lear. Biographically-minded critics have even suggested that the emotion which Shakespeare has just been able to keep in check and express in the form of art in *Lear* has got the better of him in *Timon*, but I think that both the similarity and the differences can readily be explained on artistic grounds. Timon like Lear 'hath ever but slenderly known himself'. He will not listen to the truth—'he will not hear till feel', says Flavius (2. 2. 7)—and when Flavius tries to enlighten him he retorts, 'Come, sermon me no further' (2. 2. 178). The difference between him and Lear after their falls is that Lear learns by his misfortune as Timon does not. That does not mean that there is no substance in his tirades—much of them consists of the stock-in-trade of the traditional moral satirist—but there is no hint of insight or wisdom behind them. One might express the difference between Lear and Timon by saying that Lear in affliction comes to *see* as he never did before; Timon does not undergo the ultimate ordeal of madness, and the utmost he attains to is to *see through* particular shams and injustices. Unlike Lear, who finally welcomes and values love, he grudges it when the disinterested affection of Flavius forces him to modify his wholesale condemnation of mankind (4. 3.

498–504). When, a few lines earlier, he has said, 'I never had honest man about me, I; all | I kept were knaves, to serve in meat to villains' (ll. 480–1), he has not merely exaggerated, he has been utterly wrong, since at the risk of undue simplification Shakespeare has insisted that all Timon's servants, in contrast to his flatterers, are faithful to him and have a genuine affection for him (4. 2). This picture is perhaps modified by the curious incomplete suggestions of a wisdom by withdrawal to be achieved only in death, but there is no direct connection between that and his sufferings— it is 'nothing' that brings him 'all things' (5. 1. 187). Even here, the effect is partly counteracted by the more satiric and less mysteriously resonant lines (ll. 219–22) which are appended to Timon's description of his choice of a grave, and whose tone recurs in the epitaphs from Plutarch used in the final scene. In the last instance, it is perhaps the possibility of taking these over unchanged, and so remaining within the stock-character framework of 'Timon Misanthropus', that best shows how Shakespeare has stopped short of a genuinely tragic remoulding of the traditional figure.

Shakespeare has evidently relied on the contrast between Timon and Alcibiades and between Timon and Apemantus to convey much of his meaning, and it is perhaps here that we are most conscious of the incompleteness of the draft. Most critics have seen the importance of the contrast between Timon and Alcibiades and their respective responses to Athenian baseness.[1] Collins has given perhaps the best account of what Alcibiades means for the play, in stressing how in 3. 5, 'a real man has pleaded for his friend',[2] and how,

[1] See for example F. S. Boas, *Shakspere and his Predecessors* (1896), p. 501. This book has one of the best short treatments of the play in general works on Shakespeare.

[2] *Review of English Studies*, XXII (1946), 104.

at the end of the play with Alcibiades's return to Athens, 'sanity, with common decency is restored; there shall be human-heartedness again';[1] but he destroys some of the effect of his criticism by exaggerating the contrast in technique between the handling of Timon and that of Alcibiades—the criticism of Timon that is implied in the figure of Alcibiades is much more telling than it would be if Timon were, as Collins writes, an 'abstract Virtue almost ready to be transformed to a similarly abstract Vice'.[2] In fact it is hard to see how a play could successfully work simultaneously on those two levels. The contrast is not, as Collins holds,[3] between Idealism and Realism, but between an inhuman excess and a balanced humanity. Alcibiades can see what is wrong with Athens—'banish usury' (3. 5. 101), and he is not provoked to indiscriminate[4] hatred, 'I will use the olive with my sword' (5. 4. 82). Only the outlines of the theme are indicated, but the intention is clear. The other exemplar of human-heartedness in the play, the steward Flavius, is treated in more detail, in several of Shakespeare's most tenderly beautiful scenes. (I find it significant that Campbell, in making out the treatment to be satirical throughout, is led to ignore the roles of both Flavius and Alcibiades in the play.) In him, and in Timon's other servants, we see genuine personal affection, contrasting strongly with Timon's more equivocal 'bounty'. It is noteworthy that Shakespeare seems to have been much more certain what the most significant scene involving Alcibiades, 3. 5, was to represent in the play's system of values than what its place in the action was to be. Its main function in the

---

[1] *Ibid.* p. 107.   [2] *Ibid.* p. 104.   [3] *Ibid.* p. 90.
[4] Timon is indiscriminate in both halves of the play: 'thou'rt an Athenian, therefore welcome' (1. 2. 34–5), and 'The gods confound—hear me, you good gods all— | Th'Athenians both within and out that wall.' (4. 1. 37–8).

plot is, of course, to give the occasion for Alcibiades's banishment, but it would surely have been more closely integrated into the action in a final version. To me, as to Ellis-Fermor,[1] the scene reads like a vigorous roughing-out, of particular interest for the study of a theme taking shape under Shakespeare's hands. The lack of final shaping is perhaps even more to be regretted in 4. 3, when Timon and Alcibiades meet for the last time. As the scene stands, the presence of Phrynia and Timandra provides an occasion for Timon's invective, but scarcely helps to elucidate the Alcibiades theme. I should be reluctant to regard it as intended to indicate that the claims of Alcibiades in the final scene to regenerate Athens are to be taken cynically.

In the absence of a full development of the Alcibiades theme, the other main contrast of the play, that between Timon and Apemantus, perhaps assumes undue prominence. Here there is no doubt that, especially in Act 4, this part of the play is relatively near completion. There is less of Apemantus in the first three acts, but perhaps about as much as Shakespeare meant there to be. In the earlier scenes, Apemantus falls easily enough under the type of 'scurrilous and profane jester' first introduced by Jonson in *Every Man out of his Humour* in the person of Carlo Buffone. No radical criticism of a specific kind is conveyed by his railing. In Act 4 he is able to argue with Timon on equal terms, and is given some of the most impressive poetry of the play. In spite of this, and in spite of the superficially keen play of dialectic, he seems even more ineffective than before. The audience knows that he is arguing on false premises, since Timon has discovered his new store of gold, and does not act the misanthrope 'enforcedly'

[1] *Review of English Studies*, XVIII (1942). I can see no plausibility in Ellis-Fermor's conjecture that the unknown soldier might have been intended to be Timon himself.

(4. 3. 242). But even if this were not so, we can see
that Timon would still be right in saying 'thou
flatter'st misery,' (l. 235). Apemantus's speech beginning 'Thou hast cast away thyself' (l. 221) is such a
characteristic piece of Shakespeare's mature verse that
we tend to overlook how unnecessary it is for Timon
to have all this pointed out to him. It is not only
unnecessary, it becomes clear as the scene proceeds that
from Timon's point of view it is a falsely romantic
picture. Apemantus for all his cynicism has a picture
of a finely incorruptible 'Nature' refusing to flatter
man—a picture made in his own image, and one to
which, in turn, he strives to approximate even more
closely. The core of Timon's criticism of cynicism is
in the long speech beginning at l. 329, 'A beastly
ambition'. The real animal world, in contrast to Apemantus's idealized picture, is just as full of conflict and
inequality as the human—'what beast couldst thou be
that were not subject to a beast?'. If Timon himself
later wishes 'that beasts may have the world in empire',
it is from pure hatred of mankind, not from any idealiza-
tion of beasts. All this does not mean that we are asked
to share Timon's total vision—I have already commented
on the failure of insight shown in the speech, 'The
sun's a thief'—but it does dispose of Apemantus's
essentially sentimental and self-indulgent cynicism.

It would be natural to hope to follow up a piecemeal treatment of themes by an attempt to see them
together in a coherent picture, and it is the radical
criticism to be made of the play that, unless I have
badly failed to read it aright, this is not possible. At
a highly abstract level, it is easier to summarize without
serious distortion than any other of the plays. To say
that it is a study of a potentially noble but unbalanced
and prodigal nature, corrupted by a usurious and
materialistic society with its flattery, and thrown off his

balance and plunged into an equally extreme and indiscriminate misanthropy when the loss of his wealth
discovers the falsehood of his friends—to say this is
probably a less hopelessly inadequate account of 'what
the play is about' than could be given for any other
important play of Shakespeare. But once we descend
from such generalities, and attempt an analysis in terms
of individual themes, there seems to be less over and
above, or rather encompassing, those themes than in the
greatest works. Each is worked out with passion and
brilliance,[1] though to different degrees of completeness;
yet whole-hearted encomiums of the play always give
the impression of special pleading, and attempts to
make it out to be all of a piece are unduly schematic and
incomplete. Nor does this mean simply that the play
is too rich and varied to be brought under a systematic
description. On the contrary one feels that it is a play
that ought to have been neat and shapely—it aims more
at the formal qualities of *Coriolanus* than at those of
Antony and Cleopatra or of *King Lear*. If he wrote it
before *King Lear*, it is easy for us to see after the event
that what is most profound in the play called for
development on the vaster stage which he was presently
to call into being. But Hazlitt's claim for it as a play
in which he is 'in earnest throughout' may still be
upheld, and the sight of Shakespeare at the height of
his powers struggling with material which even for him
proves recalcitrant is more instructive than the successes
of most dramatists.

J. C. M.

December 1956

[1] The interviews with the false friends—variations on a
single theme, but wittily differentiated—are, I think, often
underrated. Their merits were recognized by P. Stapfer,
Shakespeare and Classical Antiquity (1880), p. 238, who
found in them some of the spirit of Molière.

THE STAGE-HISTORY OF
TIMON OF ATHENS

No record of any performance is known prior to the closing of the theatres in 1642; and the original, if it ever appeared on the Restoration stage, was soon displaced by adaptations till well into the nineteenth century. The principal one, Thomas Shadwell's *Timon of Athens, the Man-hater*, so captured the public taste that it was shown most of the years, 1701–45. After that it disappeared from the stage, and apart from attempts at modified versions in three or four different years London saw no *Timon* again till 1816. The genius of Kean in that year and of Phelps in the mid-century failed to restore the play to favour; but the present century has witnessed some noteworthy revivals.

Timon was one of three Shakespeare plays the sole acting rights in which were 'allowed' to the Duke's company by a royal warrant of 20 August 1668; but no record has been found of their performing it. In February 1678 Shadwell published his version, which was acted by the Duke's company in their Dorset Garden Theatre. Betterton played Timon, while his wife and Mrs Shadwell took the parts of the two new women characters, Timon's mistress Evandra, and his fiancée, Melissa; Harris was Apemantus, Smith Alcibiades, Medbourne Demetrius (=Shakespeare's Flavius), and Alcibiades's two mistresses (in Shadwell 'Thais' and 'Phrinias') were given to Mrs Seymour and Mrs LeGrand.[1] Downes reports that the play was

[1] See John Genest, *Some Account of the English Stage,* 1660–1830 (1832), I, 247–8. The full cast is printed in only one of the two 1678 Quartos; and in Montague Summers's

xliv TIMON OF ATHENS

'very well Acted, and the Musick in't well Performed;
it wonderfully pleas'd the Court and City, being an
Excellent Moral'.[1] We have no record of any further
revival till 1701, though there is contemporary evidence
of frequent performance before this,[2] and Purcell composed music for *Timon* in 1694.[3] That this was the
making of the play is implied in the epilogue to *The
Jew of Venice*, by George Granville, Lord Lans-
downe, acted 1701:

> Shakespeare's sublime in vain entic'd the Throng,
> Without the charm of *Purcell's* Syren Song.

The main feature of Shadwell's *Timon* was the introduction of the theme of love into the one play in the
canon in which women play no significant part. This
was doubtless the chief cause of its popularity. Timon
has a devoted mistress, Evandra, who follows him into
exile and stabs herself when Timon dies.[4] At the outset
he is about to marry Melissa, a heartless fortune-seeker,
modelled largely on Restoration coquettes, but loved
both by Timon and Alcibiades. Having deserted her

edition of *Timon* (*The Complete Works of Shadwell*, 1927,
III, 183–273), p. 197.

[1] John Downes, *Roscius Anglicanus* (1708) (ed. Montague
Summers, 1928), p. 37.

[2] 'This Play...has been reviv'd with alterations, by Mr.
Shadwell, and for a few Years past, as often acted at the
Theatre Royal, as any Tragedy I know' (Charles Gildon,
writing in 1698; see John Munro, *The Shakspere Allusion-
Book* (1909), II, 421).

[3] Grove's *Dictionary of Music*, 5th ed. (1954), VI, 1011.

[4] Perhaps from taking poison, though this is not quite
clear. 'I have taken the best Cordial, Death, which now |
Kindly begins to work about my Vitals', Timon replies
to Evandra's 'I have a Cordial which | Will much revive
thy Spirits'; thirty-eight lines later he dies.

fiancé in his adversity, she visits him outside Athens on hearing of his find of gold. Spurned by him, she turns up again in the final scene to welcome the victorious Alcibiades whom she had refused to see when he was banished, but is in turn rejected by him. Thus the love-interest binds into closer unity the main and subsidiary plots. The picture of Alcibiades is filled out with details drawn from Plutarch's *Life*, and the dénouement exhibits him as the overthrower of tyranny and the re-establisher of democracy. In Shadwell a self-seeking steward, Demetrius, deprives Shakespeare's play of its one appealing character, Flavius, however much Evandra fills the gap. Nor is he effectively worked out. After announcing in a soliloquy opening the play his intention to 'rise' by Timon's 'ruin', he proceeds, as Flavius did in Shakespeare, repeatedly to speak of his unheeded warnings (largely in Shakespeare's words). When the crash comes, he merely disappears from the action; and though, unlike Flavius, he does not seek out Timon in his self-banishment, he is not shown as having gained anything. But the reconstruction shows an eye for dramatic effects, and gives some support to Shadwell's claim, in an epistolary dedication to George Villiers, Duke of Buckingham (author of *The Rehearsal*), to 'have made' the original 'into a Play'. More modestly the epilogue hoped that this '*Scien* grafted upon *Shakespear's* Stock...might thrive, | Kept by the vertue of his sap alive'; English judges might 'for *Shakespear's* part forgive the rest'. There is much to forgive in its tame and halting verse, though it does not deserve Dryden's taunt that 'Shadwell never deviates into sense'; his additions rarely lack point.[1]

[1]. See the analysis in C. B. Hogan's *Shakespeare in the Theatre, 1701–1800: London, 1701–50* (1952), p. 437; the accounts in Genest, *op. cit.* I, 248–53; G. C. D. Odell,

Till 1745 only nine of the years were without a performance of this hybrid play on the London stage. The first known cast (June 1707) shows Mills as acting Timon and Barton Booth Alcibiades at the two-year old Queen's Theatre in the Haymarket; Mrs Bradshaw was Melissa and Mrs Knight Evandra. Mills was Timon again in 1708 at Drury Lane; from 1709 to 1714 Powell took over the part to Booth's Alcibiades. But from 1715 to 1726 Booth played Timon, and was the most famous actor of the period in this role. Mills, who had been Apemantus in ten productions between 1711 and 1726, became Timon again in three of the years, 1729–33; in May that year Milward appeared in the part at Covent Garden, and thereafter was the Drury Lane Timon from 1735 till the Lane's last production in May 1741. In 1711 and 1720 Penkethman had played the Poet at Drury Lane; on his retirement Theophilus Cibber was seen in the part from 1725 to 1731, and finally in the Covent Garden revival of 1745. Mrs Porter (till May 1720), and Mrs Thurmond (from December 1720 to 1737) were the principal Evandras of the time; but Mrs Pritchard, who had been the Lane's Melissa from November 1736 to 1741, figured as Timon's devoted mistress in the Garden's 1745 revival. Mrs Bradshaw acted Melissa at Drury Lane till 1714; Mrs Horton took on the part from 1720 to 1729; in 1733 she twice acted Evandra. Chloe, the companion of Melissa, was personated by

Shakespeare from Betterton to Irving (1921), I, 46–8; Hazelton Spencer, *Shakespeare Improved* (1927), pp. 281–7; and an admirable article in *The Times Educational Supplement*, 30 May 1952, on this and subsequent versions, including some in German. Adaptations in German, French and Japanese, as well as the English versions, are described in S. T. Williams, 'Some Versions of *Timon of Athens*' (*Modern Philology*, XVIII (1920–1), 269–85).

Mrs Mills in 1707 and 1708, while her husband was playing Timon; at the end of the half-century Miss Hippisley performed the part—in 1741 at Goodman's Fields, and in the final showing at Covent Garden in 1745.

To Dublin almost certainly must be assigned the honour of staging the only revival of Shakespeare's play in the eighteenth century. We know of no performance of it in London or Richmond, Surrey. But Mr Hogan of Yale has discovered a playbill of a *Timon*, 'as written by Shakespeare', at the Smock Alley Theatre on 3 June 1761; the cast includes 'Phrynia' and 'Timandra' as the only woman characters, while Timon's steward is named 'Flavius'. This appears sufficient proof of its claim to be Shakespeare's play. Mossop acted Timon.[1] Six years later, a new version of the Shakespeare-Shadwell play by James Love was acted at Richmond— seven times in the summer, and again three times from June to August 1768.[2] The same year it was published but never again staged. Love, whose real name was Dance,[3] played Apemantus to Aikin's Timon and Cautherley's Alcibiades. Mrs Stephens was Evandra.[4] He followed Shadwell's plan, but named the steward Flavius, and restored many of Shakespeare's lines, writing few of his own. Melissa remained in the plot, but, though frequently spoken of, never appeared.[5] In 1771 Richard Cumberland made a new pattern out of Shadwell's patchwork, and Garrick staged this version at Drury Lane eleven times from 4 December to

[1] I owe all this information to Mr Hogan.

[2] Exact dates from Mr Hogan.

[3] See *Biographia Dramatica* (originally D. Erskine Baker's *Companion to the Playhouse*, 1764) with the additions by Isaac Reed, 1782, and by Stephen Jones, 1812.

[4] See the full cast in Genest, *op. cit.* v, 320–1.

[5] See details in S. T. Williams, *loc. cit.* pp. 271–2.

6 February, providing it with fine scenery. The cast included Barry (Timon), Bannister (Apemantus), and Croft (Alcibiades); Mrs Barry played Evanthe, Timon's daughter, whom Cumberland substituted for Evandra, omitting Melissa. She and Alcibiades (whose mistresses disappear) are lovers, and their union is sanctioned by Timon's joining their hands as he dies. As a set-off against this touching climax we have Lucius and Lucullus also wooing Evanthe as well as battening on Timon's prodigality; both meet with poetic justice when the gold which Lucullus has buried is that found by Timon in the woods, and Lucius's house in Athens is looted by Alcibiades's soldiery. But though these bright ideas compel Cumberland to re-write much, he retains Shakespeare's language when the action coincides. Thomas Davies, who thought Cumberland's 'a miserable alteration', acutely argues that his invention of Evanthe was the ruin of Shakespeare's play; it 'destroys all probability as well as extinguishes commiseration' to find Timon squandering on his guests 'the wealth that should be reserved for her portion'.[1] A *Timon* was produced in Kemble's last season in Dublin at the Smock Alley Theatre on 3 March 1783, 'for Kemble's benefit'. The playbill says '(Altered from Shakespeare)', and names Kemble first among the actors of 'the Principal Characters', without stating their parts, Mrs Inchbald being the only woman.[2] This must therefore have been Cumberland's version, and Kemble will have played Timon.

---

[1] For Cumberland's version see Genest, *op. cit.* V, 317–19; Hogan, *Shakespeare in the Theatre, 1701–1800: London, 1751–1800* (1957), pp. 654–5; Odell, *op. cit.* II, 382–4; S. T. Williams, *loc. cit.* p. 272, wrongly states that Cumberland omitted Apemantus's part. For Davies's criticism see his *Memoirs of Garrick* (1780), II, 278–80.

[2] Mr Hogan is the discoverer of this bill also.

No record is known of his having acted the part in
London where he made his debut in September,
though an engraving, dated 21 September 1785, now
in the Victoria and Albert Museum, depicts Timon
with his gold; underneath, 'Mr KEMBLE as TIMON'.[1]
Yet another adaptation was shown at Covent Garden
on 13 May 1786 for Hull's benefit. According to the
Biographia Dramatica of 1812, Hull was the author
of the version. Genest thought this 'infinitely better
than any' of the previous; but the *European Magazine*
for May 1786 declared that it 'ought to be consigned
to oblivion'. Hull acted Flavius to Holman's Timon;
Farren was Alcibiades, Wroughton Apemantus, and
Mrs Inchbald Melissa. Evandra the bills assigned to
'a Young Lady, 1st appearance'. She was Mrs Duill,
later the wife of John Taylor, the newspaper editor.[2]

There is no further record of an eighteenth-century
Timon in England. In the new century the genuine
play emerges from the dust-heaps of extraneous matter
in which it had been embedded for more than a hundred years. In his version acted at Drury Lane on
28 October 1816, the Honourable George Lamb
claimed that he had restored Shakespeare with 'no
other omissions than the refinement of manners has

[1] Mr G. W. Nash in a letter suggests that 'Kemble's
face and name were added to a studio portrait....The
costume looks too scant for that time.' Mr Hogan comments: 'This practice was not at all uncommon in the
18th century', and cites the instance in Bell's *Shakespeare*
(1773), of a portrait of Weston as Costard in *Love's Labour's
Lost*, though that play was not acted until 1839. He doubts
whether 'Kemble's one performance of Timon at a time
when he was entirely unknown to London audiences would
be the occasion of a portrait of him in that part'. Mr Nash
is inclined to agree with him.

[2] Cast in Genest, *op. cit.* VI, 402; Hogan, *op. cit.* p. 657
(also private information).

rendered necessary'. These were mainly of the cour-
tezans, so that no women but the Amazons were now
left in the play; but actually he also threw overboard
much of Shakespeare's dialogue. The Amazons carried
swords and shields instead of Shakespeare's lutes;
'lutes', commented Leigh Hunt, 'would make them
more human'.[1] Edmund Kean's Timon shed a brief
lustre on the production; Bengough was Apemantus,
Wallack Alcibiades, and Holland Flavius; Harley and
S. Penley took Lucius and Lucullus. There was much
praise in the reviews,[2] but Leigh Hunt expressed doubts
of a long run for the revival, and in fact after seven
performances it was finally withdrawn. Hunt's judgment on it was balanced between blame and praise.
Kean he thought 'too stately and tragic' in the first
part of the play; later he tended 'to mistake vehemence
for intenseness', but his handling of the scene with
Alcibiades Hunt admired without reservation. He had
never seen 'the force of contrast... more truly pathetic.
It is the encounter of hope with despair.' His strictures
on the version were severe, especially for Lamb's cur-
tailment of 'profound and poetical' passages, the play's
'main beauty'.[3]

The next revivals were not thus impaired. Samuel
Phelps at Sadler's Wells in 1851 and 1856 reproduced
Shakespeare's text with few cuts. The play was mounted
with Phelps's usual lavish splendour and attempt at
antiquarian fidelity; but Professor Henry Morley after
the second revival claimed that the scenery (by Fenton)
did not 'draw attention from the poet', being 'in the
most perfect harmony' with his 'whole conception'.

[1] See Hunt's critique (*Examiner*, 4 November 1816)
reprinted in L. H. and C. W. Houtchen's *Leigh Hunt's
Dramatic Criticism*, 1808–31 (1949), pp. 138–9.

[2] See lengthy extracts in S. T. Williams, *loc. cit.* pp. 273–5.

[3] Leigh Hunt, *op. cit.* pp. 135–9.

The same sets were used apparently for both productions, though 'much' was 'new painted', again by Fenton. They included 'Greek interiors', 'classical landscapes', and a wonderful moving picture of the march to Athens of Alcibiades and his forces. The play was shown forty nights between 15 September and Christmas 1851, and was a great success. 'Better than Kean's' was the verdict on Phelps's Timon by playgoers who had seen the former in 1816; and he was well supported by George Bennett as Apemantus and Henry Marston as Alcibiades.[1] Phelps again revived the play on 11 October 1856. Marston now took over Apemantus, Rayner played Alcibiades, and Ray Flavius. Marston's reading of his new part 'helped much', wrote Morley, 'to secure a right understanding of the play'; 'the play is a poem' and it became this to the audiences, while the actors had all been taught to treat each part, great and small, with equal care. Oxenford, writing in *The Times*, declared Timon 'one of Mr Phelps's most effective characters'; and he approved of the rest also. Yet the play had a much shorter run than five years previously; it was the chief item in the Sadler's Wells repertory till 15 November, and thereafter was seen no more.[2] We next hear of the play in Manchester. Here Charles Calvert in 1871 produced it as a three-act play at the Prince's Theatre, and acted Timon himself. He cut out the two women characters and confined the action to Timon and his false friends; but while retaining the dances in 1. 2, he also added

[1] See W. May Phelps and J. Forbes-Robertson, *Life and Life-work of Samuel Phelps* (1886), p. 121; playbill with the cast is on p. 273; description of scenery on p. 223. For Morley's account (from the *Examiner*, 18 October 1856) see his *Journal of a London Playgoer* (1866), pp. 152–5, and Phelps and Forbes-Robertson, *op. cit.* pp. 152–4.

[2] See *op. cit.* pp. 150–4 and 222–4.

'dances and choruses' to the later banquet scene. The production ran for 'some four or five weeks' in the early summer, and used the scenery and costumes of his 1869 *Winter's Tale*.[1]

In 1892 Benson chose *Timon* for three performances in Stratford, the first on 22 April, and two more on the 23rd, Shakespeare's birthday. He gave it as a three-act play, himself playing Timon—'I love the play and the part', he wrote in a letter of 1919—William Mollison, Apemantus, and E. Lyall Swete, Flavius. George R. Weir acted Lucullus, while Mrs Benson was an all but silent Phrynia, but she also danced in the masque. The limited appeal of the play defeated the skill of the production, and it evoked little interest.[2] Yet Bridges-Adams, greatly daring, produced the tragedy once more as the Birthday play in 1928 in the Greenhill Street picture house. Wilfrid Walter took the title part; George Hayes, new to Stratford, was assigned Apemantus, and Eric Maxon Alcibiades; Roy Byford was Lucullus, Kenneth Wicksteed Flavius, and Dorothy Massingham played Timandra. This time the revival won a more favourable reception.[3]

This response in 1928 was in fact symptomatic of the changed attitude to the play in recent times; the present century has seen more *Timons* than any period since the disappearance of Shadwell's perversion. As early as 1904 J. H. Leigh presented the play at the

[1] See Mrs Charles Calvert, *Sixty Years on the Stage* (1911), pp. 89–90.

[2] See M. C. Day and J. C. Trewin, *The Shakespeare Memorial Theatre* (1932), pp. 72–3; T. C. Kemp and J. C. Trewin, *The Stratford Festival* (1953), p. 33; the full cast in Ruth Ellis, *The Shakespeare Memorial Theatre* (1948), p. 133. For Benson's letter see S. T. Williams, p. 277n.

[3] See Day and Trewin, *op. cit.* p. 205; full cast in Ruth Ellis, *op. cit.* p. 149, and Kemp and Trewin, *op. cit.* p. 144.

Court Theatre in a version largely based on Benson's, according to *The Athenaeum* of 28 May. Beginning on the 18th, it was performed every night till the 28th, with *matinées* on the 21st and 28th. Leigh in the view of *The Times* of 19 May was a 'painstaking, if slightly *gauche*' Timon, Hermann Vezin's Apemantus 'drily humorous', and Frank Cooper an 'orotund and picturesque' Alcibiades. Timandra and Phrynia were almost dumb figures; the masque was 'a lovely ballet'.[1] A revival for the Old Vic company had also preceded the second in Stratford; Robert Atkins produced it for them on 1 May 1922, the later Stratford Timon, Wilfrid Walter, playing Alcibiades, and designing the settings. Atkins was Timon, Rupert Harvey Apemantus, and Andrew Leigh Flavius. The *Times* reviewer, regarding the drama as a long drawn-out argument for pessimism, commended the actors as doing their utmost to redeem it from 'the charge of dullness', and singled out the Timon and the Flavius in particular; Florence Buckton and Esther Whitehouse also, he said, 'gave all possible effect' to their meagre roles as the two mistresses. Nine years later, the Norwich Players under Tyrone Guthrie performed *Timon* in the Maddermarket Theatre, the last but three of their series of Shakespeare's plays, which by 1933 had completed the canon. On 18 November 1935 Ernest Milton appeared as principal in a production by Nugent Monck at the Westminster Theatre.[2] The revival is memorable for the special music composed for it by a young man of twenty-one, Benjamin Britten, his first work for the theatre. In 1947 the Birmingham Repertory Theatre staged the drama in modern dress, with Willard Stoker producing, and John Phillips as Timon; and their production was repeated for a single

[1] See S. T. Williams, *loc. cit.* p. 278, and the *Times* critique.
[2] See U. M. Ellis-Fermor, *English*, I (1936–7), 64.

performance in August at Stratford in the Conference Hall during the second annual Shakespeare Conference there.[1] In 1952 Guthrie again produced the play for the Old Vic with André Morell as Timon. John Phillips was now Lucullus, Leo McKern Apemantus, Peter Coke Alcibiades and Will Leighton Flavius. A comic flavour was imparted to the sombre drama in John Blatchley's rendering of the Poet, by the make-up and accents of the Senators, and in the horse-play of the wind-up of the banquet—mistakenly in the view of some critics[2] in these later instances. The décor was by Tanya Moiseiwitsch.[3] In September 1956, Michael Benthall, with Sir Ralph Richardson playing the lead, produced the Old Vic's third *Timon* in pursuance of its plan of presenting all Shakespeare's plays in five years.

Few theatres in America have ventured on the play. In April 1839 an adaptation by N. H. Bannister was presented at the Franklin Theatre, New York, but it did not survive, as far as Professor Odell can discover, beyond a second night.[4] In June 1936 Shakespeare's play was chosen at the Pasadena Playhouse as the second of its series of his 'Greco-Roman' plays. In January 1940, it was produced at Yale; and in July–September 1953, at Antioch Area Theatre, Ohio (nine performances).[5]

C. B. YOUNG

May 1957

[1] See T. C. Kemp, *The Birmingham Repertory Theatre*, 2nd ed. (1948), pp. 134–5.

[2] E.g. T. C. Worsley in *The New Statesman* and J. C. Trewin in *The Observer*.

[3] On the 1952 revival see also Gordon Crosse, *Shakespearean Playgoing, 1890–1952* (1953), pp. 132, 136–7.

[4] G. C. D. Odell, *Annals of the New York Stage* (1909–, still in progress), IV, 312.

[5] *Shakespeare Quarterly*, V (1954), 67.

TO THE READER

The following typographical conventions should be noted:

A single bracket at the beginning of a speech signifies an 'aside'.

An obelisk (†) implies probable corruption, and suggests a reference to the Notes.

Stage-directions taken verbatim from the First Folio are enclosed in single inverted commas.

The reference number for the first line is given at the head of each page. Numerals in square brackets are placed at the beginning of the traditional acts and scenes.

THE LIFE OF
TIMON OF ATHENS

The scene: Athens and neighbourhood

CHARACTERS IN THE PLAY

TIMON, a noble Athenian
LUCIUS ⎫
LUCULLUS ⎬ flattering lords
SEMPRONIUS ⎭
VENTIDIUS, one of Timon's false friends
ALCIBIADES, an Athenian captain
APEMANTUS, a churlish philosopher
FLAVIUS, steward to Timon
Poet, Painter, Jeweller, and Merchant
An old Athenian
FLAMINIUS ⎫
LUCILIUS ⎬ servants to Timon
SERVILIUS ⎭
CAPHIS ⎫
PHILOTUS ⎪
TITUS ⎬ servants to Timon's creditors and to the
HORTENSIUS ⎪   Lords
And others ⎭
A Page. A Fool. Three Strangers
PHRYNIA ⎫ mistresses to Alcibiades
TIMANDRA ⎭
Cupid and Amazons in the masque
Other Lords, Senators, Officers, Banditti, and
   Attendants

TIMON OF ATHENS

[I. I.]   *Athens. A hall in Timon's house*

'*Enter Poet, Painter, Jeweller, Merchant,*' *and others,*
'*at several doors*'

Poet. Good day, sir.
Painter.   I am glad you're well.
Poet. I have not seen you long; how goes the world?
Painter. It wears, sir, as it grows.
Poet.   Ay, that's well known.
But what particular rarity? what strange,
Which manifold record not matches? See,
Magic of bounty, all these spirits thy power
Hath conjured to attend. I know the merchant.
    Painter. I know them both; th'other's a jeweller.
    Merchant. O, 'tis a worthy lord!
    Jeweller.   Nay, that's most fixed.
    Merchant. A most incomparable man, breathed, as
        it were,   10
To an untirable and continuate goodness.
He passes.
    Jeweller. I have a jewel here.
    Merchant. O, pray, let's see't. For the Lord
        Timon, sir?
    Jeweller. If he will touch the estimate. But for that—
    Poet [*reciting to himself*]. 'When we for recompense
        have praised the vile,
It stains the glory in that happy verse
Which aptly sings the good.'

Merchant. 'Tis a good form.

20 *Jeweller.* And rich. Here is a water, look ye.

Painter. You are rapt, sir, in some work,
    some dedication

To the great lord.

Poet.   A thing slipped idly from me.

Our poesy is as a gum which oozes

From whence 'tis nourished. The fire i'th'flint

Shows not till it be struck: our gentle flame

Provokes itself, and like the current flies

Each bound it chafes. What have you there?

Painter. A picture, sir. When comes your book forth?

Poet. Upon the heels of my presentment, sir.

30 Let's see your piece.

Painter. 'Tis a good piece.

Poet. So 'tis; this comes off well and excellent.

Painter. Indifferent.

Poet.   Admirable. How this grace

Speaks his own standing! what a mental power

This eye shoots forth! how big imagination

Moves in this lip! to th'dumbness of the gesture

One might interpret.

Painter. It is a pretty mocking of the life.

Here is a touch; is't good?

Poet.   I will say of it,

40 It tutors nature; artificial strife

Lives in these touches, livelier than life.

      '*Enter certain Senators*', *and pass by*

Painter. How this lord is followed!

Poet. The senators of Athens—happy man!

Painter. Look, moe!

Poet. You see this confluence, this great flood
    of visitors:

I have in this rough work shaped out a man
Whom this beneath world doth embrace and hug
With amplest entertainment. My free drift
Halts not particularly, but moves itself
In a wide sea of wax; no levelled malice   50
Infects one comma in the course I hold,
But flies an eagle flight, bold and forth on,
Leaving no tract behind.

   Painter. How shall I understand you?

   Poet.   I will unbolt to you.
You see how all conditions, how all minds,
As well of glib and slipp'ry creatures as
Of grave and austere quality, tender down
Their services to Lord Timon. His large fortune,
Upon his good and gracious nature hanging,
Subdues and properties to his love and tendance   60
All sorts of hearts; yea, from the glass-faced flatterer
To Apemantus, that few things loves better
Than to abhor himself; even he drops down
The knee before him, and returns in peace
Most rich in Timon's nod.

   'Painter.   I saw them speak together.

   Poet. Sir, I have upon a high and pleasant hill
Feigned Fortune to be throned. The base o'th'mount
Is ranked with all deserts, all kind of natures,
That labour on the bosom of this sphere
To propagate their states; amongst them all   70
Whose eyes are on this sovereign lady fixed
One do I personate of Lord Timon's frame,
Whom Fortune with her ivory hand wafts to her,
Whose present grace to present slaves and servants
Translates his rivals.

   Painter.   'Tis conceived to scope.
This throne, this Fortune, and this hill, methinks,

With one man beckoned from the rest below,
Bowing his head against the steepy mount
To climb his happiness, would be well expressed
80 In our condition.
   Poet.   Nay, sir, but hear me on.
All those which were his fellows but of late,
Some better than his value, on the moment
Follow his strides, his lobbies fill with tendance,
Rain sacrificial whisperings in his ear,
Make sacred even his stirrup, and through him
Drink the free air.
   Painter.   Ay, marry, what of these?
   Poet. When Fortune in her shift and change of mood
Spurns down her late beloved, all his dependants,
Which laboured after him to the mountain's top
90 Even on their knees and hands, let him slip down,
Not one accompanying his declining foot.
   Painter. 'Tis common:
A thousand moral paintings I can show,
That shall demonstrate these quick blows
     of Fortune's
More pregnantly than words. Yet you do well
To show Lord Timon that mean eyes have seen
The foot above the head.

'*Trumpets sound. Enter* LORD TIMON, *addressing him-self courteously to every' suitor'; a Messenger from* VENTIDIUS *talking with him;* LUCILIUS *and other servants following*

   Timon.   Imprisoned is he, say you?
   Messenger. Ay, my good lord; five talents is
     his debt,
His means most short, his creditors most strait.
100 Your honourable letter he desires

To those have shut him up, which failing
Periods his comfort.

Timon.   Noble Ventidius! Well.
I am not of that feather to shake off
My friend when he must need me. I do know him
A gentleman that well deserves a help,
Which he shall have. I'll pay the debt and free him.

Messenger. Your lordship ever binds him.

Timon. Commend me to him; I will send his ransom;
And, being enfranchiséd, bid him come to me.
'Tis not enough to help the feeble up,   110
But to support him after. Fare you well.   n.b. real charity

Messenger. All happiness to your honour!   [*goes*

'*Enter an old Athenian*'

Athenian. Lord Timon, hear me speak.

Timon.   Freely, good father.

Athenian. Thou hast a servant named Lucilius.

Timon. I have so; what of him?

Athenian. Most noble Timon, call the man
     before thee.

Timon. Attends he here, or no? Lucilius!

Lucilius. Here, at your lordship's service.

Athenian. This fellow here, Lord Timon, this
     thy creature,
By night frequents my house. I am a man   120
That from my first have been inclined to thrift,
And my estate deserves an heir more raised
Than one which holds a trencher.

Timon.   Well; what further?

Athenian. One only daughter have I, no kin else,
On whom I may confer what I have got.
The maid is fair, o'th'youngest for a bride,
And I have bred her at my dearest cost

In qualities of the best. This man of thine
Attempts her love; I prithee, noble lord,
130 Join with me to forbid him her resort;
Myself have spoke in vain.

Timon.   The man is honest.

Athenian. Therefore he will be, Timon.
His honesty rewards him in itself;
It must not bear my daughter.

Timon.   Does she love him?

Athenian. She is young and apt.
Our own precedent passions do instruct us
What levity's in youth.

Timon [*to Lucilius*]. Love you the maid?

Lucilius. Ay, my good lord, and she accepts of it.

Athenian. If in her marriage my consent
    be missing,
140 I call the gods to witness, I will choose
Mine heir from forth the beggars of the world,
And dispossess her all.

Timon.   How shall she be endowéd,
If she be mated with an equal husband?

Athenian. Three talents on the present; in
    future, all.

Timon. This gentleman of mine hath served
    me long;
To build his fortune I will strain a little,
For 'tis a bond in men. Give him thy daughter:
What you bestow, in him I'll counterpoise,
And make him weigh with her.

Athenian.   Most noble lord,
150 Pawn me to this your honour, she is his.

Timon. My hand to thee; mine honour on
    my promise.

Lucilius. Humbly I thank your lordship; never may

That state or fortune fall into my keeping
Which is not owed to you!

[*Lucilius and Old Athenian go*

Poet. Vouchsafe my labour, and long live
   your lordship!

Timon. I thank you; you shall hear from me anon.
Go not away. What have you there, my friend?

Painter. A piece of painting, which I do beseech
Your lordship to accept.

Timon.   Painting is welcome.
The painting is almost the natural man;   160
For since dishonour traffics with man's nature,
He is but outside; these pencilled figures are
Even such as they give out. I like your work,
And you shall find I like it; wait attendance
Till you hear further from me.

Painter.   The gods preserve ye!

Timon. Well fare you, gentleman. Give me
   your hand;
We must needs dine together. Sir, your jewel
Hath sufferéd under praise.

Jeweller.   What, my lord, dispraise?

Timon. A mere satiety of commendations.
If I should pay you for't as 'tis extolled,   170
It would unclew me quite.

Jeweller.   My lord, 'tis rated
As those which sell would give; but you well know,
Things of like value, differing in the owners,
Are prizéd by their masters. Believe't, dear lord,
You mend the jewel by the wearing it.

Timon. Well mocked.

Merchant. No, my good lord; he speaks the
   common tongue
Which all men speak with him.

Timon. Look who comes here; will you be chid?

Enter APEMANTUS

180 *Jeweller.* We'll bear, with your lordship.
     Merchant.   He'll spare none.
     Timon. Good morrow to thee, gentle Apemantus.
     Apemantus. Till I be gentle, stay thou for thy
          good morrow;
When thou art Timon's dog, and these knaves honest.
     Timon. Why dost thou call them knaves? thou
          know'st them not.
     Apemantus. Are they not Athenians?
     Timon. Yes.
     Apemantus. Then I repent not.
     Jeweller. You know me, Apemantus?
     Apemantus. Thou know'st I do; I called thee by
          thy name.
190 *Timon.* Thou art proud, Apemantus.
     Apemantus. Of nothing so much as that I am not
          like Timon.
     Timon. Whither art going?
     Apemantus. To knock out an honest Athenian's
          brains.
     Timon. That's a deed thou'lt die for.
     Apemantus. Right, if doing nothing be death by
          th'law.
     Timon. How lik'st thou this picture, Apemantus?
     Apemantus. The best, for the innocence.
     Timon. Wrought he not well that painted it?
     Apemantus. He wrought better that made the
200 painter; and yet he's but a filthy piece of work.
     Painter. You're a dog.
     Apemantus. Thy mother's of my generation; what's
     she, if I be a dog?

Timon. Wilt dine with me, Apemantus?

Apemantus. No; I eat not lords.

Timon. An thou shouldst, thou'ldst anger ladies.

Apemantus. O, they eat lords; so they come by great bellies.

Timon. That's a lascivious apprehension.

Apemantus. So thou apprehend'st it; take it for thy 210 labour.

Timon. How dost thou like this jewel, Apemantus?

Apemantus. Not so well as plain-dealing, which will not cost a man a doit.

Timon. What dost thou think 'tis worth?

Apemantus. Not worth my thinking. How now, poet!

Poet. How now, philosopher!

Apemantus. Thou liest.

Poet. Art not one?

Apemantus. Yes. 220

Poet. Then I lie not.

Apemantus. Art not a poet?

Poet. Yes.

Apemantus. Then thou liest. Look in thy last work, where thou hast feigned him a worthy fellow.

Poet. That's not feigned; he is so.

Apemantus. Yes, he is worthy of thee, and to pay thee for thy labour. He that loves to be flattered is worthy o'th'flatterer. Heavens, that I were a lord!

Timon. What wouldst do then, Apemantus? 230

Apemantus. E'en as Apemantus does now: hate a lord with my heart.

Timon. What, thyself?

Apemantus. Ay.

Timon. Wherefore?

Apemantus. That I had no angry wit to be a lord. Art not thou a merchant?

Merchant. Ay, Apemantus.

Apemantus. Traffic confound thee, if the gods will not!

240 *Merchant.* If traffic do it, the gods do it.

Apemantus. Traffic's thy god, and thy god confound thee!

'*Trumpet sounds. Enter a Messenger*'

Timon. What trumpet's that?

Messenger. 'Tis Alcibiades, and some twenty horse,
All of companionship.

Timon. Pray, entertain them; give them guide to us.

[*some attendants go*

You must needs dine with me. Go not you hence
Till I have thanked you. When dinner's done,
Show me this piece. I am joyful of your sights.

'*Enter ALCIBIADES, with the rest*'

Most welcome, sir!

Apemantus.   So, so, there!

250 Achës contract and starve your supple joints!
That there should be small love amongst these
          sweet knaves,
And all this courtesy! The strain of man's bred out
Into baboon and monkey.

Alcibiades. Sir, you have saved my longing, and
          I feed
Most hungerly on your sight.

Timon.   Right welcome, sir!
Ere we depart, we'll share a bounteous time
In different pleasures. Pray you, let us in.

[*all but Apemantus go*

'*Enter two Lords*'

1 *Lord.* What time o' day is't, Apemantus?

Apemantus. Time to be honest.

1 *Lord.* That time serves still.   260

Apemantus. The more acccurséd thou that still
    omit'st it.

2 *Lord.* Thou art going to Lord Timon's feast?

Apemantus. Ay, to see meat fill knaves and wine
    heat fools.

2 *Lord.* Fare thee well, fare thee well.

Apemantus. Thou art a fool to bid me farewell twice.

2 *Lord.* Why, Apemantus?

Apemantus. Shouldst have kept one to thyself, for I
mean to give thee none.

1 *Lord.* Hang thyself.

Apemantus. No, I will do nothing at thy bidding; 270
make thy requests to thy friend.

2 *Lord.* Away, unpeaceable dog, or I'll spurn thee
hence.

Apemantus. I will fly, like a dog, the heels o'th'ass.

                                        [*goes*

1 *Lord.* He's opposite to humanity.
Come, shall we in,
And taste Lord Timon's bounty? he outgoes
The very heart of kindness.

2 *Lord.* He pours it out. Plutus, the god of gold,
Is but his steward; no meed, but he repays   280
Sevenfold above itself; no gift to him
But breeds the giver a return exceeding
All use of quittance.

1 *Lord.*   The noblest mind he carries
That ever governed man.

2 *Lord.* Long may he live in fortunes! Shall we in?

1 *Lord.* I'll keep you company.   [*they go*

[1. 2.]   *A banqueting-room in Timon's house*

'*Hautboys playing loud music. A great banquet served in*'; FLAVIUS *and others attending;* '*and then enter* LORD TIMON', ALCIBIADES, *Lords, Senators, and* VENTIDIUS. '*Then comes, dropping after all,* APEMANTUS, *discontentedly, like himself.*'

Ventidius. Most honouréd Timon,
It hath pleased the gods to remember my father's age,
And call him to long peace.
He is gone happy, and has left me rich.
Then, as in grateful virtue I am bound
To your free heart, I do return those talents,
Doubled with thanks and service, from whose help
I derived liberty.
Timon.   O, by no means,
Honest Ventidius; you mistake my love;
10 I gave it freely ever, and there's none
Can truly say he gives, if he receives.
If our betters play at that game, we must not dare
To imitate them; faults that are rich are fair.
Ventidius. A noble spirit!
Timon. Nay, my lords, ceremony was but devised at first
To set a gloss on faint deeds, hollow welcomes,
Recanting goodness, sorry ere 'tis shown;
But where there is true friendship, there needs none.
Pray, sit; more welcome are ye to my fortunes
20 Than my fortunes to me.   [*they sit*
  1 *Lord.* My lord, we always have confessed it.
  Apemantus. Ho, ho, confessed it? hanged it, have
     you not?
  Timon. O, Apemantus, you are welcome.
  Apemantus.   No;

You shall not make me welcome.
I come to have thee thrust me out of doors.

Timon. Fie, thou'rt a churl; ye've got a
humour there
Does not become a man; 'tis much to blame.
They say, my lords, 'ira furor brevis est'; but yond man
is ever angry. Go, let him have a table by himself; for
he does neither affect company, nor is he fit for't 30
indeed.

Apemantus. Let me stay at thine apperil, Timon.
I come to observe, I give thee warning on't.

Timon. I take no heed of thee; thou'rt an Athenian,
therefore welcome; I myself would have no power—
prithee let my meat make thee silent.

Apemantus. I scorn thy meat; 'twould choke me, for
I should ne'er flatter thee. O you gods, what a number
of men eats Timon, and he sees 'em not! It grieves me
to see so many dip their meat in one man's blood; and 40
all the madness is, he cheers them up too.
I wonder men dare trust themselves with men.
Methinks they should invite them without knives:
Good for their meat, and safer for their lives.
There's much example for't; the fellow that sits next
him, now parts bread with him, pledges the breath of
him in a divided draught, is the readiest man to kill
him: 't has been proved. If I were a huge man, I should
fear to drink at meals,
Lest they should spy my windpipe's dangerous notes. 50
Great men should drink with harness on their throats.

Timon. My lord, in heart; and let the health go round.

2 Lord. Let it flow this way, my good lord.

Apemantus. Flow this way? A brave fellow. He
keeps his tides well. Those healths will make thee and
thy state look ill, Timon.

Here's that which is too weak to be a sinner,
Honest water, which ne'er left man i'th'mire.
This and my food are equals; there's no odds.
60 Feasts are too proud to give thanks to the gods.

'*Apemantus' Grace*'

Immortal gods, I crave no pelf;
I pray for no man but myself;
Grant I may never prove so fond
To trust man on his oath or bond,
Or a harlot for her weeping,
Or a dog that seems a-sleeping,
Or a keeper with my freedom,
Or my friends if I should need 'em..
Amen. So fall to't:
70   Rich men sin, and I eat root.

[*eats and drinks*

Much good dich thy good heart, Apemantus!

Timon. Captain Alcibiades, your heart's in the field now.

Alcibiades. My heart is ever at your service, my lord.

Timon. You had rather be at a breakfast of enemies than a-dinner of friends.

Alcibiades. So they were bleeding-new, my lord; there's no meat like 'em; I could wish my best friend 80 at such a feast.

Apemantus. Would all those flatterers were thine enemies, then, that then thou mightst kill 'em—and bid me to 'em!

1 *Lord.* Might we but have that happiness, my lord, that you would once use our hearts, whereby we might express some part of our zeals, we should think ourselves for ever perfect.

Timon. O, no doubt, my good friends, but the gods
themselves have provided that I shall have much help
from you: how had you been my friends else? Why 90
have you that charitable title from thousands, did not
you chiefly belong to my heart? I have told more of
you to myself than you can with modesty speak in your
own behalf; and thus far I confirm you. O you gods,
think I, what need we have any friends, if we should
ne'er have need of 'em? they were the most needless
creatures living, should we ne'er have use for 'em; and
would most resemble sweet instruments hung up in
cases, that keeps their sounds to themselves. Why, I
have often wished myself poorer, that I might come 100
nearer to you. We are born to do benefits; and what
better or properer can we call our own than the riches
of our friends? O, what a precious comfort 'tis to
have so many like brothers commanding one another's
fortunes! O joy, e'en made away ere't can be born!
Mine eyes cannot hold out water, methinks. To forget
their faults, I drink to you.

Apemantus. Thou weep'st to make them drink,
Timon.

2 *Lord.* Joy had the like conception in our eyes, 110
And at that instant like a babe sprung up.

Apemantus. Ho, ho! I laugh to think that babe
     a bastard.

3 *Lord.* I promise you, my lord, you moved me much.
Apemantus. Much!   ['*Tucket*' *heard*
Timon. What means that trump?

          '*Enter*' *a* '*Servant*'

                    How now?
Servant. Please you, my lord, there are certain ladies
most desirous of admittance.

N.S.T.A.—5

Timon. Ladies? what are their wills?

Servant. There comes with them a forerunner,
120 my lord, which bears that office to signify their
pleasures.

Timon. I pray let them be admitted.

Enter Cupid

Cupid. Hail to thee, worthy Timon, and to all
That of his bounties taste! The five best senses
Acknowledge thee their patron, and come freely
To gratulate thy plenteous bosom. Th'ear,
Taste, touch, smell, all pleased from thy table rise;
They only now come but to feast thine eyes.

Timon. They're welcome all; let 'em have
    kind admittance.
130 Music make their welcome!   [*Cupid goes*
    1 *Lord.* You see, my lord, how ample
        you're beloved.

*Music. Re-enter Cupid, with a 'masque of Ladies' as
'Amazons, with lutes in their hands, dancing and
playing'*

Apemantus. Hoy-day, what a sweep of vanity comes
    this way!
They dance? they are madwomen.
Like madness is the glory of this life
As this pomp shows to a little oil and root.
We make ourselves fools, to disport ourselves,
And spend our flatteries to drink those men
Upon whose age we void it up again
With poisonous spite and envy.
140 Who lives that's not depravéd or depraves?
Who dies that bears not one spurn to their graves
Of their friends' gift?

I should fear those that dance before me now
Would one day stamp upon me. 'T has been done;
Men shut their doors against a setting sun.

'*The Lords rise from table, with much adoring of* TIMON,
*and to show their loves, each single out an Amazon, and
all dance, men with women, a lofty strain or two to the
hautboys, and cease*'

Timon. You have done our pleasures much grace,
    fair ladies,
Set a fair fashion on our entertainment,
Which was not half so beautiful and kind;
You have added worth unto't and lustre,
And entertained me with mine own device.   150
I am to thank you for't.
  1 *Lady.* My lord, you take us even at the best.
  Apemantus. Faith, for the worst is filthy, and would
not hold taking, I doubt me.
  Timon. Ladies, there is an idle banquet attends you,
Please you to dispose yourselves.
  All Ladies. Most thankfully, my lord.
                      [*Cupid and Ladies go*
  Timon. Flavius!
  Flavius. My lord?
  Timon.   The little casket bring me hither.
  Flavius. Yes, my lord. [*aside*] More jewels yet!   160
There is no crossing him in's humour,
Else I should tell him well, i' faith I should;
When all's spent, he'ld be crossed then, an he could.
'Tis pity bounty had not eyes behind,
That man might ne'er be wretched for his mind.
                             [*goes*
  1 *Lord.* Where be our men?
  Servant. Here, my lord, in readiness.

2 *Lord.* Our horses!

Re-enter FLAVIUS, *with the casket*

Timon. O my friends,
170 I have one word to say to you. Look you, my
        good lord,
I must entreat you honour me so much
As to advance this jewel; accept it and wear it,
Kind my lord.
        1 *Lord.* I am so far already in your gifts.
        All. So are we all.

'*Enter a Servant*'

Servant. My lord, there are certain nobles of the
senate newly alighted and come to visit you.
        Timon. They are fairly welcome.
        Flavius. I beseech your honour, vouchsafe me a
180 word; it does concern you near.
        Timon. Near? why, then, another time I'll hear
thee. I prithee let's be provided to show them entertainment.
        (*Flavius.* I scarce know how.

'*Enter another Servant*'

2 *Servant.* May it please your honour, Lord Lucius,
Out of his free love, hath presented to you
Four milk-white horses, trapped in silver.
        Timon. I shall accept them fairly. Let the presents
Be worthily entertained.

'*Enter a third Servant*'

                        How now? what news?
190 3 *Servant.* Please you, my lord, that honourable
gentleman, Lord Lucullus, entreats your company

to-morrow to hunt with him, and has sent your honour
two brace of greyhounds.

   Timon. I'll hunt with him; and let them be received,
Not without fair reward.

   (*Flavius.*   What will this come to?
He commands us to provide and give great gifts,
And all out of an empty coffer;
Nor will he know his purse, or yield me this,
To show him what a beggar his heart is,
Being of no power to make his wishes good.   200
His promises fly so beyond his state
That what he speaks is all in debt, he owes
For every word. He is so kind that he now
Pays interest for't; his land's put to their books.
Well, would I were gently put out of office,
Before I were forced out!
.Happier is he that has no friend to feed
Than such that do e'en enemies exceed.
I bleed inwardly for my lord.   *[goes*

   Timon. You do yourselves much wrong.   210
You bate too much of your own merits.
Here, my lord, a trifle of our love.

   2 Lord. With more than common thanks I will
      receive it.

   3 Lord. O, he's the very soul of bounty!

   Timon. And now I remember, my lord, you gave
good words the other day of a bay courser I rode on.
'Tis yours because you liked it.

   3 Lord. O, I beseech you pardon me, my lord, in that.

   Timon. You may take my word, my lord; I know no
man can justly praise but what he does affect. I weigh 220
my friend's affection with mine own. I'll tell you true,
I'll call to you.

   All Lords. O, none so welcome.

Timon. I take all and your several visitations
So kind to heart, 'tis not enough to give;
Methinks I could deal kingdoms to my friends,
And ne'er be weary. Alcibiades,
Thou art a soldier, therefore seldom rich.
It comes in charity to thee; for all thy living
230 Is 'mongst the dead, and all the lands thou hast
Lie in a pitched field.

Alcibiades. Ay, defiled land, my lord.

1 *Lord.* We are so virtuously bound—

Timon. And so am I to you.

2 *Lord.* So infinitely endeared—

Timon. All to you. Lights, more lights!

1 *Lord.* The best of happiness, honour and fortunes,
Keep with you, Lord Timon!

Timon. Ready for his friends.

> [*all leave but Apemantus and Timon*

Apemantus. What a coil's here!
240 Serving of becks and jutting-out of bums!
I doubt whether their legs be worth the sums
That are given for 'em. Friendship's full of dregs:
Methinks false hearts should never have sound legs.
Thus honest fools lay out their wealth on curtsies.

Timon. Now, Apemantus, if thou wert not sullen,
I would be good to thee.

Apemantus. No, I'll nothing; for if I should be
bribed too, there would be none left to rail upon thee,
and then thou wouldst sin the faster. Thou giv'st
250 so long, Timon, I fear me thou wilt give away thyself
in paper shortly. What needs these feasts, pomps and
vainglories?

Timon. Nay, an you begin to rail on society once, I
am sworn not to give regard to you. Farewell, and
come with better music. [*goes*

Apemantus. So. Thou wilt not hear me now; thou
shalt not then. I'll lock thy heaven from thee.
O, that men's ears should be
To counsel deaf, but not to flattery!   [*goes*

[2. 1.]   *A Senator's house*

'*Enter a Senator*', *with papers in his hand*

Senator. And late five thousand; to Varro and to Isidore
He owes nine thousand, besides my former sum,
Which makes it five and twenty. Still in motion
Of raging waste? It cannot hold; it will not.
If I want gold, steal but a beggar's dog
And give it Timon, why, the dog coins gold.
If I would sell my horse and buy twenty moe
Better than he, why, give my horse to Timon,
Ask nothing, give it him, it foals me straight,
And able horses. No porter at his gate,   10
But rather one that smiles, and still invites
All that pass by. It cannot hold; no reason
Can sound his state in safety. Caphis, ho!
Caphis, I say!   '*Enter* CAPHIS'

Caphis.   Here, sir; what is your pleasure?
Senator. Get on your cloak, and haste you to
        Lord Timon;
Importune him for my moneys; be not ceased
With slight denial; nor then silenced when
'Commend me to your master' and the cap
Plays in the right hand, thus; but tell him
My uses cry to me, I must serve my turn   20
Out of mine own; his days and times are past,

And my reliances on his fracted dates
Have smit my credit. I love and honour him,
But must not break my back to heal his finger.
Immediate are my needs, and my relief
Must not be tossed and turned to me in words,
But find supply immediate. Get you gone;
Put on a most importunate aspect,
A visage of demand; for I do fear,
30 When every feather sticks in his own wing,
Lord Timon will be left a naked gull,
Which flashes now a phoenix. Get you gone.
  Caphis. I go, sir.
  Senator.   Take the bonds along with you,
And have the dates in compt.
  Caphis.   I will, sir.
  Senator.   Go.   *[they go*

[2. 2.]   *Before Timon's house*

  '*Enter*' FLAVIUS, '*with many bills in his hand*'

  Flavius. No care, no stop, so senseless of expense
That he will neither know how to maintain it,
Nor cease his flow of riot; takes no account
How things go from him, nor resumes no care
Of what is to continue; never mind
Was to be so unwise to be so kind.
What shall be done? he will not hear till feel.
I must be round with him, now he comes from hunting.
Fie, fie, fie, fie!

    '*Enter* CAPHIS', *with the Servants of* 'ISIDORE
              and VARRO'

  Caphis. Good even, Varro. What, you come
10   for money?
  Varro's Servant. Is't not your business too?

Caphis. It is; and yours too, Isidore?

Isidore's Servant. It is so.

Caphis. Would we were all discharged!

Varro's Servant. I fear it.

Caphis. Here comes the lord.

'*Enter* TIMON *and his Train*', *with* ALCIBIADES

Timon. So soon as dinner's done, we'll forth again,
My Alcibiades. With me? What is your will?

  Caphis. My lord, here is a note of certain dues.

  Timon. Dues? Whence are you?

  Caphis.   Of Athens here, my lord. 20

  Timon. Go to my steward.

  Caphis. Please it your lordship, he hath put me off
To the succession of new days this month.
My master is awaked by great occasion
To call upon his own, and humbly prays you
That with your other noble parts you'll suit
In giving him his right.

  Timon.   Mine honest friend,
I prithee but repair to me next morning.

  Caphis. Nay, good my lord—

  Timon.   Contain thyself, good friend.

  Varro's Servant. One Varro's servant, my good lord— 30

  Isidore's Servant. From Isidore; he humbly prays
your speedy payment.

  Caphis. If you did know, my lord, my
      master's wants,—

  Varro's Servant. 'Twas due on forfeiture, my lord,
six weeks and past.

  Isidore's Servant. Your steward puts me off, my lord,
      and I
Am sent expressly to your lordship.

  Timon. Give me breath.

I do beseech you, good my lords, keep on;
40 I'll wait upon you instantly.

                    [*Alcibiades, Lords and others go*
                    [*to Flavius*] Come hither. Pray you,
How goes the world, that I am thus encount'red
With clamorous demands of broken bonds,
And the detention of long-since-due debts
Against my honour?
  Flavius.   Please you, gentlemen,
The time is unagreeable to this business.
Your importunacy cease till after dinner,
That I may make his lordship understand
Wherefore you are not paid.
  Timon. Do so, my friends. See them well entertained.
                                        [*he goes*
50 *Flavius.* Pray draw near.   [*he goes*

           '*Enter* APEMANTUS *and Fool*'

  Caphis. Stay, stay, here comes the fool with Ape-
mantus. Let's ha' some sport with 'em.
  Varro's Servant. Hang him, he'll abuse us.
  Isidore's Servant. A plague upon him, dog!
  Varro's Servant. How dost, fool?
  Apemantus. Dost dialogue with thy shadow?
  Varro's Servant. I speak not to thee.
  Apemantus. No, 'tis to thy self. [*to the Fool*] Come
away.
60 *Isidore's Servant.* There's the fool hangs on your back
already.
  Apemantus. No, thou stand'st single, thou'rt not on
him yet.
  Caphis. Where's the fool now?
  Apemantus. He last asked the question. Poor rogues,
and usurers' men, bawds between gold and want!

All Servants. What are we, Apemantus?

Apemantus. Asses.

All Servants. Why?

Apemantus. That you ask me what you are, and do 70
not know yourselves. Speak to 'em, fool.

Fool. How do you, gentlemen?

All Servants. Gramercies, good fool. How does
your mistress?

Fool. She's e'en setting on water to scald such chickens
as you are. Would we could see you at Corinth!

Apemantus. Good, gramercy.

'Enter Page'

Fool. Look you, here comes my mistress' page.

Page [to the Fool]. Why, how now, captain? what do
you in this wise company? How dost thou, Apemantus? 80

Apemantus. Would I had a rod in my mouth, that I
might answer thee profitably.

Page. Prithee, Apemantus, read me the superscription of these letters. I know not which is which.

Apemantus. Canst not read?

Page. No.

Apemantus. There will little learning die then, that
day thou art hanged. This is to Lord Timon; this to
Alcibiades. Go, thou wast born a bastard, and thou'lt
die a bawd.   90

Page. Thou wast whelped a dog, and thou shalt
famish a dog's death. Answer not, I am gone.   [*goes*

Apemantus. E'en so thou outrun'st grace. Fool, I
will go with you to Lord Timon's.

Fool. Will you leave me there?

Apemantus. If Timon stay at home. You three serve
three usurers?

All Servants. Ay; would they served us!

Apemantus. So would I—as good a trick as ever
100 hangman served thief.

Fool. Are you three usurers' men?

All Servants. Ay, fool.

Fool. I think no usurer but has a fool to his servant.
My mistress is one, and I am her fool. When men come
to borrow of your masters, they approach sadly and go
away merry; but they enter my mistress' house merrily
and go away sadly. The reason of this?

Varro's Servant. I could render one.

Apemantus. Do it then, that we may account thee a
110 whoremaster and a knave; which notwithstanding,
thou shalt be no less esteemed.

Varro's Servant. What is a whoremaster, fool?

Fool. A fool in good clothes, and something like
thee. 'Tis a spirit. Sometime 't appears like a lord,
sometime like a lawyer, sometime like a philosopher,
with two stones moe than 's artificial one. He is very
often like a knight; and generally, in all shapes that
man goes up and down in, from fourscore to thirteen,
this spirit walks in.

120 *Varro's Servant.* Thou art not altogether a fool.

Fool. Nor thou altogether a wise man: as much
foolery as I have, so much wit thou lack'st.

Apemantus. That answer might have become Apemantus.

All Servants. Aside, aside; here comes Lord Timon.

Re-enter TIMON *and* FLAVIUS

Apemantus. Come with me, fool, come.

Fool. I do not always follow lover, elder brother,
and woman; sometime the philosopher.   [*they go*

Flavius. Pray you, walk near: I'll speak with you
     anon.   [*Servants withdraw*

Timon. You make me marvel wherefore ere
  this time   130
Had you not fully laid my state before me,
That I might so have rated my expense
As I had leave of means.
  Flavius.   You would not hear me.
At many leisures I proposed—
  Timon.   Go to.
Perchance some single vantages you took
When my indisposition put you back,
And that unaptness made your minister
Thus to excuse yourself.
  Flavius.   O my good lord,
At many times I brought in my accounts,
Laid them before you; you would throw them off,   140
And say you found them in mine honesty.
When for some trifling present you have bid me
Return so much, I have shook my head and wept;
Yea, 'gainst th'authority of manners prayed you
To hold your hand more close. I did endure
Not seldom, nor no slight checks, when I have
Prompted you in the ebb of your estate
And your great flow of debts. My loved lord—
Though you hear now too late, yet now's a time—
The greatest of your having lacks a half   150
To pay your present debts.
  Timon.   Let all my land be sold.
  Flavius. 'Tis all engaged, some forfeited and gone,
And what remains will hardly stop the mouth
Of present dues. The future comes apace;
What shall defend the interim? and at length
How goes our reck'ning?
  Timon. To Lacedæmon did my land extend.
  Flavius. O my good lord, the world is but a word;

Were it all yours to give it in a breath,
160 How quickly were it gone!
    Timon.   You tell me true.
    Flavius. If you suspect my husbandry or falsehood,
Call me before th'exactest auditors,
And set me on the proof. So the gods bless me,
When all our offices have been oppressed
With riotous feeders, when our vaults have wept
With drunken spilth of wine, when every room
Hath blazed with lights and brayed with minstrelsy,
I have retired me to a wasteful cock,
And set mine eyes at flow.
    Timon.   Prithee no more.
170   *Flavius.* Heavens, have I said, the bounty of
      this lord!
How many prodigal bits have slaves and peasants
This night englutted! Who is not Timon's?
What heart, head, sword, force, means, but is
      Lord Timon's?
Great Timon, noble, worthy, royal Timon!
Ah, when the means are gone that buy this praise,
The breath is gone whereof this praise is made.
Feast-won, fast-lost; one cloud of winter showers,
These flies are couched.
    Timon.   Come, sermon me no further.
No villainous bounty yet hath passed my heart;
180 Unwisely, not ignobly, have I given.
Why dost thou weep? Canst thou the conscience lack
To think I shall lack friends? Secure thy heart;
If I would broach the vessels of my love,
And try the argument of hearts, by borrowing,
Men and men's fortunes could I frankly use
As I can bid thee speak.
    Flavius.   Assurance bless your thoughts!

Timon. And in some sort these wants of mine
    are crowned,
That I account them blessings; for by these
Shall I try friends:
You shall perceive how you mistake my fortunes;   190
I am wealthy in my friends.
†Within there! Flaminius! Servilius!

Enter FLAMINIUS, SERVILIUS, and another Servant

Servants. My lord, my lord?
Timon. I will dispatch you severally. You to Lord
Lucius, to Lord Lucullus you—I hunted with his
honour to-day—you to Sempronius, commend me to
their loves; and I am proud, say, that my occasions have
found time to use 'em toward a supply of money. Let
the request be fifty talents.
   Flaminius. As you have said, my Lord.   200
   (*Flavius.* Lord Lucius and Lucullus? hum!
   Timon. Go you, sir, to the senators,
Of whom, even to the state's best health, I have
Deserved this hearing; bid 'em send o'th'instant
A thousand talents to me.
   Flavius.   I have been bold,
For that I knew it the most general way,
To them to use your signet and your name;
But they do shake their heads, and I am here
No richer in return.
   Timon.   Is't true? can't be?
   Flavius. They answer, in a joint and corporate voice, 210
That now they are at fall, want treasure, cannot
Do what they would; are sorry—you are honourable—
But yet they could have wished—they know not—
Something hath been amiss—a noble nature
May catch a wrench—would all were well—'tis pity;

And so, intending other serious matters,
After distasteful looks, and these hard fractions,
With certain half-caps and cold-moving nods
They froze me into silence.
   Timon.   You gods, reward them!
220 Prithee, man, look cheerly. These old fellows
Have their ingratitude in them hereditary.
Their blood is caked, 'tis cold, it seldom flows;
'Tis lack of kindly warmth they are not kind;
And nature, as it grows again toward earth,
Is fashioned for the journey, dull and heavy.
Go to Ventidius. Prithee, be not sad;
Thou art true and honest; ingeniously I speak,
No blame belongs to thee. Ventidius lately
Buried his father, by whose death he's stepped
230 Into a great estate. When he was poor,
Imprisoned, and in scarcity of friends,
I cleared him with five talents. Greet him from me;
Bid him suppose some good necessity
Touches his friend, which craves to be rememb'red
With those five talents. That had, give't these fellows
To whom 'tis instant due. Ne'er speak or think
That Timon's fortunes 'mong his friends can sink.
   Flavius. I would I could not think it.
That thought is bounty's foe;
240 Being free itself, it thinks all others so.   *[they go*

[3. 1.]   *A room in Lucullus's house*

'*FLAMINIUS waiting to speak with*' LUCULLUS '*from his master, enters a Servant to him*'

Servant. I have told my lord of you; he is coming down to you.

Flaminius. I thank you, sir.

'*Enter* LUCULLUS'

Servant. Here's my lord.

(*Lucullus.* One of Lord Timon's men? a gift, I warrant. Why, this hits right; I dreamt of a silver basin and ewer to-night. [*aloud*] Flaminius, honest Flaminius, you are very respectively welcome, sir. Fill me some wine. [*Servant goes*] And how does that honourable, complete, free-hearted gentleman of Athens, thy very 10 bountiful good lord and master?

Flaminius. His health is well, sir.

Lucullus. I am right glad that his health is well, sir. And what hast thou there under thy cloak, pretty Flaminius?

Flaminius. Faith, nothing but an empty box, sir, which in my lord's behalf I come to entreat your honour to supply; who, having great and instant occasion to use fifty talents, hath sent to your lordship to furnish him, nothing doubting your present assistance 20 therein.

Lucullus. La, la, la, la! 'Nothing doubting', says he? Alas, good lord! a noble gentleman 'tis, if he would not keep so good a house. Many a time and often I ha' dined with him, and told him on't, and come again to supper to him of purpose to have him spend less, and yet he would embrace no counsel, take no warning by

my coming. Every man has his fault, and honesty is his.
I ha' told him on't, but I could ne'er get him from't.

Re-enter 'Servant, with wine'

30 *Servant.* Please your lordship, here is the wine.
Lucullus. Flaminius, I have noted thee always wise.
Here's to thee.
Flaminius. Your lordship speaks your pleasure.
Lucullus. I have observed thee always for a towardly
prompt spirit, give thee thy due, and one that knows
what belongs to reason; and canst use the time well, if
the time use thee well. Good parts in thee. [*to Servant*]
Get you gone, sirrah. [*Servant goes*] Draw nearer,
honest Flaminius. Thy lord's a bountiful gentleman;
40 but thou art wise, and thou know'st well enough,
although thou com'st to me, that this is no time to lend
money, especially upon bare friendship without
security. Here's three solidares for thee. Good boy,
wink at me, and say thou saw'st me not. Fare thee
well.
    Flaminius. Is't possible the world should so
        much differ,
And we alive that lived? Fly, damnéd baseness,
To him that worships thee! [*throwing back the money*
    Lucullus. Ha! now I see thou art a fool, and fit for
50 thy master.   [*goes*
    Flaminius. May these add to the number that may
        scald thee!
Let molten coin be thy damnation,
Thou disease of a friend, and not himself!
Has friendship such a faint and milky heart,
It turns in less than two nights? O you gods,
I feel my master's passion! this slave,
Unto this hour, has my lord's meat in him;

Why should it thrive and turn to nutriment,
When he is turn'd to poison?
O, may diseases only work upon't!   60
And when he's sick to death, let not that part
     of nature
Which my lord paid for be of any power
To expel sickness, but prolong his hour!   [*goes*

[3. 2.]   *A public place*

'*Enter LUCIUS, with three Strangers*'

Lucius. Who, the Lord Timon? he is my very good
friend, and an honourable gentleman.

1 *Stranger.* We know him for no less, though we are
but strangers to him. But I can tell you one thing, my
lord, and which I hear from common rumours: now
Lord Timon's happy hours are done and past, and his
estate shrinks from him.

Lucius. Fie, no, do not believe it; he cannot want
for money.

2 *Stranger.* But believe you this, my lord, that not 10
long ago one of his men was with the Lord Lucullus to
borrow so many talents; nay, urged extremely for't,
and showed what necessity belonged to't, and yet was
denied.

Lucius. How?

2 *Stranger.* I tell you, denied, my lord.

Lucius. What a strange case was that! now, before
the gods, I am ashamed on't. Denied that honourable
man? there was very little honour showed in't. For
my own part, I must needs confess, I have received 20
some small kindnesses from him, as money, plate,
jewels, and such-like trifles, nothing comparing to his;

yet, had he mistook him and sent to me, I should ne'er have denied his occasion so many talents.

'*Enter SERVILIUS*'

Servilius. See, by good hap, yonder's my lord; I have sweat to see his honour. My honoured lord!

Lucius. Servilius? you are kindly met, sir. Fare thee well; commend me to thy honourable virtuous lord, my very exquisite friend.

30 *Servilius.* May it please your honour, my lord hath sent—

Lucius. Ha! what has he sent? I am so much endeared to that lord; he's ever sending. How shall I thank him, think'st thou? And what has he sent now?

Servilius. Has only sent his present occasion now, my lord; requesting your lordship to supply his instant use with so many talents.

Lucius. I know his lordship is but merry with me; He cannot want fifty five hundred talents.

40 *Servilius.* But in the mean time he wants less,
    my lord.
If his occasion were not virtuous,
I should not urge it half so faithfully.

Lucius. Dost thou speak seriously, Servilius?

Servilius. Upon my soul, 'tis true, sir.

Lucius. What a wicked beast was I to disfurnish myself against such a good time, when I might ha' shown myself honourable! how unluckily it happ'ned that I should purchase the day before †for a little part, and undo a great deal of honour! Servilius, now before 50 the gods, I am not able to do—the more beast, I say—I was sending to use Lord Timon myself, these gentlemen can witness; but I would not, for the wealth of Athens, I had done't now. Commend me bountifully to his

good lordship, and I hope his honour will conceive the
fairest of me, because I have no power to be kind.
And tell him this from me, I count it one of my
greatest afflictions, say, that I cannot pleasure such an
honourable gentleman. Good Servilius, will you be-
friend me so far as to use mine own words to him?

Servilius. Yes, sir, I shall.   60

Lucius. I'll look you out a good turn, Servilius.

                                         [*Servilius goes*

True, as you said, Timon is shrunk indeed,

And he that's once denied will hardly speed.   [*goes*

  1 *Stranger.* Do you observe this, Hostilius?

  2 *Stranger.*   Ay, too well.

  1 *Stranger.* Why, this is the world's soul; and just of
      the same piece

Is every flatterer's spirit. Who can call him his friend

That dips in the same dish? for, in my knowing,

Timon has been this lord's father,

And kept his credit with his purse;

Supported his estate; nay, Timon's money   70

Has paid his men their wages. He ne'er drinks

But Timon's silver treads upon his lip;

And yet—O, see the monstrousness of man

When he looks out in an ungrateful shape—

He does deny him, in respect of his,

What charitable men afford to beggars.

  3 *Stranger.* Religion groans at it.

  1 *Stranger.*   For mine own part,

I never tasted Timon in my life,

Nor came any of his bounties over me,

To mark me for his friend. Yet I protest,   80

For his right noble mind, illustrious virtue,

And honourable carriage,

Had his necessity made use of me,

I would have put my wealth into donation,
And the best half should have returned to him,
So much I love his heart. But I perceive,
Men must learn now with pity to dispense,
For policy sits above conscience.   [*they go*

[3. 3.]   *A room in Sempronius's house*

Enter SEMPRONIUS, *and a Servant of* TIMON'S

Sempronius. Must he needs trouble me in't—hum!
     —'bove all others?
He might have tried Lord Lucius or Lucullus;
And now Ventidius is wealthy too,
Whom he redeemed from prison. All these
Owe their estates unto him.
     Servant.   My lord,
They have all been touched and found base metal, for
They have all denied him.
     Sempronius.   How? have they denied him?
Has Ventidius and Lucullus denied him,
And does he send to me? Three? hum!
10 It shows but little love or judgement in him.
Must I be his last refuge? His friends, like physicians,
Thrice give him over: must I take th'cure upon me?
Has much disgraced me in't; I'm angry at him,
That might have known my place. I see no sense for't,
But his occasions might have wooed me first;
For, in my conscience, I was the first man
That e'er receivéd gift from him.
And does he think so backwardly of me now,
That I'll requite it last? No;
20 So it may prove an argument of laughter
To th'rest, and I 'mongst lords be thought a fool.

I'd rather than the worth of thrice the sum
Had sent to me first, but for my mind's sake;
I'd such a courage to do him good. But now return,
And with their faint reply this answer join:
Who bates mine honour shall not know my coin.

[goes

  Servant. Excellent. Your lordship's a goodly villain.
The devil knew not what he did when he made man
politic; he crossed himself by't; and I cannot think but
in the end the villainies of man will set him clear. How 30
fairly this lord strives to appear foul! takes virtuous
copies to be wicked; like those that under hot ardent
zeal would set whole realms on fire:
Of such a nature is his politic love.
This was my lord's best hope; now all are fled,
Save only the gods. Now his friends are dead,
Doors that were ne'er acquainted with their wards
Many a bounteous year must be employed
Now to guard sure their master.
And this is all a liberal course allows;   .40
Who cannot keep his wealth must keep his house.

[goes

[3. 4.]   *A hall in Timon's house*

*Enter two Servants of VARRO, and the Servant of LUCIUS,
meeting TITUS, HORTENSIUS, and other Servants of
Timon's creditors, waiting his coming out*

  1 *Varro's Servant.* Well met; good morrow, Titus
    and Hortensius.
  Titus. The like to you, kind Varro.
  Hortensius.   Lucius;
What, do we meet together?
  Lucius's Servant.   Ay, and I think

One business does command us all;
For mine is money.
    Titus.   So is theirs and ours.

             '*Enter* PHILOTUS'

Lucius's Servant. And Sir Philotus too!
Philotus.   Good day at once.
Lucius's Servant. Welcome, good brother. What
    do you think the hour?
Philotus. Labouring for nine.
Lucius's Servant. So much?
Philotus.   Is not my lord seen yet?
Lucius's Servant.   Not yet.
10 *Philotus.* I wonder on't; he was wont to shine
    at seven.
  Lucius's Servant. Ay, but the days are waxed
    shorter with him;
You must consider that a prodigal course
Is like the sun's, but not, like his, recoverable.
I fear
'Tis deepest winter in Lord Timon's purse;
That is,
One may reach deep enough and yet find little.
  Philotus. I am of your fear for that.
  Titus. I'll show you how t'observe a strange event.
20 Your lord sends now for money?
  Hortensius.   Most true, he does.
  Titus. And he wears jewels now of Timon's gift,
For which I wait for money.
  Hortensius. It is against my heart.
  Lucius's Servant.   Mark, how strange it shows
Timon in this should pay more than he owes;
And e'en as if your lord should wear rich jewels
And send for money for 'em.

1.2.144

Hortensius. I'm weary of this charge, the gods
    can witness;
I know my lord hath spent of Timon's wealth,
And now ingratitude makes it worse than stealth.
  1 *Varro's Servant.* Yes, mine's three thousand crowns;
    what's yours?   30
  Lucius's Servant. Five thousand mine.
  1 *Varro's Servant.* 'Tis much deep; and it should
    seem by th'sum
Your master's confidence was above mine,
Else, surely, his had equalled.

           '*Enter FLAMINIUS*'

Titus. One of Lord Timon's men.
  Lucius's Servant. Flaminius? Sir, a word. Pray,
is my lord ready to come forth?
  Flaminius. No, indeed he is not.
  Titus. We attend his lordship; pray signify so much.
  Flaminius. I need not tell him that; he knows you 40
are too diligent.   [*goes*

    '*Enter*' FLAVIUS '*in a cloak, muffled*'

Lucius's Servant. Ha, is not that his steward
    muffled so?
He goes away in a cloud. Call him, call him.
  Titus. Do you hear, sir?
  2 *Varro's Servant.* By your leave, sir.
  Flavius. What do ye ask of me, my friend?
  Titus. We wait for certain money here, sir.
  Flavius.   Ay,
If money were as certain as your waiting,
'Twere sure enough.
Why then preferred you not your sums and bills,   50
When your false masters ate of my lord's meat?

Then they could smile and fawn upon his debts,
And take down th'interest into their glutt'nous maws.
You do yourselves but wrong to stir me up;
Let me pass quietly.
Believe't, my lord and I have made an end;
I have no more to reckon, he to spend.
   Lucius's Servant. Ay, but this answer will
      not serve.
   Flavius. If 'twill not serve, 'tis not so base as you,
60 For you serve knaves.   [*goes*
   1 *Varro's Servant.* How? what does his cashiered
worship mutter?
   2 *Varro's Servant.* No matter what; he's poor, and
that's revenge enough. Who can speak broader than he
that has no house to put his head in? such may rail
against great buildings.

       '*Enter SERVILIUS*'

   Titus. O, here's Servilius; now we shall know some
answer.
   Servilius. If I might beseech you, gentlemen, to
70 repair some other hour, I should derive much from't;
for, take't of my soul, my lord leans wondrously to
discontent. His comfortable temper has forsook him;
he's much out of health and keeps his chamber.
   Lucius's Servant. Many do keep their chambers
      are not sick;
And if it be so far beyond his health,
Methinks he should the sooner pay his debts,
And make a clear way to the gods.
   Servilius.   Good gods!
   Titus. We cannot take this for an answer, sir.
   Flaminius ['*within*']. Servilius, help! My lord,
      my lord!

'*Enter TIMON, in a rage*', FLAMINIUS *following*

Timon. What, are my doors opposed against
    my passage? 80
Have I been ever free, and must my house
Be my retentive enemy, my gaol?
The place which I have feasted, does it now,
Like all mankind, show me an iron heart?

Lucius's Servant. Put in now, Titus.

Titus. My lord, here is my bill.

Lucius's Servant. Here's mine.

Hortensius. And mine, my lord.

Both Varro's Servants. And ours, my lord.

Philotus. All our bills. 90

Timon. Knock me down with 'em; cleave me to
    the girdle.

Lucius's Servant. Alas, my lord—

Timon. Cut my heart in sums.

Titus. Mine, fifty talents.

Timon. Tell out my blood.

Lucius's Servant. Five thousand crowns, my lord.

Timon. Five thousand drops pays that. What yours?
    and yours?

1 Varro's Servant. My lord—

2 Varro's Servant. My lord—

Timon. Tear me, take me, and the gods fall
    upon you! [*goes* 100

Hortensius. Faith, I perceive our masters may throw
their caps at their money; these debts may well be
called desperate ones, for a madman owes 'em. [*they go*

Re-enter TIMON *and* FLAVIUS

Timon. They have e'en put my breath from me,
    the slaves.

Creditors? devils!

Flavius. My dear lord—

Timon. What if it should be so?

Flavius. My lord—

Timon. I'll have it so. My steward!

110 *Flavius.* Here, my lord.

Timon. So fitly! Go, bid all my friends again,
Lucius, Lucullus, and Sempronius—all.
I'll once more feast the rascals.

  Flavius.   O my lord,
You only speak from your distracted soul;
There is not so much left, to furnish out
A moderate table.

  Timon.   Be it not in thy care;
Go,
I charge thee, invite them all: let in the tide
Of knaves once more; my cook and I'll provide.

                            [they go

[3. 5.]   *The Senate-house*

'*Enter three Senators*'; ALCIBIADES, *attended, at the door*

  1 *Senator.* My lord, you have my voice to't; the
      fault's bloody;
'Tis necessary he should die:
Nothing emboldens sin so much as mercy.

  2 *Senator.* Most true; the law shall bruise him.

        ALCIBIADES *is brought forward*

  Alcibiades. Honour, health, and compassion to
      the senate!

  1 *Senator.* Now, captain?

  Alcibiades. I am an humble suitor to your virtues;
For pity is the virtue of the law,

And none but tyrants use it cruelly.
It pleases time and fortune to lie heavy   10
Upon a friend of mine, who in hot blood
Hath stepped into the law, which is past depth
To those that without heed do plunge into't.
He is a man, setting this fault aside,
Of comely virtues;
Nor did he soil the fact with cowardice—
An honour in him which buys out his fault—
But with a noble fury and fair spirit,
Seeing his reputation touched to death,
He did oppose his foe;   20
And with such sober and unnoted passion
He did behove his anger, ere 'twas spent,
As if he had but proved an argument.

  1 *Senator.* You undergo too strict a paradox,
Striving to make an ugly deed look fair;
Your words have took such pains as if they laboured
To bring manslaughter into form, and set quarrelling
Upon the head of valour; which indeed
Is valour misbegot, and came into the world
When sects and factions were newly born.   30
He's truly valiant that can wisely suffer
The worst that man can breathe,
And make his wrongs his outsides,
To wear them like his raiment, carelessly,
And ne'er prefer his injuries to his heart,
To bring it into danger.
If wrongs be evils and enforce us kill,
What folly 'tis to hazard life for ill!

  Alcibiades. My lord—

  1 *Senator.*   You cannot make gross sins look clear:
To revenge is no valour, but to bear.   40

  Alcibiades. My lords, then, under favour, pardon me

If I speak like a captain.
Why do fond men expose themselves to battle,
And not endure all threats? sleep upòn't,
And let the foes quietly cut their throats,
Without repugnancy? If there be
Such valour in the bearing, what make we
Abroad? why then women are more valiant
That stay at home, if bearing carry it,
50 And the ass more captain than the lion,
The felon loaden with irons wiser than the judge,
If wisdom be in suffering. O my lords,
As you are great, be pitifully good.
Who cannot condemn rashness in cold blood?
To kill, I grant, is sin's extremest gust;
But in defence, by Mercy, 'tis most just.
To be in anger is impiety;
But who is man that is not angry?
Weigh but the crime with this.
60 *2 Senator.* You breathe in vain.
 Alcibiades.   In vain? His service done
At Lacedæmon and Byzantium
Were a sufficient briber for his life.
 1 Senator. What's that?
 Alcibiades.   Why, I say, my lords, has done
  fair service,
And slain in fight many of your enemies;
How full of valour did he bear himself
In the last conflict, and made plenteous wounds!
 2 Senator. He has made too much plenty with 'em.
He's a sworn rioter; he has a sin
That often drowns him and takes his valour prisoner.
70 If there were no foes, that were enough
To overcome him. In that beastly fury
He has been known to commit outrages

And cherish factions. 'Tis inferred to us,
His days are foul and his drink dangerous.

  1 Sen. He dies.

  Alcibiades.   Hard fate! he might have died in war.
My lords, if not for any parts in him—
Though his right arm might purchase his own time
And be in debt to none—yet, more to move you,
Take my deserts to his and join 'em both;
And, for I know   80
Your reverend ages love security,
I'll pawn my victories, all my honour to you,
Upon his good returns.
If by this crime he owes the law his life,
Why, let the war receive't in valiant gore,
For law is strict, and war is nothing more.

  1 Senator. We are for law: he dies; urge it no more,
On height of our displeasure. Friend or brother,
He forfeits his own blood that spills another.

  Alcibiades. Must it be so? it must not be. My lords, 90
I do beseech you, know me.

  2 Senator. How?

  Alcibiades. Call me to your remembrances.

  3 Senator. What?

  Alcibiades. I cannot think but your age has
      forgot me;
It could not else be I should prove so base
To sue and be denied such common grace.
My wounds ache at you.

  1 Senator.   Do you dare our anger?
'Tis in few words, but spacious in effect:
We banish thee for ever.

  Alcibiades.   Banish me?   100
Banish your dotage, banish usury,
That makes the senate ugly.

1 Senator. If, after two days' shine, Athens
    contain thee,
Attend our weightier judgement. And, not to swell
    our spirit,
He shall be executed presently.   [*Senators go*
  Alcibiades. Now the gods keep you old enough, that
    you may live
Only in bone, that none may look on you!
I'm worse than mad; I have kept back their foes,
While they have told their money and let out
110 Their coin upon large interest, I myself
Rich only in large hurts. All those for this?
Is this the balsam that the usuring senate
Pours into captains' wounds? Banishment!
It comes not ill; I hate not to be banished;
It is a cause worthy my spleen and fury,
That I may strike at Athens. I'll cheer up
My discontented troops, and lay for hearts.
'Tis honour with most lands to be at odds;
Soldiers should brook as little wrongs as gods.   [*goes*

n.b

[3. 6.]   *A banqueting-room in Timon's house*

Music. Tables set out; Servants attending. 'Enter divers'
  Lords, Senators and others, 'at several doors'

  1 Lord. The good time of day to you, sir.
  2 Lord. I also wish it to you. I think this honourable
lord did but try us this other day.
  1 Lord. Upon that were my thoughts tiring when
we encount'red. I hope it is not so low with him as he
made it seem in the trial of his several friends.
  2 Lord. It should not be, by the persuasion of his
new feasting.

1 Lord. I should think so. He hath sent me an earnest inviting, which many my near occasions did 10 urge me to put off; but he hath conjured me beyond them, and I must needs appear.

2 Lord. In like manner was I in debt to my importunate business, but he would not hear my excuse. I am sorry, when he sent to borrow of me, that my provision was out.

1 Lord. I am sick of that grief too, as I understand how all things go.

2 Lord. Every man here's so. What would he have borrowed of you? 20

1 Lord. A thousand pieces.

2 Lord. A thousand pieces?

1 Lord. What of you?

2 Lord. He sent to me, sir—Here he comes.

'*Enter* TIMON *and Attendants*'

Timon. With all my heart, gentlemen both; and how fare you?

1 Lord. Ever at the best, hearing well of your lordship.

2 Lord. The swallow follows not summer more willing than we your lordship.

(*Timon.* Nor more willingly leaves winter; such 30 summer birds are men. [*aloud*] Gentlemen, our dinner will not recompense this long stay; feast your ears with the music awhile, if they will fare so harshly o'th'trumpet's sound; we shall to't presently.

1 Lord. I hope it remains not unkindly with your lordship, that I returned you an empty messenger.

Timon. O, sir, let it not trouble you.

2 Lord. My noble lord,—

Timon. Ah, my good friend, what cheer?

2 Lord. My most honourable lord, I am e'en sick of 40

N.S.T.A.—7

shame that when your lordship this other day sent to me I was so unfortunate a beggar.

Timon. Think not on't, sir.

2 Lord. If you had sent but two hours before—

Timon. Let it not cumber your better remembrance. [*the banquet brought in*] Come, bring in all together.

2 Lord. All covered dishes.

1 Lord. Royal cheer, I warrant you.

3 Lord. Doubt not that, if money and the season can 50 yield it.

1 Lord. How do you? What's the news?

3 Lord. Alcibiades is banished. Hear you of it?

1 and 2 Lords. Alcibiades banished?

3 Lord. 'Tis so, be sure of it.

1 Lord. How? how?

2 Lord. I pray you, upon what?

Timon. My worthy friends, will you draw near?

3 Lord. I'll tell you more anon. Here's a noble feast toward.

60 *2 Lord.* This is the old man still.

3 Lord. Will't hold? will't hold?

2 Lord. It does; but time will—and so—

3 Lord. I do conceive.

Timon. Each man to his stool, with that spur as he would to the lip of his mistress; your diet shall be in all places alike. Make not a city feast of it, to let the meat cool ere we can agree upon the first place. Sit, sit. The gods require our thanks.

You great benefactors, sprinkle our society with 70 thankfulness. For your own gifts, make yourselves praised; but reserve still to give, lest your deities be despised. Lend to each man enough, that one need not lend to another; for, were your godheads to borrow of men, men would forsake the gods. Make the meat be

beloved more than the man that gives it. Let no
assembly of twenty be without a score of villains. If
there sit twelve women at the table, let a dozen of
them be—as they are. The rest of your fees, O gods—the
senators of Athens, together with the common lag of
people—what is amiss in them, you gods, make suitable 80
for destruction. For these my present friends, as they
are to me nothing, so in nothing bless them, and to
nothing are they welcome.
Uncover, dogs, and lap.

[*the dishes are uncovered and seen to be full of warm*
water and stones

'*Some speak.*' What does his lordship mean?
'*Some other.*' I know not.
Timon. May you a better feast never behold,
You knot of mouth-friends! smoke and lukewarm water
Is your perfection. This is Timon's last,
Who, stuck and spangled with your flatteries, 90
Washes it off, and sprinkles in your faces
Your reeking villainy. [*throwing the water in their faces*]
    Live loathed and long,
Most smiling, smooth, detested parasites,
Courteous destroyers, affable wolves, meek bears,
You fools of fortune, trencher-friends, time's flies,
Cap-and-knee slaves, vapours, and minute-jacks!
Of man and beast the infinite malady
Crust you quite o'er! What, dost thou go?
Soft, take thy physic first; thou too, and thou.
Stay, I will lend thee money, borrow none. 100
        [*throws the stones at them, and drives them out*
What, all in motion? Henceforth be no feast,
Whereat a villain's not a welcome guest.
Burn house! sink Athens! henceforth hated be
Of Timon man and all humanity!   [*goes*

Re-enter the Lords, Senators, etc.

1 *Lord.* How now, my lords!

2 *Lord.* Know you the quality of Lord Timon's fury?

3 *Lord.* Push! did you see my cap?

4 *Lord.* I have lost my gown.

110   1 *Lord.* He's but a mad lord, and nought but humours sways him. He gave me a jewel th'other day, and now he has beat it out of my hat. Did you see my jewel?

3 *Lord.* Did you see my cap?

2 *Lord.* Here 'tis.

4 *Lord.* Here lies my gown.

1 *Lord.* Let's make no stay.

2 *Lord.* Lord Timon's mad.

3 *Lord.*   I feel't upon my bones.

4 *Lord.* One day he gives us diamonds, next
    day stones.   [*they go*

[4. 1.]   *Without the walls of Athens*

'*Enter* TIMON'

Timon. Let me look back upon thee. O thou wall
That girdles in those wolves, dive in the earth,
And fence not Athens. Matrons, turn incontinent.
Obedience fail in children. Slaves and fools
Pluck the grave wrinkled senate from the bench,
And minister in their steads. To general filths
Convert o'th'instant, green virginity.
Do't in your parents' eyes. Bankrupts, hold fast;
Rather than render back, out with your knives,

And cut your trusters' throats. Bound servants, steal: 10
Large-handed robbers your grave masters are,
And pill by law. Maid, to thy master's bed:
Thy mistress is o'th'brothel. Son of sixteen,
Pluck the lined crutch from thy old limping sire,
With it beat out his brains. Piety and fear,
Religion to the gods, peace, justice, truth,
Domestic awe, night-rest, and neighbourhood,
Instruction, manners, mysteries and trades,
Degrees, observances, customs and laws,
Decline to your confounding contraries,   20
And yet confusion live. Plagues incident to men,
Your potent and infectious fevers heap
On Athens, ripe for stroke. Thou cold sciatica,
Cripple our senators, that their limbs may halt
As lamely as their manners. Lust and liberty
Creep in the minds and marrows of our youth,
That 'gainst the stream of virtue they may strive,
And drown themselves in riot. Itches, blains,
Sow all th'Athenian bosoms, and their crop
Be general leprosy! Breath infect breath,   30
That their society, as their friendship, may
Be merely poison! Nothing I'll bear from thee
But nakedness, thou detestable town;
Take thou that too, with multiplying bans.
Timon will to the woods, where he shall find
Th'unkindest beast more kinder than mankind.
The gods confound—hear me, you good gods all—
Th'Athenians both within and out that wall.
And grant, as Timon grows, his hate may grow
To the whole race of mankind, high and low.   40
Amen.   [goes

[4. 2.]   *Athens. Timon's house*

    '*Enter*' FLAVIUS, '*with two or three Servants*'

  1 *Servant*. Hear you, master steward, where's
        our master?
Are we undone? cast off? nothing remaining?
  Flavius. Alack, my fellows, what should I say to you?
Let me be recorded by the righteous gods,
I am as poor as you.
  1 *Servant*.   Such a house broke?
So noble a master fall'n; all gone, and not
One friend to take his fortune by the arm,
And go along with him?
  2 *Servant*.   As we do turn our backs
From our companion thrown into his grave,
10 So his familiars to his buried fortunes
Slink all away; leave their false vows with him,
Like empty purses picked; and his poor self,
A dedicated beggar to the air,
With his disease of all-shunned poverty,
Walks like contempt alone. More of our fellows.

            '*Enter other Servants*'

  Flavius. All broken implements of a ruined house.
  3 *Servant*. Yet do our hearts wear Timon's livery,
That see I by our faces; we are fellows still,
Serving alike in sorrow. Leaked is our bark,
20 And we, poor mates, stand on the dying deck,
Hearing the surges threat; we must all part
Into this sea of air.
  Flavius.   Good fellows all,
The latest of my wealth I'll share amongst you.
Wherever we shall meet, for Timon's sake

Let's yet be fellows; let's shake our heads, and say,
As 'twere a knell unto our master's fortunes,
'We have seen better days'. Let each take some.
Nay, put out all your hands. Not one word more:
Thus part we rich in sorrow, parting poor.

　　　　　　[*Servants 'embrace, and part several ways'*
O the fierce wretchedness that glory brings us!　　　30
Who would not wish to be from wealth exempt,
Since riches point to misery and contempt?
Who would be so mocked with glory, or to live
But in a dream of friendship,
To have his pomp and all what state compounds
But only painted, like his varnished friends?
Poor honest lord, brought low by his own heart,
Undone by goodness: strange, unusual blood,
When man's worst sin is, he does too much good.
Who then dares to be half so kind again?　　　40
For bounty, that makes gods, does still mar men.
My dearest lord, blest to be most accursed,
Rich only to be wretched, thy great fortunes
Are made thy chief afflictions. Alas, kind lord,
He's flung in rage from this ingrateful seat
Of monstrous friends;
Nor has he with him to supply his life,
Or that which can command it.
I'll follow, and inquire him out.
I'll ever serve his mind with my best will;　　　50
Whilst I have gold, I'll be his steward still.　　[*goes*

[4. 3.] *Woods and cave, near the sea-shore*

Enter TIMON, *from the cave*

Timon. O blessed breeding sun, draw from the earth
Rotten humidity; below thy sister's orb
Infect the air. Twinned brothers of one womb,
Whose procreation, residence, and birth,
Scarce is dividant, touch them with several fortunes,
The greater scorns the lesser. Not nature,
To whom all sores lay siege, can bear great fortune
But by contempt of nature.
Raise me this beggar and deject that lord,
10 The senator shall bear contempt hereditary,
The beggar native honour.
It is the pasture lards the wether's sides,
The want that makes him lean. Who dares, who dares,
In purity of manhood stand upright,
And say, 'This man's a flatterer'? If one be,
So are they all; for every grise of fortune
Is smoothed by that below. The learnéd pate
Ducks to the golden fool. All's obliquy;
There's nothing level in our curséd natures
20 But direct villainy. Therefore be abhorred
All feasts, societies and throngs of men.
His semblable, yea, himself, Timon disdains;
Destruction fang mankind. Earth, yield me roots.

[*digging*

Who seeks for better of thee, sauce his palate
With thy most operant poison. What is here?
Gold? yellow, glittering, precious gold?
No, gods, I am no idle votarist:
Roots, you clear heavens! thus much of this will make
Black white, foul fair, wrong right,

Base noble, old young, coward valiant.   30
Ha, you gods! why this? what this, you gods? Why, this
Will lug your priests and servants from your sides,
Pluck stout men's pillows from below their heads.
This yellow slave
Will knit and break religions; bless th'accursed;
Make the hoar leprosy adored; place thieves,
And give them title, knee and approbation
With senators on the bench. This is it
That makes the wappered widow wed again;
She whom the spital-house and ulcerous sores   40
Would cast the gorge at, this embalms and spices
To th'April day again. Come, damnéd earth,
Thou common whore of mankind, that puts odds
Among the rout of nations, I will make thee
Do thy right nature. ['*march afar off*'] Ha, a drum?
    Thou'rt quick,
But yet I'll bury thee. Thou'lt go, strong thief,
When gouty keepers of thee cannot stand.
Nay, stay thou out for earnest.   [*keeping some gold*

'*Enter* ALCIBIADES, *with drum and fife, in warlike
    manner; and* PHRYNIA *and* TIMANDRA'

Alcibiades.   What art thou there? speak.
Timon. A beast, as thou art. The canker gnaw thy heart
For showing me again the eyes of man!   50
    Alcibiades. What is thy name? Is man so hateful
    to thee,
That art thyself a man?
    Timon. I am Misanthropos, and hate mankind.
For thy part, I do wish thou wert a dog,
That I might love thee something.
    Alcibiades.   I know thee well;
But in thy fortunes am unlearned and strange.

Timon. I know thee too, and more than that I
    know thee
I not desire to know. Follow thy drum;
With man's blood paint the ground, gules, gules.
60 Religious canons, civil laws are cruel;
Then what should war be? This fell whore of thine
Hath in her more destruction than thy sword,
For all her cherubin look.
    Phrynia.   Thy lips rot off!
    Timon. I will not kiss thee; then the rot returns
To thine own lips again.
    Alcibiades. How came the noble Timon to
      this change?
    Timon. As the moon does, by wanting light to give.
But then renew I could not like the moon;
There were no suns to borrow of.
70 *Alcibiades.* Noble Timon, what friendship may I
      do thee?
    Timon. None, but to maintain my opinion.
    Alcibiades. What is it, Timon?
    Timon. Promise me friendship, but perform none.
If thou wilt not promise, the gods plague thee, for
thou art a man! If thou dost perform, confound thee,
for thou art a man!
    Alcibiades. I have heard in some sort of thy miseries.
    Timon. Thou saw'st them when I had prosperity.
    Alcibiades. I see them now; then was a blessed time.
80 *Timon.* As thine is now, held with a brace of harlots.
    Timandra. Is this th'Athenian minion whom the world
Voiced so regardfully?
    Timon.   Art thou Timandra?
    Timandra. Yes.
    Timon. Be a whore still; they love thee not that
      use thee;

Give them diseases, leaving with thee their lust.
Make use of thy salt hours. Season the slaves
For tubs and baths; bring down rose-cheeked youth
To the tub-fast and the diet.
  Timandra.   Hang thee, monster!
  Alcibiades. Pardon him, sweet Timandra, for
     his wits
Are drowned and lost in his calamities.   90
I have but little gold of late, brave Timon,
The want whereof doth daily make revolt
In my penurious band. I have heard, and grieved,
How cursèd Athens, mindless of thy worth,
Forgetting thy great deeds, when neighbour states,
But for thy sword and fortune, trod upon them—
  Timon. I prithee beat thy drum and get thee gone.
  Alcibiades. I am thy friend, and pity thee,
     dear Timon.
  Timon. How dost thou pity him whom thou
     dost trouble?
I had rather be alone.
  Alcibiades.   Why, fare thee well;   100
Here is some gold for thee.
  Timon.   Keep it, I cannot eat it.
  Alcibiades. When I have laid proud Athens on
     a heap—
  Timon. Warr'st thou 'gainst Athens?
  Alcibiades.   Ay, Timon, and have cause.
  Timon. The gods confound them all in thy conquest,
And thee after, when thou hast conquered!
  Alcibiades. Why me, Timon?
  Timon.   That by killing of villains
Thou wast born to conquer my country.
Put up thy gold. Go on, here's gold, go on;
Be as a planetary plague, when Jove

110 Will o'er some high-viced city hang his poison
In the sick air: let not thy sword skip one;
Pity not honoured age for his white beard;
He is an usurer. Strike me the counterfeit matron:
It is her habit only that is honest,
Herself's a bawd. Let not the virgin's cheek
Make soft thy trenchant sword; for those milk-paps
That through the window-bars bore at men's eyes
Are not within the leaf of pity writ,
But set them down horrible traitors. Spare not
    the babe
120 Whose dimpled smiles from fools exhaust their mercy;
Think it a bastard whom the oracle
Hath doubtfully pronounced thy throat shall cut,
And mince it sans remorse. Swear against objects;
Put armour on thine ears and on thine eyes,
Whose proof nor yells of mothers, maids, nor babes,
Nor sight of priests in holy vestments bleeding,
Shall pierce a jot. There's gold to pay thy soldiers;
Make large confusion; and, thy fury spent,
Confounded be thyself. Speak not, be gone.
130   *Alcibiades.* Hast thou gold yet? I'll take the gold
    thou givest me,
Not all thy counsel.
    Timon. Dost thou or dost thou not, heaven's curse
      upon thee!
    Phrynia and Timandra. Give us some gold, good
      Timon; hast thou more?
    Timon. Enough to make a whore forswear
      her trade,
And to make whores, a bawd. Hold up, you sluts,
Your aprons mountant; you are not oathable,
Although, I know, you'll swear, terribly swear,
Into strong shudders and to heavenly agues,

Th'immortal gods that hear you. Spare your oaths;
I'll trust to your conditions. Be whores still;   140
And he whose pious breath seeks to convert you,
Be strong in whore, allure him, burn him up;
Let your close fire predominate his smoke,
And be no turncoats. Yet may your pains six months
Be quite contrary: and thatch
Your poor thin roofs with burdens of the dead—
Some that were hanged, no matter:
Wear them, betray with them; whore still;
Paint till a horse may mire upon your face.
A pox of wrinkles!

   Phrynia and Timandra. Well, more gold.
      What then?   150
Believe't that we'll do any thing for gold.
   Timon. Consumptions sow
In hollow bones of man; strike their sharp shins,
And mar men's spurring. Crack the lawyer's voice,
That he may never more false title plead,
Nor sound his quillets shrilly. Hoar the flamen,
That scolds against the quality of flesh
And not believes himself. Down with the nose,
Down with it flat, take the bridge quite away
Of him that his particular to foresee   160
Smells from the general weal. Make curled-pate
    ruffians bald;
And let the unscarred braggarts of the war
Derive some pain from you. Plague all,
That your activity may defeat and quell
The source of all erection. There's more gold.
Do you damn others, and let this damn you,
And ditches grave you all!

   Phrynia and Timandra. More counsel with more
    money, bounteous Timon.

Timon. More whore, more mischief first; I have
    given you earnest.
170 *Alcibiades.* Strike up the drum towards Athens.
    Farewell, Timon;
If I thrive well, I'll visit thee again.
  Timon. If I hope well, I'll never see thee more.
  Alcibiades. I never did thee harm.
  Timon. Yes, thou spok'st well of me.
  Alcibiades.   Call'st thou that harm?
  Timon. Men daily find it. Get thee away, and take
Thy beagles with thee.
  Alcibiades.   We but offend him. Strike!
          [*Drum beats. Alcibiades, Phrynia,*
                       and Timandra go
  Timon. That nature, being sick of man's unkindness,
Should yet be hungry! Common mother, thou,
                         [*digging*
Whose womb unmeasurable and infinite breast
180 Teems, and feeds all; whose selfsame mettle,
Whereof thy proud child, arrogant man, is puffed,
Engenders the black toad and adder blue,
The gilded newt and eyeless venomed worm,
With all th'abhorréd births below crisp heaven
Whereon Hyperion's quick'ning fire doth shine;
Yield him, who all thy human sons doth hate,
From forth thy plenteous bosom, one poor root.
Ensear thy fertile and conceptious womb;
Let it no more bring out ingrateful man.
190 Go great with tigers, dragons, wolves and bears,
Teem with new monsters, whom thy upward face
Hath to the marbléd mansion all above
Never presented. O, a root, dear thanks!
Dry up thy marrows, vines and plough-torn leas,
Whereof ingrateful man with liquorish draughts

And morsels unctuous greases his pure mind,
That from it all consideration slips!

'*Enter APEMANTUS*'

More man? plague, plague!
Apemantus. I was directed hither. Men report
Thou dost affect my manners, and dost use them.   200
   Timon. 'Tis, then, because thou dost not keep a dog,
Whom I would imitate. Consumption catch thee!
   Apemantus. This is in thee a nature but infected,
A poor unmanly melancholy sprung
From change of fortune. Why this spade? this place?
This slave-like habit and these looks of care?
Thy flatterers yet wear silk, drink wine, lie soft,
Hug their diseased perfumes, and have forgot
That ever Timon was. Shame not these woods
By putting on the cunning of a carper.   210
Be thou a flatterer now, and seek to thrive
By that which has undone thee; hinge thy knee
And let his very breath whom thou'lt observe
Blow off thy cap; praise his most vicious strain
And call it excellent. Thou wast told thus;
Thou gav'st thine ears like tapsters that
        bade welcome
To knaves and all approachers. 'Tis most just
That thou turn rascal; hadst thou wealth again,
Rascals should have't. Do not assume my likeness.
   Timon. Were I like thee, I'ld throw away myself.   220
   Apemantus. Thou hast cast away thyself, being
        like thyself;
A madman so long, now a fool. What, think'st
That the bleak air, thy boisterous chamberlain,
Will put thy shirt on warm? will these mossed trees,
That have outlived the eagle, page thy heels,

And skip where thou point'st out? will the cold brook,
Candied with ice, caudle thy morning taste,
To cure thy o'ernight's surfeit? Call the creatures
Whose naked natures live in all the spite
230 Of wreakful heaven, whose bare unhouséd trunks,
To the conflicting elements exposed,
Answer mere nature; bid them flatter thee;
O, thou shalt find—
　　Timon.　　　　　A fool of thee. Depart.
　　Apemantus. I love thee better now than e'er I did.
　　Timon. I hate thee worse.
　　Apemantus.　　　　　Why?
　　Timon.　　　　　　　Thou flatter'st misery.
　　Apemantus. I flatter not, but say thou art a caitiff.
　　Timon. Why dost thou seek me out?
　　Apemantus.　　　　　　To vex thee.
　　Timon. Always a villain's office or a fool's.
Dost please thyself in't?
　　Apemantus.　　　Ay.
　　Timon.　　　　　What, a knave too?
240 *Apemantus.* If thou didst put this sour, cold habit on
To castigate thy pride, 'twere well; but thou
Dost it enforcedly. Thou'ldst courtier be again,
Wert thou not beggar. Willing misery
Outlives incertain pomp, is crowned before;
The one is filling still, never complete,
The other at high wish; best state, contentless,
Hath a distracted and most wretched being,
Worse than the worst, content.
Thou shouldst desire to die, being miserable.
250 *Timon.* Not by his breath that is more miserable.
Thou art a slave whom Fortune's tender arm
With favour never clasped, but bred a dog.
Hadst thou like us from our first swath proceeded

The sweet degrees that this brief world affords
To such as may the passive drugs of it
Freely command, thou wouldst have plunged thyself
In general riot, melted down thy youth
In different beds of lust, and never learned
The icy precepts of respect, but followed
The sug'red game before thee. But myself,   260
Who had the world as my confectionary,
The mouths, the tongues, the eyes and hearts of men
At duty, more than I could frame employment;
That numberless upon me stuck, as leaves
Do on the oak, have with one winter's brush
Fell from their boughs, and left me open, bare
For every storm that blows—I to bear this,
That never knew but better, is some burden.
Thy nature did commence in sufferance, time
Hath made thee hard in't. Why shouldst thou hate men? 270
They never flattered thee. What hast thou given?
If thou wilt curse, thy father, that poor rag,
Must be thy subject; who in spite put stuff
To some she-beggar and compounded thee
Poor rogue hereditary. Hence, be gone.
If thou hadst not been born the worst of men,
Thou hadst been a knave and flatterer.
  Apemantus. Art thou proud yet?
  Timon.   Ay, that I am not thee.
  Apemantus. I, that I was no prodigal.
  Timon. I, that I am one now.   280
Were all the wealth I have shut up in thee,
I'ld give thee leave to hang it. Get thee gone.
That the whole life of Athens were in this!
Thus would I eat it.   [*eating a root*
  Apemantus.   Here, I will mend thy feast.
                              [*offering him another*

Timon. First mend my company; take away thyself.

Apemantus. So I shall mend mine own, by th'lack
of thine.

Timon. 'Tis not well mended so, it is but botched;
If not, I would it were.

Apemantus. What wouldst thou have to Athens?

290 *Timon.* Thee thither in a whirlwind. If thou wilt,
Tell them there I have gold; look, so I have.

Apemantus. Here is no use for gold.

Timon. The best and truest;
For here it sleeps, and does no hiréd harm.

Apemantus. Where liest a-nights, Timon?

Timon. Under that's above me.
Where feed'st thou a-days, Apemantus?

Apemantus. Where my stomach finds meat; or, rather,
where I eat it.

Timon. Would poison were obedient, and knew my
300 mind!

Apemantus. Where wouldst thou send it?

Timon. To sauce thy dishes.

Apemantus. The middle of humanity thou never
knewest, but the extremity of both ends. When thou
wast in thy gilt and thy perfume, they mocked thee for
too much curiosity; in thy rags thou know'st none, but
art despised for the contrary. There's a medlar for
thee; eat it.

Timon. On what I hate I feed not.

310 *Apemantus.* Dost hate a medlar?

Timon. Ay, though it look like thee.

Apemantus. An thou'dst hated meddlers sooner, thou
shouldst have loved thyself better now. What man didst
thou ever know unthrift that was beloved after his means?

Timon. Who, without those means thou talk'st of,
didst thou ever know beloved?

Apemantus. Myself.

Timon. I understand thee; thou hadst some means to keep a dog.

Apemantus. What things in the world canst thou 320 nearest compare to thy flatterers?

Timon. Women nearest; but men—men are the things themselves. What wouldst thou do with the world, Apemantus, if it lay in thy power?

Apemantus. Give it the beasts, to be rid of the men.   *Swift*

Timon. Wouldst thou have thyself fall in the confusion of men, and remain a beast with the beasts?

Apemantus. Ay, Timon.

Timon. A beastly ambition, which the gods grant thee t'attain to! If thou wert the lion, the fox would beguile 330 thee; if thou wert the lamb, the fox would eat thee; if thou wert the fox, the lion would suspect thee when peradventure thou wert accused by the ass; if thou wert the ass, thy dulness would torment thee, and still thou livedst but as a breakfast to the wolf; if thou wert the wolf, thy greediness would afflict thee, and oft thou shouldst hazard thy life for thy dinner; wert thou the unicorn, pride and wrath would confound thee and make thine own self the conquest of thy fury; wert thou a bear, thou wouldst be killed by the horse; wert 340 thou a horse, thou wouldst be seized by the leopard; wert thou a leopard, thou wert german to the lion, and the spots of thy kindred were jurors on thy life; all thy safety were remotion, and thy defence absence. What beast couldst thou be that were not subject to a beast? and what a beast art thou already, that seest not thy loss in transformation!

Apemantus. If thou couldst please me with speaking to me, thou mightst have hit upon it here. The commonwealth of Athens is become a forest of beasts. 350

Timon. How has the ass broke the wall, that thou art out of the city?

Apemantus. Yonder comes a poet and a painter; the plague of company light upon thee! I will fear to catch it, and give way. When I know not what else to do, I'll see thee again.

Timon. When there is nothing living but thee, thou shalt be welcome. I had rather be a beggar's dog than Apemantus.

360 *Apemantus.* Thou art the cap of all the fools alive.

Timon. Would thou wert clean enough to spit upon!

Apemantus. A plague on thee! thou art too bad to curse.

Timon. All villains that do stand by thee are pure.

Apemantus. There is no leprosy but what thou speak'st.

Timon. If I name thee.

I'ld beat thee, but I should infect my hands.

Apemantus. I would my tongue could rot them off.

Timon. Away, thou issue of a mangy dog!

Choler does kill me that thou art alive;

370 I swoon to see thee.

Apemantus. Would thou wouldst burst!

Timon.   Away, thou tedious rogue!

I am sorry I shall lose a stone by thee.

                              [*throws a stone at him*

Apemantus. Beast!

Timon. Slave!

Apemantus. Toad!

Timon. Rogue, rogue, rogue!

I am sick of this false world, and will love nought

But even the mere necessities upon't.

Then, Timon, presently prepare thy grave;

380 Lie where the light foam of the sea may beat

Thy grave-stone daily; make thine epitaph,
That death in me at others' lives may laugh.
[*To the gold*] O thou sweet king-killer, and dear divorce
'Twixt natural son and sire, thou bright defiler
Of Hymen's purest bed, thou valiant Mars,
Thou ever young, fresh, loved, and delicate wooer,
Whose blush doth thaw the consecrated snow
That lies on Dian's lap, thou visible god,
That sold'rest close impossibilities,
And mak'st them kiss; that speak'st with every tongue, 390
To every purpose! O thou touch of hearts!
Think thy slave man rebels; and by thy virtue
Set them into confounding odds, that beasts
May have the world in empire.

Apemantus.   Would 'twere so,
But not till I am dead. I'll say thou'st gold.
Thou wilt be thronged to shortly.

Timon.   Thronged to?

Apemantus.   Ay.

Timon. Thy back, I prithee.

Apemantus.   Live, and love thy misery.

Timon. Long live so, and so die. [*Apemantus goes*] I
    am quit.
Moe things like men? Eat, Timon, and abhor them.

Enter three Bandits

1 *Bandit.* Where should he have this gold? It is some 400
poor fragment, some slender ort of his remainder. The
mere want of gold, and the falling-from of his friends,
drove him into this melancholy.

2 *Bandit.* It is noised he hath a mass of treasure.

3 *Bandit.* Let us make the assay upon him; if he care
not for't, he will supply us easily; if he covetously
reserve it, how shall's get it?

2 Bandit. True; for he bears it not about him; 'tis hid.

1 Bandit. Is not this he?

410 *3 Bandit.* Where?

2 Bandit. 'Tis his description.

3 Bandit. He? I know him.

Bandits. Save thee, Timon.

Timon. Now, thieves?

Bandits. Soldiers, not thieves.

Timon. Both two, and women's sons.

Bandits. We are not thieves, but men that much
    do want.

Timon. Your greatest want is, you want much of meat.
Why should you want? Behold, the earth hath roots;
420 Within this mile break forth a hundred springs;
The oaks bear mast, the briers scarlet hips;
The bounteous housewife Nature on each bush
Lays her full mess before you. Want? why want?

1 Bandit. We cannot live on grass, on berries, water,
As beasts and birds and fishes.

Timon. Nor on the beasts themselves, the birds
    and fishes;
You must eat men. Yet thanks I must you con
That you are thieves professed, that you work not
In holier shapes; for there is boundless theft
430 In limited professions. Rascal thieves,
Here's gold. Go, suck the subtle blood o'th'grape,
Till the high fever seethe your blood to froth,
And so 'scape hanging. Trust not the physician;
His antidotes are poison, and he slays
Moe than you rob, takes wealth and lives together.
Do villainy, do, since you protest to do't,
Like workmen. I'll example you with thievery:
The sun's a thief, and with his great attraction
Robs the vast sea; the moon's an arrant thief,

And her pale fire she snatches from the sun;   440
The sea's a thief, whose liquid surge resolves
The moon into salt tears; the earth's a thief,
That feeds and breeds by a composture stol'n
From gen'ral excrement—each thing's a thief.
The laws, your curb and whip, in their rough power
Has unchecked theft. Love not yourselves; away,
Rob one another. There's more gold. Cut throats;
All that you meet are thieves; to Athens go,
Break open shops; nothing can you steal,
But thieves do lose it; steal less for this I give you,   450
And gold confound you howsoe'er. Amen.

  3 *Bandit.* Has almost charmed me from my profession by persuading me to it.

  1 *Bandit.* 'Tis in the malice of mankind that he thus advises us, not to have us thrive in our mystery.

  2 *Bandit.* I'll believe him as an enemy, and give over my trade.

  1 *Bandit.* Let us first see peace in Athens; there is no time so miserable but a man may be true.   [*Bandits go*

Enter FLAVIUS

Flavius. O you gods!   460
Is yond despised and ruinous man my lord?
Full of decay and failing? O monument
And wonder of good deeds evilly bestowed!
What an alteration of honour has desp'rate
    · want made!
What viler thing upon the earth than friends,
Who can bring noblest minds to basest ends!
How rarely does it meet with this time's guise,
When man was wished to love his enemies!
Grant I may ever love, and rather woo
Those that would mischief me than those that do!   470

Has caught me in his eye;
I will present my honest grief unto him,
And as my lord still serve him with my life.
My dearest master!
  Timon. Away! what art thou?
  Flavius.   Have you forgot me, sir?
  Timon. Why dost ask that? I have forgot all men.
Then, if thou grant'st thou'rt a man, I have forgot thee.
  Flavius. An honest poor servant of yours.
  Timon. Then I know thee not;
480 I never had honest man about me, I; all
I kept were knaves, to serve in meat to villains.
  Flavius. The gods are witness,
Ne'er did poor steward wear a truer grief
For his undone lord than mine eyes for you.
  Timon. What, dost thou weep? come nearer; then I
    love thee,
Because thou art a woman, and disclaim'st
Flinty mankind, whose eyes do never give
But thorough lust and laughter. Pity's sleeping.
Strange times, that weep with laughing, not
    with weeping!
490 *Flavius.* I beg of you to know me, good my lord,
T'accept my grief, and whilst this poor wealth lasts
To entertain me as your steward still.
  Timon. Had I a steward
So true, so just, and now so comfortable?
It almost turns my dangerous nature mild.
Let me behold thy face. Surely this man
Was born of woman.
Forgive my general and exceptless rashness,
You perpetual-sober gods! I do proclaim
500 One honest man—mistake me not, but one;
No more, I pray—and he's a steward.

How fain would I have hated all mankind,
And thou redeem'st thyself. But all save thee
I fell with curses.
Methinks thou art more honest now than wise;
For, by oppressing and betraying me,
Thou mightst have sooner got another service;
For many so arrive at second masters,
Upon their first lord's neck. But tell me true—
For I must ever doubt, though ne'er so sure—　　510
Is not thy kindness subtle-covetous,
A usuring kindness, as rich men deal gifts,
Expecting in return twenty for one?
　Flavius. No, my most worthy master, in
　　　whose breast
Doubt and suspect, alas, are placed too late.
You should have feared false times when you
　　　did feast:
Suspect still comes where an estate is least.
That which I show, heaven knows, is merely love,
Duty and zeal to your unmatchéd mind,
Care of your food and living; and believe it,　　520
My most honoured lord,
For any benefit that points to me,
Either in hope or present, I'ld exchange
For this one wish, that you had power and wealth
To requite me by making rich yourself.
　Timon. Look thee, 'tis so. Thou singly honest man,
Here, take. The gods, out of my misery,
Have sent thee treasure. Go, live rich and happy,
But thus conditioned: thou shalt build from men,
Hate all, curse all, show charity to none,　　530
But let the famished flesh slide from the bone
Ere thou relieve the beggar. Give to dogs
What thou deniest to men. Let prisons swallow 'em,

Debts wither 'em to nothing; be men like
    blasted woods,
And may diseases lick up their false bloods!
And so farewell, and thrive.
  Flavius. O, let me stay and comfort you, my master.
  Timon. If thou hat'st curses
Stay not; fly, whilst thou art blest and free;
540 Ne'er see thou man, and let me ne'er see thee.

                             [they depart severally

[5. 1.]   *The woods. Before Timon's cave*

   '*Enter Poet and Painter*'; TIMON *listens from*
             his cave, unseen

  Painter. As I took note of the place, it cannot be far
where he abides.
  Poet. What's to be thought of him? does the rumour
hold for true, that he's so full of gold?
  Painter. Certain. Alcibiades reports it; Phrynia and
Timandra had gold of him. He likewise enriched poor
straggling soldiers with great quantity. 'Tis said he
gave unto his steward a mighty sum.
  Poet. Then this breaking of his has been but a try for
10 his friends.
  Painter. Nothing else. You shall see him a palm in
Athens again, and flourish with the highest. Therefore
'tis not amiss we tender our loves to him in this supposed distress of his; it will show honestly in us, and is
very likely to load our purposes with what they travail
for, if it be a just and true report that goes of his having.
  Poet. What have you now to present unto him?
  Painter. Nothing at this time but my visitation; only
I will promise him an excellent piece.

Poet. I must serve him so too, tell him of an intent 20
that's coming toward him.

Painter. Good as the best. Promising is the very air
o'th'time; it opens the eyes of expectation. Performance is ever the duller for his act, and but in the
plainer and simpler kind of people the deed of saying is
quite out of use. To promise is most courtly and
fashionable; performance is a kind of will or testament
which argues a great sickness in his judgement that
makes it.

(*Timon.* Excellent workman! thou canst not paint 30
a man so bad as is thyself.

Poet. I am thinking what I shall say I have provided
for him. It must be a personating of himself; a satire
against the softness of prosperity, with a discovery of the
infinite flatteries that follow youth and opulency.

(*Timon.* Must thou needs stand for a villain in thine
own work? wilt thou whip thine own faults in other
men? Do so, I have gold for thee.

Poet. Nay, let's seek him.
Then do we sin against our own estate,   40
When we may profit meet, and come too-late.

Painter. True.
When the day serves, before black-cornered night,
Find what thou want'st by free and offered light.
Come.

(*Timon.* I'll meet you at the turn. What a god's gold,
That he is worshipped in a baser temple
Than where swine feed!
'Tis thou that rigg'st the bark and plough'st the foam,
Settlest admiréd reverence in a slave.   50
To thee be worship, and thy saints for aye
Be crowned with plagues, that thee alone obey!
Fit I meet them.   [*coming forward*

Poet. Hail, worthy Timon!

Painter.   Our late noble master!

Timon. Have I once lived to see two honest men?

Poet. Sir,
Having often of your open bounty tasted,
Hearing you were retired, your friends fall'n off,
Whose thankless natures—O abhorréd spirits!—
60 Not all the whips of heaven are large enough—
What, to you,
Whose star-like nobleness gave life and influence
To their whole being! I am rapt, and cannot cover
The monstrous bulk of this ingratitude
With any size of words.

  Timon. Let it go naked, men may see't the better.
You that are honest, by being what you are,
Make them best seen and known.

    Painter.   He and myself
Have travelled in the great shower of your gifts,
70 And sweetly felt it.

    Timon.   Ay, you are honest men.

    Painter. We are hither come to offer you
      our service.

    Timon. Most honest men. Why, how shall I
      requite you?
Can you eat roots, and drink cold water? no?

  Both. What we can do, we'll do, to do you service.

  Timon. Ye're honest men: ye've heard that I
      have gold;
I am sure you have. Speak truth; ye're honest men.

  Painter. So it is said, my noble lord, but therefore
Came not my friend nor I.

    Timon. Good honest men. Thou draw'st a counterfeit
80 Best in all Athens; thou'rt indeed the best;
Thou counterfeit'st most lively.

Painter.   So so, my lord.
Timon. E'en so, sir, as I say. And for thy fiction,
Why, thy verse swells with stuff so fine and smooth
That thou art even natural in thine art.
But for all this, my honest-natured friends,
I must needs say you have a little fault;
Marry, 'tis not monstrous in you, neither wish I
You take much pains to mend.
Both.   Beseech your honour
To make it known to us.
Timon.   You'll take it ill.
Both. Most thankfully, my lord.
Timon.   Will you indeed?   90
Both. Doubt it not, worthy lord.
Timon. There's never a one of you but trusts
      a knave
That mightily deceives you.
Both.   Do we, my lord?
Timon. Ay, and you hear him cog, see
      him dissemble,
Know his gross patchery, love him, feed him,
Keep in your bosom; yet remain assured
That he's a made-up villain.
Painter. I know none such, my lord.
Poet.   Nor I.
Timon. Look you, I love you well; I'll give
      you gold,
Rid me these villains from your companies.   100
Hang them or stab them, drown them in a draught,
Confound them by some course, and come to me,
I'll give you gold enough.
Both. Name them, my lord, let's know them.
Timon. You that way, and you this—but two
      in company—

Each man apart, all single and alone,
Yet an arch-villain keeps him company.
If, where thou art, two villains shall not be,
Come not near him. If thou wouldst not reside
110 But where one villain is, then him abandon.
Hence, pack, there's gold; you came for gold,
        ye slaves.
[*to Painter*] You have work for me; there's
        payment. Hence!
[*to Poet*] You are an alchemist, make gold of that.
Out, rascal dogs!   [*he beats them out, and retires into
                                    his cave*

'*Enter*' FLAVIUS '*and two Senators*'

Flavius. It is in vain that you would speak
        with Timon;
For he is set so only to himself
That nothing but himself which looks like man
Is friendly with him.
    1 *Senator*.   Bring us to his cave:
It is our part and promise to th'Athenians
120 To speak with Timon.
    2 *Senator*.   At all times alike
Men are not still the same; 'twas time and griefs
That framed him thus. Time, with his fairer hand,
Offering the fortunes of his former days,
The former man may make him. Bring us to him,
And chance it as it may.
    Flavius.   Here is his cave.
Peace and content be here! Lord Timon, Timon,
Look out, and speak to friends. Th'Athenians
By two of their most reverend senate greet thee.
Speak to them, noble Timon.

        TIMON comes from his cave

Timon. Thou sun, that comforts, burn! Speak and
      be hanged.   130
For each true word a blister, and each false
Be as a cantherizing to the root o'th'tongue,
Consuming it with speaking!
  1 *Senator.*   Worthy Timon—
  Timon. Of none but such as you, and you of Timon.
  1 *Senator.* The senators of Athens greet thee, Timon.
  Timon. I thank them, and would send them back
      the plague,
Could I but catch it for them.
  1 *Senator.*   O, forget
What we are sorry for ourselves in thee.
The senators with one consent of love
Entreat thee back to Athens, who have thought   140
On special dignities, which vacant lie
For thy best use and wearing.
  2 *Senator.*   They confess
Toward thee forgetfulness too general-gross;
Which now the public body, which doth seldom
Play the recanter, feeling in itself
A lack of Timon's aid, hath sense withal
Of it own fail, restraining aid to Timon;
And send forth us, to make their sorrowéd render,
Together with a recompense more fruitful
Than their offence can weigh down by the dram;   150
Ay, even such heaps and sums of love and wealth
As shall to thee blot out what wrongs were theirs,
And write in thee the figures of their love,
Ever to read them thine.
  Timon.   You witch me in it;
Surprise me to the very brink of tears.
Lend me a fool's heart and a woman's eyes,
And I'll beweep these comforts, worthy senators.

1 *Senator.* Therefore so please thee to return
   with us,
And of our Athens, thine and ours, to take
160 The captainship, thou shalt be met with thanks,
Allowed with absolute power, and thy good name
Live with authority: so soon we shall drive back
Of Alcibiades th'approaches wild,
Who like a boar too savage doth root up
His country's peace.

   2 *Senator.*   And shakes his threat'ning sword
Against the walls of Athens.

   1 *Senator.*   Therefore, Timon—

   Timon. Well, sir, I will—therefore I will, sir, thus:
If Alcibiades kill my countrymen,
Let Alcibiades know this of Timon,
170 That Timon cares not. But if he sack fair Athens,
And take our goodly agéd men by th'beards,
Giving our holy virgins to the stain
Of contumelious, beastly, mad-brained war;
Then let him know, and tell him Timon speaks it,
In pity of our agéd and our youth,
I cannot choose but tell him that I care not,
And let him take't at worst; for their knives care not,
While you have throats to answer; for myself,
There's not a whittle in th'unruly camp
180 But I do prize it at my love before
The reverend'st throat in Athens. So I leave you
To the protection of the prosperous gods,
As thieves to keepers.

   Flavius.   Stay not, all's in vain.

   Timon. Why, I was writing of my epitaph;
It will be seen to-morrow. My long sickness
Of health and living now begins to mend,
And nothing brings me all things. Go, live still;

Be Alcibiades your plague, you his,
And last so long enough!

  1 *Senator.*   We speak in vain.

  Timon. But yet I love my country, and am not   **190**
One that rejoices in the common wreck,
As common bruit doth put it.

  1 *Senator.*   That's well spoke.

  Timon. Commend me to my loving countrymen—

  1 *Senator.* These words become your lips as they pass
     through them.

  2 *Senator.* And enter in our ears like great triumphers
In their applauding gates.

  Timon.   Commend me to them,
And tell them that, to ease them of their griefs,
Their fears of hostile strokes, their achës, losses,
Their pangs of love, with other incident throes
That nature's fragile vessel doth sustain   **200**
In life's uncertain voyage, I will some kindness
     do them;
I'll teach them to prevent wild Alcibiades' wrath.

  1 *Senator.* I like this well; he will return again.

  Timon. I have a tree, which grows here in my close,
That mine own use invites me to cut down,
And shortly must I fell it. Tell my friends,
Tell Athens, in the sequence of degree
From high to low throughout, that whoso please
To stop affliction, let him take his haste,
Come hither ere my tree hath felt the axe,   **210**
And hang himself. I pray you do my greeting.

  Flavius. Trouble him no further; thus you still shall
     find him.

  Timon. Come not to me again, but say to Athens,
Timon hath made his everlasting mansion
Upon the beachéd verge of the salt flood,

Who once a day with his embosséd froth
The turbulent surge shall cover; thither come,
And let my grave-stone be your oracle.
Lips, let four words go by, and language end:
220 What is amiss, plague and infection mend!
Graves only be men's works, and death their gain!
Sun, hide thy beams; Timon hath done his reign.

                                              [retires to his cave

  1 *Senator.* His discontents are unremovably
Coupled to nature.
  2 *Senator.* Our hope in him is dead. Let us return,
And strain what other means is left unto us
In our dear peril.
  1 *Senator.*   It requires swift foot.   *[they go*

[5. 2.]   *Before the walls of Athens*

    '*Enter two other Senators, with a Messenger*'

  3 *Senator.* Thou hast painfully discovered; are his files
As full as thy report?
  Messenger.   I have spoke the least.
Besides, his expedition promises
Present approach.
  4 *Senator.* We stand much hazard if they bring
    not Timon.
  Messenger. I met a courier, one mine ancient friend,
Whom, though in general part we were opposed,
Yet our old love made a particular force,
And made us speak like friends. This man was riding
10 From Alcibiades to Timon's cave
With letters of entreaty, which imported
His fellowship i'th'cause against your city,
In part for his sake moved.

3 *Senator.*   Here come our brothers.

'Enter the other Senators' from TIMON.

1 *Senator.* No talk of Timon, nothing of him expect.
The enemy's drum is heard, and fearful scouring
Doth choke the air with dust: in, and prepare.
Ours is the fall, I fear, our foe's the snare.   [*they go*

[5. 3.] *The woods. Timon's cave, and a rude tomb seen*

'Enter a Soldier, seeking TIMON*'*

Soldier. By all description this should be the place.
Who's here? speak, ho! No answer? What is this?
[*reads*] 'Timon is dead, who hath outstretched his span;
Some beast read this; there does not live a man.'
Dead, sure, and this his grave. What's on this tomb
I cannot read; the character I'll take with wax;
Our captain hath in every figure skill,
An aged interpreter, though young in days;
Before proud Athens he's set down by this,
Whose fall the mark of his ambition is.   [*he goes* 10

[5. 4.]   *Before the walls of Athens*

'Trumpets sound. Enter ALCIBIADES *with his powers'*

Alcibiades. Sound to this coward and lascivious town
Our terrible approach.   [*'sounds a parley'*

'The Senators appear upon the walls'

Till now you have gone on and filled the time
With all licentious measure, making your wills
The scope of justice. Till now, myself and such

As stepped within the shadow of your power
Have wandered with our traversed arms and breathed
Our sufferance vainly; now the time is flush,
When crouching marrow in the bearer strong
10 Cries of itself 'No more'; now breathless wrong
Shall sit and pant in your great chairs of ease,
And pursy insolence shall break his wind
With fear and horrid flight.

   1 *Senator.*   Noble and young,
When thy first griefs were but a mere conceit,
Ere thou hadst power or we had cause of fear,
We sent to thee, to give thy rages balm,
To wipe out our ingratitude with loves
Above their quantity.

   2 *Senator.*   So did we woo
Transforméd Timon to our city's love
20 By humble message and by promised means;
We were not all unkind, nor all deserve
The common stroke of war.

   1 *Senator.*   These walls of ours
Were not erected by their hands from whom
You have received your griefs; nor are they such
That these great towers, trophies, and schools should fall
For private faults in them.

   2 *Senator.*   Nor are they living
Who were the motives that you first went out;
Shame, that they wanted cunning, in excess
Hath broke their hearts. March, noble lord,
30 Into our city with thy banners spread;
By decimation and a tithéd death,
If thy revenges hunger for that food
Which nature loathes, take thou the destined tenth,
And by the hazard of the spotted die
Let die the spotted.

1 *Senator.*   All have not offended;
For those that were, it is not square to take,
On those that are, revenges; crimes like lands
Are not inherited. Then, dear countryman,
Bring in thy ranks, but leave without thy rage;
Spare thy Athenian cradle and those kin   40
Which, in the bluster of thy wrath, must fall
With those that have offended. Like a shepherd
Approach the fold and cull th'infected forth,
But kill not all together.

2 *Senator.*   What thou wilt,
Thou rather shalt enforce it with thy smile
Than hew to't with thy sword.

1 *Senator.*   Set but thy foot
Against our rampired gates, and they shall ope;
So thou wilt send thy gentle heart before,
To say thou'lt enter friendly.

2 *Senator.*   Throw thy glove,
Or any token of thine honour else,   50
That thou wilt use the wars as thy redress
And not as our confusion, all thy powers
Shall make their harbour in our town, till we
Have sealed thy full desire.

Alcibiades.   Then there's my glove;
Descend, and open your unchargéd ports;
Those enemies of Timon's, and mine own,
Whom you yourselves shall set out for reproof,
Fall, and no more; and, to atone your fears
With my more noble meaning, not a man
Shall pass his quarter, or offend the stream   60
Of regular justice in your city's bounds,
But shall be rendered to your public laws
At heaviest answer.

Both.   'Tis most nobly spoken.

Alcibiades. Descend, and keep your words.
> [*the Senators descend, and open the gates*

Enter Soldier

Soldier. My noble general, Timon is dead,
Entombed upon the very hem o'th'sea,
And on his grave-stone this insculpture, which
With wax I brought away, whose soft impression
Interprets for my poor ignorance.

70　*Alcibiades* [*reads*]. 'Here lies a wretched corse, of
　　　wretched soul bereft;
Seek not my name: a plague consume you wicked
　　　caitiffs left!
Here lie I, Timon, who alive all living men did hate;
Pass by and curse thy fill, but pass, and stay not here
　　　thy gait.'
These well express in thee thy latter spirits.
Though thou abhorredst in us our human griefs,
Scornedst our brain's flow, and those our
　　　droplets which
From niggard nature fall, yet rich conceit
Taught thee to make vast Neptune weep for aye
On thy low grave, on faults forgiven. Dead
80　Is noble Timon, of whose memory
Hereafter more. Bring me into your city,
And I will use the olive with my sword,
Make war breed peace, make peace stint war,
　　　make each
Prescribe to other, as each other's leech.
Let our drums strike.　　　　　　　　　　[*they go*

THE COPY FOR
TIMON OF ATHENS, 1623

The bibliographical facts of the printing of *Timon* in the Folio show that it was not originally intended to occupy its present position—perhaps not to be printed at all. It occupies the space left by the withdrawal, as a result of copyright difficulties, of *Troilus and Cressida*, and even with the addition of the list of 'Actors Names' on a separate page with blank verso, there is a gap in the signatures between hh 6 and kk, and in the pagination between 98 and 109.[1]

In the Introduction, I have given reasons for accepting what is now the orthodox view that the source of the Folio *Timon* is Shakespeare's incomplete draft. Whether such a draft was actually the printer's copy, it is not so easy to be sure. Recent scholars have generally believed that it was, notably Sir Walter Greg, who has 'no doubt that F was printed from foul papers that had never been reduced to anything like order'.[2] But Professor Fredson Bowers in *On Editing Shakespeare and the Elizabethan Dramatists* (1955) has attacked the tendency to assume 'foul papers' copy too readily, and writes of certain 'finer-grained evidence' used by the late Philip Williams: 'When on such evidence Dr Williams can confidently pronounce the *Timon of Athens* printer's copy to have been scribal rather than

[1] W. W. Greg, *The Shakespeare First Folio* (1955), pp. 445–6. The facts about *Timon* were first correctly set out, apart from a few details for which see Greg, pp. 464–5, by J. Q. Adams, *Journal of English and Germanic Philology*, VII (1907–8), i, 53–63.

[2] *The Shakespeare First Folio*, p. 411.

unfinished author's foul papers, as conjectured by Greg, chaos has come again in the question of Shakespearian printer's copy'.[1] Unfortunately, although in his last pronouncement on the subject Dr Williams refers to 'my belief that [*Timon*] was set from a fair transcript made by the same scribe who prepared the manuscript from which the folio text of *Coriolanus* was set',[2] he does not produce his evidence. The mere fact that such an acute scholar held this view is important, but all I can do is to record my own failure to discover anything that helps to decide the question.

If what lies behind the Folio text, either immediately or with a transcript intervening, is a rough draft, there is little that need surprise us in that text. The compositor is the notoriously peccant B,[3] and he has certainly contributed his quota of errors, but the general impression is of an honest and fairly successful attempt to reproduce what must have been a very difficult copy, even if a transcriber has shouldered some of the burden (and fallen into some of the pitfalls) of deciphering it.

The more puzzling anomalies and loose ends of the action obviously go back to the copy; one of the most interesting, the treatment of sums reckoned in talents, calls for separate discussion, which it will receive at the end of this note. As in some of the completed plays,[4] there are a few places where the Folio text is most readily explained as reproducing false starts or alternative versions that Shakespeare failed to cancel (I. 2.

[1] P. 110; 'unfinished' can scarcely, as it seems to do, attribute to Dr Williams the view that Shakespeare's draft was *not* unfinished.

[2] *Studies in Bibliography*, VIII (1956), 6.

[3] See Alice Walker, *Textual Problems of the First Folio* (1953), pp. 11–12.

[4] See, e.g., *Romeo and Juliet*, p. 113 in this edition

95–7; 2. 2. 42; 4. 3. 31, 512; 5. 4. 70–3). There is
a fair, but not an immoderate, sprinkling of literal
errors, among which those involving *n:u* and *r:t* as
usual predominate. The play is not particularly rich in
what are often (perhaps over-confidently) described as
'Shakespearian' spellings, but there are some anomalies
that seem to go back to Shakespeare. Two proper
names furnish the most interesting examples. Besides
the normal spelling *Ventidius*, we find *Ventigius, Ventidgius* and *Ventiddius*, each consistently used in a
separate scene. The variation between *Ventidius* and
Ventigius also occurs in *Antony and Cleopatra*, with
Ventigius similarly confined to a single scene. Shakespeare has evidently followed the whim of the moment
—the *g* and *dg*[1] spellings are phonetic—and neither
transcriber (if any) nor compositor has made any
attempt to correct him. The other significantly varying
name is *Apemantus*, which frequently appears as *Apermantus* in Acts 1–2. This spelling also occurs in Thomas
Lodge's *Wits Miserie* (1596), p. 100. The distribution
suggests that here, in contrast to the case of *Ventidius*,
an attempt was being made to normalize—as it might
well be, since the *r* is intrusive and anomalous. The
bibliographical incidence of the two spellings is rather
puzzling. Up to the end of gg 3 (1. 2. 252), the variations correspond exactly to Folio pages, 1ᵛ and 2ᵛ
(1. 1. 1–76; 1. 1. 182–1. 2. 9) having only *Apemantus*,[2]
and 2ʳ, 3ʳ and 3ᵛ (1. 1. 77–181; 1. 2. 10–252) only
Apermantus. The transition from 2ʳ to 2ᵛ is particularly
striking, with *Apermantus* in the last line of text of 2ʳ,
and catchword prefix *Aper.* followed by prefix *Ape.*,
and so consistently through the next page, along with
Apemantus in the text. If we are to suppose that in this

[1] Cf. F's 'hindge' at 4. 3. 212, and *Cor.* 5. 6. 40,
'wadg'd'.

[2] Only once on 1ᵛ.

part of the play *Apemantus* represents a correction of a MS. *Apermantus*, no readily intelligible system can be traced. According to the possible orders of setting up a quire described by C. Hinman,[1] the two pages which consistently spell *Apemantus* (2 and 4 of the quire) have between them an *Apermantus* page ($2^r = 3$ of the quire). That is to say, the decision to correct cannot have been taken after part of the quire had already been set up, and then carried out thoroughly. When we pass on to 4^r (1. 2. 253–2. 2. 74), we meet a variation that, unlike the earlier ones, looks as if it went back to copy. Near the beginning of that page we have the prefix *Aper.* (1. 2. 256), as in the earlier part of the scene. Then towards the end of the page, in a new scene, we have 'Enter Apemantus' (2. 2. 50) and this spelling continues in text and prefixes to the end of this page and throughout 4^v (2. 2. 75–192), with the one exception of *Apermantus* in the text of 2. 2. 80. In the second half of the play, *Apemantus* is invariable. I think it is consistent with the evidence to conjecture that Shakespeare used the form *Apermantus* up to the end of Act 1 (near the beginning of 4^r), but began to use the correct form in 2. 2. The backsliding at 2. 2. 80 could then be due either to him or to the compositor, who had become familiar with the other form. If this is so, the two earlier pages with *Apemantus* only must be the result of a haphazard attempt, with the page as the unit, to normalize in the printing-house.

No other spellings raise anything like so interesting or difficult problems. A few have some indication of manuscript origin: 1. 2. 216, 'rod', 3. 5. 112, 'Senat' and 2. 6. 13–14, 'importunat';[2] 5. 1. 109, 'recide'

---

[1] *Shakespeare Quarterly*, VI (1955), 261.

[2] See J. Dover Wilson, *The Manuscript of Shakespeare's Hamlet*, p. 114.

(see note); 1. 1. 264 (twice), 'farthee'.[1] The confusion of 'there' and 'their' occurs several times: 1. 2. 40, 44 ('there' and 'their' in the same line), 99.

There are a number of errors that can be traced to familiar types of misreading, which I classify on the general lines of *The Manuscript of Shakespeare's Hamlet*, and of the *Antony and Cleopatra* Note on the Copy:

Minim errors (*m, n, u, v, i, w, c, r*)—1. 1. 23 Gowne (gum=gomme: Pope); 3. 1. 57 Honor (hour: Pope); 3. 3. 12 Thriue (Thrice: Johnson); 3. 5. 51 fellow (felon: Theobald); 4. 1. 13 Some (Son: F 2); 4. 3. 9 deny't (deject: Arrowsmith); 4. 3. 13 leaue (lean: F 2); 4. 3. 39 wappen'd (wapper'd: Malone); 4. 3. 205 future (fortune: Shadwell *et al.*); 4. 3. 436 Villaine (villainy: Rowe); 4. 3. 495 wilde (mild: Thirlby); 5. 4. 62 remedied (render'd: Chedworth).

f:s errors—1. 1. 27 chases (chafes: Theobald); 2. 2. 141 sound (found, F 2); 4. 3. 384 fire (sire: Rowe); 5. 4. 55 Defend (Descend: F 2).

a:o error—1. 1. 214 cast (cost: F 3).

a:u error—4. 3. 477 grunt'st (grant'st: Southern MS.).

e:d error—2. 2. 134 propose (propos'd: F 2).

l:t error—5. 4. 6 slept (stept: Danchin).

Miscellaneous misreadings—the correction is not always certain—are probably to be found at 1. 1. 23; 1. 2. 29; 2. 1. 34; 2 2. 78, 106; 3. 2. 66; 3. 5. 14; 4. 3. 12; 5. 1. 146. Most of the other obvious or probable errors belong to classes of which this compositor is frequently guilty when setting up from printed

[1] *Ibid.*, citing 'farwell'; for the probability that this in *Merchant of Venice* (Q 1) and *Hamlet* (Q 2) goes back to MS., cf. J. R. Brown, *Studies in Bibliography*, VII (1955), 38—but it is by no means an uncommon spelling in printed texts. Cf. also *Julius Caesar*, 4. 3. 236, 'farwell', and 5. 3. 99, 'far thee well'.

copy:[1] substitution of one short word for another
(1. 1. 43, 90, 261; 4. 2. 41; 4. 3. 122, 186; 5. 1. 70);
anticipation or repetition (4. 3. 88, 285); confusion of
inflexional endings (4. 3. 157; 5. 1. 51); transposition
(3. 6. 90); omission or addition of s (1. 1. 90, 276;
1. 2. 105; 4. 3. 10; 5. 4. 24, 37); omission of a short
word (3. 2. 21; 3. 4. 78; 3. 5. 63; 5. 1. 115). A peculiarity—scarcely an error and therefore not usually
recorded in the notes—that is more than usually common in this play, and may reflect a tendency to follow
a difficult copy faithfully, is the omission of the apo-
strophe before s=is (1. 1. 137, 202, 241, 242, 253;
1. 2. 72, 239; 2. 2. 17, 149; 3. 1. 39; 3. 2. 25; 3. 5. 1;
3. 6. 19; 4. 3. 15, 438; 5. 1. 46), and there is one
instance of the similar whose=who's (5. 3. 2).

At first sight, the lineation of *Timon* appears very
defective, but closer examination suggests that the compositor probably made quite a good job of interpreting
his copy. There are many instances of the characteristic
Folio practice[2] of dividing lines to avoid a turnover,
and this is quite often done even when a turnover
would not in fact have been necessary. There is one
patch where a series of not particularly long lines has
been divided (4. 3. 360–7). This passage consists
mostly of single-line speeches, and it appears that the
division of the opening line of a speech has become
almost habitual. In the light of Professor Hinman's
recent discoveries,[3] it is also possible that the need to
lose space in setting up cast-off copy may explain some
of these divisions. Apart from this peculiarity, there
are few errors of lineation in passages of verse that is

[1] See Alice Walker, *Studies in Bibliography*, VI (1953 for
1954), esp. pp. 48–53.
[2] See R. B. McKerrow, *Prolegomena for the Oxford
Shakespeare* (1939), pp. 48–9.
[3] *Shakespeare Quarterly*, VI (1955).

clearly intended to be regular—much fewer than in *Antony and Cleopatra* or *Coriolanus*. Where there is irregular verse, editors have tampered considerably with the Folio lineation, but often with no better result than to transfer the irregularity from one line to another. Where prose and verse are mixed, the Folio solution is usually not conspicuously worse than those of later editors. In some of the rougher scenes, Shakespeare had probably not decided exactly what was to be verse and what prose. There remain a few longer passages where the compositor has clearly gone wrong. He set up verse as prose at 1. 1. 249–53; 1. 2. 123–6 (to 'bosom'); 239–42 (to 'for 'em'); 4. 3. 84–8; and he made a more perverse error by cutting up what is plainly prose into irregular verse at 2. 2. 92 (from 'Answer') to 100; 4. 3. 348–50, 353–9;[1] and, worst of all, 5. 1. 3–38.

The punctuation is as a rule workmanlike. Where it is wrong, the error is sometimes accompanied by other misunderstandings or misreadings, as at 1. 1. 249–50; 1. 2. 126; 4. 3. 477. There are more perverse errors at 5. 1. 66; 5. 4. 28; and similar, though less glaring, ones at 1. 1. 75; 1. 2. 106–7; 4. 1. 6, 8–9; 4. 3. 455; 5. 4. 30–1. Questions and conditional clauses are confused at 1. 2. 91, 97 (where two alternative versions probably survived in the draft).

There remains one problem relevant to the copy: that of the talents. The references to numbers of talents in the Folio text are inconsistent, and were used as evidence by disintegrators. Thus J. M. Robertson in *Shakespeare and Chapman* (1917) attributed the passages which mention a small number of talents to Chapman, a good classical scholar, and those which

---

[1] The fact that this immediately precedes the series of divided single lines strengthens the suspicion that 'casting-off' difficulties may be involved.

mention an unplausibly large number to Shakespeare. The most recent examination is that of Professor T. J. B. Spencer, *Shakespeare Survey*, vi (1953), to which, and to private correspondence with him, I am much indebted.

The precise value of the talent need not concern us. There were different varieties of talent in the Greek world, as Shakespeare could have discovered from current works of reference, such as Cooper's *Thesaurus*, which gives for them equivalents varying from £100 to £180. Elyot's *Governour* (iii, xvii) gives £120. The main point is that it is a relatively large sum.

There are three types of reference to talents in *Timon*: (i) those in which a relatively small number, three or five, is used (1. 1. 98, 144; 2. 2. 232, 235; the reference in 1. 2. 6 to 'those talents' does not contradict these); (ii) those which clearly mention a large number, fifty (2. 2. 199; 3. 1. 19; 3. 4. 94) or a thousand (2. 2. 205); (iii) those in which the number is either inappropriately indefinite or otherwise confused—'so many' (3. 2. 12, 24, 37) and 'fifty five hundred' (3. 2. 39). Of these, the last is the most helpful as a clue. It was early recognized that a request for 'so many' talents was an absurdity,[1] and Rowe at 3. 2. 39 emended to 'fifty'; while 'fifty five hundred' is odd in itself and does not fit in with a preceding 'so many'. It seems clear that 'so many' is a stop-gap expression, and probable that, as Spencer (p. 77) puts it, 'fifty five hundred' represents Shakespeare's MS. indication for '*either* fifty *or* five hundred, according to whether the loan is for five or fifty talents; this I shall decide when I have found how much a talent was really worth'. But in 1. 1, Shakespeare had already had quite

---

[1] At a pinch, the Stranger's 'so many' at 3. 2. 12 might pass muster; he could be ignorant of the exact sum. But Lucius could scarcely answer him with 'so many'.

a good idea of the value of a talent when (to take Elyot's equivalent for the sake of convenience) he made Timon pay a debt of £600 for Ventidius and give the Old Athenian's daughter a dowry of £360 (to be followed in due course by a sum equal to the father's 'all'). Spencer therefore argues that 'in the course of writing the play Shakespeare (i) became aware that he did not know the value of a talent, (ii) found out this piece of information from some person or some book, and (iii) then in several places got his figures right'. The correction was made in 1. 1 (and in the reference back at 2. 2. 232, 235), but impossibly large figures were used in 2. 2, 3. 1 and 3. 4, and the uncertainties in 3. 2 left standing.

This is plausible, but I am not convinced that the low figures in 1. 1 need represent a correction. In support of the view that they do, Spencer, in a private letter, argues that the low numbers are 'dramatically and theatrically wrong', and that they are the result of a 'scrupulous alteration'[1] of sums which had probably originally been stated in thousands of crowns, and then turned into the vague or high numbers of talents that have survived in the later scenes. This is obviously possible, and there is something in Spencer's contention that it is odd for a writer who *starts* with the correct low figures to go on to the high ones. But I think there is an explanation of how this might have happened which avoids supposing that Shakespeare deliberately substituted the theatrically ineffective low figures for higher figures in an original draft.

It may be significant that the incidents of Ventidius's debt and of the dowry are both paralleled by passages in Lucian's *Timon* where similarly small figures are used. I think it is possible that Shakespeare took his figures

[1] Carried out, as Spencer recognizes, without leaving any irregularities of metre.

from Lucian in the first instance,[1] and then got into difficulties by turning to Plutarch for an idea of debts on the grand scale. It is true, as Spencer says, that the request to the senate for a thousand talents 'o'th'instant' is absurd when we come to work it out, as is the notion that fifty talents could be carried away in a box (3. 1. 16), but dramatically what is wanted is an impressive, large round figure, and figures of this magnitude would not, at first sight, seem extravagant for debts that arise from prodigality on a monstrous scale: in Plutarch's *Life of Caesar*, chapter 5, Shakespeare could have read that Caesar's debts at one time quite early in his career amounted to 1300 talents, and in the *Life of Antony* itself that 'in short time [Curio] brought Antonius into a marvellous great debt, and too great for one of his years, to wit, of two hundred and fifty talents'. With such references as these in mind, Shakespeare was not likely to content himself with such moderate sums as he had used in 1. 1 (which I do not imagine he would in any case have left standing in a final version). At some stage he probably became aware that his figures were incongruous. At 2. 2. 235, the five talents to be given to 'these fellows | To whom 'tis instant due' are evidently thought of as at least staving off disaster for the moment, and the difference between this sum and the 'thousand' and 'fifty' talents mentioned earlier in the same scene may well have caused him some disquiet. In 3. 1 he carries on with 'fifty' from 2. 2. 199, but it is not surprising to find his faltering confidence reflected in 'so many' and 'fifty five hundred' in 3. 2. If this was a reminder to himself to be careful, he did not consider it need be repeated at 3. 4. 94, where 'fifty talents' is evidently thought of as a sum of the same order as the following 'five thousand crowns',

[1] This was suggested by Fleay in *New Shakspere Society Transactions*, 1 (1874), 145.

whereas, giving the crown its English value and taking Elyot's equivalents, it is in fact almost five times as much.

To sum up, while I am quite sure that 3. 2 indicates uncertainty on Shakespeare's part about the appropriate figures, I do not regard as proved Spencer's theory that the low numbers are the result of revision, and think it equally possible that Shakespeare started from two different points—Lucian and Plutarch, and only realized the incongruity after he had, in different contexts, used both high and low figures.[1]

---

[1] The Bible could have furnished Shakespeare with examples of both low and high figures: the former at Matthew, xxv. 14–30 (noted by Spencer); the latter at Matthew xviii. 24, whose 'ten thousand talents' are, as Donne observed, 'more money then perchance any private man is worth' (*Sermons*, ed. Potter and Simpson, III, 6, 73–4).

NOTES

All significant departures from F are recorded, the source of the accepted reading being indicated in brackets. Square brackets about an author's name denote a general acknowledgment; round brackets mean that his actual words are quoted. Line-numeration for references to plays not yet issued in this edition is that found in Bartlett's *Concordance* (1894) and the *Globe Shakespeare*.

F stands for First Folio (1623); F 2, F 3, F 4 for Second, Third and Fourth Folios (1632, 1663, 1685); G. for Glossary; O.E.D. for the *Oxford English Dictionary*; S.D. for stage-direction; Sh. for Shakespeare or Shakespearian; sp.-pref. for speech-prefix. Common words are also usually abbreviated; e.g. sp.=spelling or spelt, prob.=probable or probably, etc.

The following is a list of other works cited in abridged form: Abbott=*A Shakespearian Grammar*, by E. A. Abbott, 3rd ed., 1870; Al.=ed. of Sh. by Peter Alexander, 1951; B.C.P.=Book of Common Prayer; Camb.=*The Cambridge Sh.*, 2nd ed., 1892; Cap.=ed. of Sh. by Edward Capell, 1768; Clarke=ed. of Sh. by Charles and Mary Cowden Clarke [1864–8] (notes chiefly by M.C.C.: cf. R. D. Altick, *The Cowden Clarkes*, 1948, p. 199); Collier=ed. of Sh. by J. P. Collier, 1842–4, 1858; Conrad=H. Conrad, 'Sh.'s Timon', *Zeitschrift für vergleichende Litteraturgeschichte*, n.f. XVII, 1907; D.=ed. by K. Deighton (*Arden Sh.*), 1905; Danchin=ed. by F. C. Danchin, 1944; Dekker=*The Dramatic Works of Thomas Dekker*, ed. by F. Bowers, 1953– ; Delius=ed. of Sh. by N. Delius, 3rd ed., 1872; Douce=*Illustrations of Sh.*, by F. Douce, 1807; Dyce=ed. of Sh. by A. Dyce, 1857, 1864–6; E.D.D.=*English Dialect Dictionary*, ed. Joseph Wright, 1898–1905; Evans = ed. by H. A. Evans (*Henry Irving Sh.*), 1890; Farnham = *Sh.'s Tragic Frontier*, by W. Farnham, 1950; Fleay = F. G. Fleay, 'The Life of Tymon of Athens as written by W. Shakspere', *New Sh. Society's Transactions*, I, 1874; Franz = *Die Sprache Shakespeares*, by W. Franz (4th ed. of *Shakespeare-Grammatik*), 1939; G.K.H. = Dr G. K. Hunter (private communications); *Globe* = ed. by W. G. Clark and W. A. Wright (*Globe Shakespeare*), 1864; Han. = ed. of Sh. by Sir Thomas Hanmer, 1743–4; Hankins = *Sh.'s Derived Imagery*, by J. E. Hankins, 1953; Heath = *Revisal of Sh.'s Text*, by B. Heath, 1765; Herford = ed. by C. H. Herford (*Eversley Sh.*), 1899; J. = ed. of Sh. by Samuel Johnson, 1765; Jonson = *Works of Ben Jonson*, ed. by C. H. Herford and Percy and Evelyn Simpson, 11 vols., 1925–52; K. = ed of Sh. by G. L. Kittredge, 1936; Kellner = *Restoring Sh.*, by L. Kellner, 1925; Kökeritz = *Sh.'s Pronunciation*, by H. Kökeritz, 1953; Mal. = ed. of Sh. by E. Malone, 1790 (notes incorporated in final form in 1821 Variorum, ed. J. Boswell); Marlowe = *Works of C. Marlowe*, ed. by Tucker Brooke *et al.*, 1930–3; Mason = *Comments on the Several Editions of Sh.'s Plays*, by J. M. Mason, 1807 (expanded from edd. 1785, 1798); Middleton = *Works of Thomas Middleton*, ed. by A. H. Bullen, 1885–6; MSH = *The Manuscript of Sh.'s 'Hamlet'*, by J. D. Wilson, 1934; M.S.R. = Malone Society Reprint; Nashe = *The Works of Thomas Nashe*, ed. by R. B. McKerrow, 5 vols., 1904–10; Neilson and Hill = ed. of Sh. by W. A. Neilson and C. J. Hill, 1942; *N. & Q.* = *Notes and Queries*; Noble = *Sh.'s Biblical Knowledge*, by R. Noble, 1935; On. = *A Sh. Glossary*, by C. T. Onions, 1911 (last corrected impression, 1946); Palingenius = *Zodiacus Vitae*, by M. Palingenius, tr. B. Googe, *Zodiacke of Life*, 1575 ed.; Pope = ed. of Sh. by Alexander Pope,

1723–5; *R.E.S.*=*Review of English Studies*; Ridley=
ed. by M. R. Ridley (*New Temple Sh.*), 1934; Ritson
=*Remarks...on the Last Edition of Sh.*, 1783; Rolfe
=ed. by W. J. Rolfe (*Friendly Edition*), 1891; Rowe=
ed. of Sh. by N. Rowe, 1709–10 (2 edd.), 1714;
S.A.B.=*Shakespeare Association Bulletin*; Schmidt=
Sh.-Lexikon, by A. Schmidt, 3rd ed., 1902; Shadwell
=*The History of Timon of Athens*, by T. Shadwell,
1678; *Sh.-Jb.*=*Jahrbuch der Deutschen Sh.-Gesell-
schaft*, later *Shakespeare Jahrbuch*; Sisson=ed. of Sh.
by C. J. Sisson [1954]; Sisson, *Readings*=*New Readings
in Sh.*, by C. J. Sisson, 1956; Staunton=ed. of Sh. by
H. Staunton, 1858–60; Steev.=ed. of J.'s Sh. by
G. Steevens, 1773 (supplemented in later edd. up to
1803); Theob.=ed. of Sh. by L. Theobald, 1733;
Tilley=*A Dictionary of the Proverbs in England in the
Sixteenth and Seventeenth Centuries*, by M. P. Tilley,
1950; Var.=Variorum ed. of Sh., ed. J. Boswell, 1821;
Warb.=ed. of Sh. by William Warburton, 1747;
Webster=*The Complete Works of John Webster*, ed.
by F. L. Lucas, 1927; Wright=*The Authorship of
Timon of Athens*, by E. H. Wright, 1910; Yale=ed. by
S. T. Williams (*Yale Sh.*), 1919.

The names of scholars cited from the Cambridge
Shakespeare for readings alone are not as a rule included
in the above list. The notes with the initials 'J.D.W.'
represent only a small fraction of what the General
Editor has done to improve all parts of the edition.

Names of the Characters. F contains, on the recto
page facing the end of the text, an imperfect list headed
'THE ACTORS NAMES'. Later editions, from Rowe on,
have supplemented it. Timon, Alcibiades and Apemantus come from Plutarch's *Life of Antony* and
Timandra from his *Life of Alcibiades*. The other
characters, with one exception, have Latin names which

are either very common (like Titus) or are to be found
in one or other of Plutarch's *Lives*, as noted by W. W.
Skeat, *Sh.'s Plutarch* (1875), pp. xvii–xviii, and, with
a few additions, R. A. Law, *Texas Studies in English*,
xxx (1951), 61–2. The exception is Phrynia. Danchin,
in his edition, suggested that Sh. might have been
influenced by the passage in the *Life of Alcibiades*
describing Alcibiades just before his death 'in a certain
village of Phrygia, with a concubine of his called
Timandra'. Law, repeating this, also suggests a conflation with the name of Phrynichus, described by
Plutarch as an enemy of Alcibiades. But the name is
probably in the first instance an adaptation of that of
the celebrated courtezan Phryne, which Shadwell
reintroduces into his version at one point, though he
elsewhere has 'Phrinias'.

Acts and Scenes. None marked in F, except for
'Actus Primus. Scæna Prima.'. I follow the divisions
of Rowe and later editors.

Punctuation. See Note on the Copy, p. 93. Apart
from the correction of positive errors, departures from
F have usually taken the form of exclamation-marks for
question-marks (which, however, I have retained oftener
than is customary), full-stops and commas, and of the
strengthening of commas which leave the construction
obscure.

Stage-directions. These are, as might be expected,
sketchy in F, though a few are more elaborately de-
scriptive (1. 1. 97; 1. 2. init., 131, 145; 3. 4. 41, 79;
4. 3. 48). Some 'are reminiscent of what may have
been jottings in the author's original plot' (Greg, *The
Shakespeare First Folio*, p. 410). For places where they
fail to indicate the exact staging, see notes on 1. 2. 114;
3. 5. init.; 5. 1. 30. For an anticipated entry, see
1. 1. 179, note. The speech-prefixes are often vague

(see notes on 1. 1. 260; 2. 2. 9; 3. 6. init.; and text, 3. 6. 85–6). Some are 'functional' (Greg, *First Folio*, pp. 113–14): except in 1. 2, Flavius is simply 'Steward', and in 1. 1, 'an old Athenian' enters at l. 112, and is 'Oldm.' (once 'Old.') in the prefixes. The 'three Strangers' appear only as such in their entry, and have numerical prefixes, though one has a name in the dialogue (3. 2. 64).

1. 1

S.D. *Loc.* (Cap. and Rowe). *Entry* (F and Mal.). After 'Merchant' F adds 'and Mercer', app. an idea which Sh. did not follow up. The prefix 'Mer.' (ll. 9, etc.) could stand for either, as Delius notes.

1. *you're* F 'y'are': so throughout.

1–97. On the relation of this dialogue to 'the "Paragone", or the quarrel and rivalry which had set the painters and poets of Italy against each other for two centuries', see A. B[lunt], *Journal of the Warburg Institute*, II (1938–9), 260–2. The relevance of this, and the latter scene involving the Poet and the Painter, to the theme of appearance and reality is discussed by W. M. Merchant, *Sh. Quarterly*, VI (1955), 249–57.

2. *how...world?* = 'how do you do?', though the Painter takes it up more literally.

3. *wears* Cf. *Lr.* 4. 6. 137–8, 'This great world | Shall so wear out to nought' [Conrad, p. 340], and T. Spencer, *Sh. and the Nature of Man* (1942), p. 26, for the widespread belief that 'the entire system of Nature was running hopelessly down'.

5. *record* Sh. usu. so stresses the noun, though the mod. 'récord' is also found.

9. *'tis* For this usage (cf. Fr. 'c'est'), where mod. Eng. has 'he is', cf. *Ant.* 3. 2. 6, *Oth.* 2. 1. 30, *Mac.* 1. 4. 58.

10. *breathed* see G. There is a suggestion of the exaggerated and unnatural in the eulogies here.

10–11. *breathed...goodness* Metaphor from horsemanship; cf. *Ado*, 1. 1. 136 and G. 'continuer' [J.D.W.].

11. *goodness* Used throughout the play with special reference to bounty; cf. Bacon, *Of Goodnesse and Goodnesse of Nature*, 'I take *Goodnesse* in this Sense, the affecting of the Weale of Men, which is that the Grecians call *Philanthropia*'. Erasmus translates Lucian's χρηστότης in *Timon*, §§ 8, 10 by 'probitas' and 'benignitas'. Boiardo, *Timone*, 1. 2. 19, talks of Timon's 'bontate'.

16. S.D. (Camb.) *vile* F 'vild', a common form.

23. *gum* (Pope)...*oozes* (J.) F 'Gowne...vfes'. The former is a minim error for 'Gomme', the latter prob. a misunderstanding of 'oufes'; cf. 'Owfe' in *H.V,* 1. 2. 164 (F).

24–5. *fire...struck* Cf. *J.C.* 4. 3. 110–12 n. [Conrad, p. 341].

26–7. *like...chafes* J. found this obscure, and thought there might have been a cut, but it is characteristic of a developing Sh. image that 'provokes itself' should generate a more elaborate image describing how the poet's imagination is stimulated by difficulties.

27. *chafes* (Theob.) F 'chafes'; elsewhere in Sh. intr. in this sense ('chafing with'='fretting against', *J.C.* 1. 2. 101).

32. *this* Pointing, no doubt, to a detail of the picture; prob., from what follows, the central figure.

33. *Indifferent* see G. Mock-modest, but not as uncomplimentary as 'indifferent' in mod. Eng.

33–4. *How...standing!* If we assume, as ll. 46–8 suggest, that the picture represents Timon, this prob. means, 'how truly the gracefulness of this figure expresses the dignity of the original' (Yale).

36–7. *to . . . interpret* Cf. *Wint.* 5. 2. 13–14, 'there was speech in their dumbness, language in their very gesture', *Tp.* 3. 3. 37–9 [G. W. Knight, *The Crown of Life* (1947), pp. 117, 248]. The primary reference is to a dumb-show, rather than, as Mal. thought, citing *Ham.* 3. 2. 245–6, a puppet-show.

38. *It . . . life* Cf. *Wint.* 5. 3. 19, 'To see the life as lively mocked' [Conrad, p. 342].

40. *artificial strife* the strife of art to outdo nature, cf. *Ven.* 289–92 [Mal.]; *Lucr.* 1377.

41. S.D. (F; after Cap.).

43. *man* (Theob.) F 'men', which seems pointless (cf. the reverse error at 5. 1. 70). As D. says, 'There would be no particular happiness in their being allowed to approach Tim., for high and low alike had that privilege; but Tim. is by the sycophant Poet deemed happy in being visited by men of the highest rank'.

44. *Look,* (Rowe) F 'Looke'.

47. *this beneath world* Cf. *Lr.* 2. 2. 170, 'this under globe' [D.].

49. *Halts not particularly* 'does not stop at any single character' (J.).

50. *sea of wax* Prob. a reference to wax writing-tablets. The phrase is strained. For an attempt to link it with an 'image-cluster' connected with 'Icarus who attached wings to his back with wax and for whom pride came before a fall', cf. E. A. Armstrong, *Sh.'s Imagination* (1946), p. 37, citing *3 H. VI*, 2. 1. 170–1. Al. prefers Staunton's conj. 'tax' (=censure), and cites (privately) *A.Y.L.* 2. 7. 86, 'my taxing like a wild-goose flies'.

52. *flies* sc. it (the course) flies. Sisson, less plausibly, makes 'no . . . hold' a parenthesis, so that 'drift' can be the subject.

55. *conditions* see G.

59. *hanging* Metaph. from clothes; cf. *Mac.* 5. 2. 21.

60. *to...tendance* to paying him loving attention.

61. *glass-faced* see G.; cf. *Cym.* 1. 1. 1–3.

63–5. *even...nod* Conflicts with 1. 2. 23 ff., 239 ff. Perh. an oversight of the rough draft; there would not be much point in a misapprehension on the Poet's part, suggested by Ritson.

65. *nod* Lucian's Timon (§ 5), as D. notes, describes his sycophants as hanging on his nod: in Erasmus's tr. 'meo de nutu pendebant'.

68. *all deserts* those whose deserts are of all different degrees.

70. *propagate...states* see G.

74. *present...present* The mod. sense 'existing now' and the sense 'immediate' are prob. both involved, and the repetition brings out the precarious nature of this sudden promotion.

75. *conceived to scope.* (J.; Theob. 'to th' scope.') F 'conceyu'd, to ſcope'.

79–80. *would...condition* App. loosely, for 'would well express [cf. 5. 4. 74] the condition of mankind'. Sh. seems to take the picture as his point of departure, and regard the human situation, which it was designed to allegorize, as in its turn an exemplification of it. So, virtually, Schmidt, 'would find a striking parallel in our state'.

83. *fill with tendance* O.E.D. glosses 'tendance' as 'attendants collectively; train or retinue'. But it is the 'fellows' themselves who form the train. The whole phrase means 'crowd and offer their services'.

84. *Rain...ear* The metaphor perh. glances at holy water rather than incense; 'rain' may be an intensification of the 'sprinkle' of 3. 6. 69 [J.D.W.].

85. *Make...stirrup* For holding the stirrup as a type of menial service, cf. *2 H. VI*, 4. 1. 53 [Clarke]; also Webster, *White Devil*, 1. 2. 306–7.

85–6. *through...air* 'would make him believe that only by his favour do they draw in that air which God has made a free gift to all' (D.). The very terms of this eulogy hint at a certain oppressiveness in Tim.'s 'goodness'.

86. *Drink...air* So *Ven.* 273, *Lucr.* 1666.

87–91. *When...foot* For a similar figure, also involving the idea of the danger the fall of the mighty can bring to lesser men, cf. *Ham.* 3. 3. 15–22, *Lr.* 2. 4. 72–4.

90. *hands* (F 2) F 'hand', defended unconvincingly by Sisson, *Readings*, on the ground that 'one hand is likely enough to have something to carry'. *slip* (Rowe) F 'fit', which fails to give the sense of motion. Delius's 'sink' is also possible.

93–7. *A thousand...head* 'A comparison in which three commonplaces of renaissance critical thought join hands: the similarity of poetry and painting, the idea of art as a vehicle of universal truth, and the idea of art as a teacher of mankind' (M. Doran, *Endeavors of Art*, 1954, p. 74).

94. *demonstrate* So stressed *Oth.* 1. 1. 62, but Sh. also has 'démonstrate' (*H. V*, 4. 2. 54). *quick* Prob. in the mod. sense, but note the collocation with 'pregnantly', also in *2 H. IV*, 1. 2. 168 [D.].

97. *foot...head* Cf. Tilley, F 562, 'Do not make the foot the head'. S.D. (F; Camb.).

98. *five talents* See Note on the Copy, pp. 93–7.

100. *Your honourable* your honour's.

103. *feather...shake off* Perh. an ironical anticipation of the image in 2. 1. 30–2; 'of that feather' = 'of such a kind' (On.).

104. *must need* F 3 'most needs', which may be right. The F text reads awkwardly, and the common expression 'must needs' might have unconsciously affected the compositor.

107. *binds* See G., and Introd. p. xxxv.

109. *enfranchiséd* F 'enfranchized'. Most edd. treat this ending as non-syllabic, but the F form gives a good line if we stress 'come tó me'; cf. *Tp.* 1. 2. 494.

111. *But to* i.e. by a natural ellipse, 'but it is necessary to'. So also Middleton, *More Dissemblers besides Women*, 1. 3. 38–9, ''Tis not enough for tapers to burn bright, | But to be seen' (cited by H. D. Sykes, *N. & Q.* 13 Ser. 1, 1923, 167, who attributes the *Tim.* passage to Middleton); Middleton, *Honourable Entertainments* (*M.S.R.*), x, 20–2; Drayton, *Muses Elizium*, VII, 2–4; and also in prose: *Admonition to Parliament*, 1572, in Frere and Douglas, *Puritan Manifestoes* (1907), p. 8, 'it is not enough to take paynes in taking away evil, but also to be occupied in placing good in the stead thereof'. *M.N.D.*, 5.1.120–21 [1966].

112. S.D. F 'Exit'.

113. Athenian. F 'Oldm.'(so below; l. 124 'Old.'); cf. 'wiseman', 'goodman', as single words; the one mod. survivor of this class is 'madman'.

123. *holds a trencher* i.e. waits at table.

132. *Therefore...Timon* Cryptic; to say that he will continue honest has little point, since the speaker is asserting that the man *does* want his daughter. Coleridge's gloss (*Sh. Criticism*, ed. T. M. Raysor, 1930, II, 82), 'for that very cause, and with no additional or extrinsic motive, he will be so', may be right, but the idea is not clearly expressed.

133. *His...itself* The earliest valid quotation for 'Virtue is its own reward' (Ovid, *Ep. ex Ponto*, II. iii. 12, 'Virtutem pretium qui putat esse sui'; Silius Italicus, *Punica*, XIII. 663, 'Ipsa quidem virtus sibimet pulcherrima merces') in Tilley, V 81 (for Spenser, *F.Q.* III. xii. 39. 5 is not to the point) is from *Caesar and Pompey* (=*Caesar's Revenge*), l. 1472 (*M.S.R.*,) 'Vertue vnto it felfe a fhure reward' (S.R. 1606,

written perh. *c.* 1595); cf. Daniel, *Musophilus*, 1599 (in *Poems*, ed. A. C. Sprague), 609–10, 'Her selfe a recompence sufficient | Vnto her selfe, to giue her owne content'.

136. *precedent* see G. Not to be confused with our 'précedent', usually sp. 'president' in Sh.

137. S.D. (J.).

142. *dispossess her all* Recalls in its rhythm and sense of 'all' *Lr.* 1. 1. 106, 'To love my father all'; cf. the adv. use of 'something', 4. 3. 55.

147. *For...men* Not clear whether Timon refers to a duty between men as men, or to one which a master specifically owes a faithful servant.

152–4. *never...you!* 'let me never henceforth consider anything that I possess, but as *owed* or *due* to you; held for your service, and at your disposal' (J.). The word 'keeping' implies that he will not think of himself as the *owner* of anything [Delius].

154. S.D. (after Theob.) F 'Exit'.

160–3. *The painting...out* Painting can almost be called natural, in comparison with the deceitfulness of human nature; a painting professes to be no other than it is; Sh. almost always uses 'outside' with an implication of false semblance, e.g. *M.V.* 1. 3. 99, 'O, what a goodly outside falsehood hath!'.

168. *suffered under praise* been overwhelmed with praise (jocular). The jeweller misunderstands.

169. *satiety* F 'faciety', cf. *Shr.* 1. 1. 24 n.

171. *unclew* This metaphor, like that in l. 103, points forward to 2. 1. 30–2.

172. *As...give* i.e. 'at cost price' (D.).

173–4. *Things...masters* Cf. *Son.* 96. 5–6, 'As on the finger of a thronéd queen | The basest jewel will be well esteemed' [Conrad, p. 341].

174. *by* see G.

177. *the common tongue* On.'s gloss, 'common

report, general opinion' is wrong; 'speaks...tongue'
is simply fig. for 'says the same thing as everyone else'.

179. *will you* 'are you prepared to' (D.). S.D.
Here Pope; F after l. 176.

180. *bear, with* (Steev.) F 'beare with'. Pope's
'bear it with' is attractive, but the absolute use possible, and the line runs well enough with a disyllabic
'bear'.

183. *When...honest* i.e. never [Mal.].

184. *Why...not* Perh. Sh. makes Tim. unconsciously admit that, if Apem. did know them, he would
have reason to call them knaves.

197. *The best, for the innocence* perfectly well,
because, being a mere picture, it can do no harm
[Delius].

201. *a dog* As being a Cynic, i.e. taking the dog as
his model. Cf. W. Empson, 'Timon's Dog' in *The
Structure of Complex Words* (1951), ch. 8.

202. *generation* see G.

205. *eat not lords* Farnham (pp. 71–2) notes how
'the beastlike men in *Timon*'—flatterers and others—
'are often devourers of each other'; cf. 1. 2. 39, 76–80,
137; 4. 3. 427.

207. *eat lords* Presumably=enjoy (sexually).

210–11. *So...labour* Punctuation and syntax dis-
puted. F has 'So,...it,', which favours taking 'So'
as an adv., as in l. 207. Staunton and others take it as
a conj., which Staunton, with no warrant, glosses 'in
whatever sense'. Others interpret 'provided that' and
by implication make it do duty a second time as an
adv.: thus D., 'since you put that interpretation on my
words'. There seems nothing wrong with 'that is how
you interpret it; take it etc.'.

213. *plain-dealing* Alluding to the prov., 'Plain
dealing is a jewel' (Tilley, P 381).

214. *cost* (F 3) F 'caſt'.

218. *Thou liest* Because 'the truest poetry is the most feigning' (*A.Y.L.* 3. 3. 17–18); Apem. turns from this commonplace to give more specific evidence that the poet lives up to the reputation of his profession.

236. *no angry wit* Prob. corrupt, but not convincingly emended. The sense required is that of the anon. conj. (*ap.* Camb.) 'no ampler wit than be'.

244. *of companionship* of the same party.

245. S.D. (after Cap.).

249–53. *So...monkey* Divided by Cap.; prose in F.

249. *So, so, there!* just look at that! [J.D.W.].

249–50. *there! Achës* (Cap.) F 'their Aches'; cf. *Shr.* 1. 1. 107 n. 'Aches' disyllabic as in 5. 1. 198 and *Tp.* 1. 2. 371.

253. *baboon and monkey* Cf. the association of 'dog-apes' with insincere compliments in *A.Y.L.* 2. 5. 24–5, and G. 'dog-ape' [G.K.H.].

257. S.D. (after Camb.) F 'Exeunt'.

260. From this line to the end of the sc., the F prefixes are simply '1' and '2'.

261. *more* (Han.) F 'moſt', which lacks adequate support, though cf. *Club Law* (ed. Moore Smith), 1730, 'the worst lucke myne'.

274. S.D. (after Han.); F om.

275–6. So lineated in F. A single (broken-backed) line in Cap.

275. *opposite to humanity* either 'hostile to mankind' or 'quite inhuman' (Tieck, 'ein Widerspiel der Menschheit').

276. *Come* (F 2) F 'Comes'.

279. *Plutus* Figures as a character in Lucian's *Timon* [D.].

280. *meed* see G.; the use of the word for both 'service' and 'reward' is well illustrated in *Tit.* 5. 3. 66, 'There's meed for meed, death for a deadly deed';

similarly, 'merit' sometimes='reward' (*R. II*, 1. 3. 156).

282. *breeds* Cf. *M.V.* 1. 3. 93 [D.]. See Introd. p. xxxii.

283. *use of quittance* 'all the customary returns made in discharge of obligations (Warb.), with a word-play on 'use'='interest'.

284. *governed* Perh. with a suggestion of the original Latin sense of 'steer' (O.E.D. 'govern', 7); cf. *Ant.* 5. 1. 31–2, 'a rarer spirit never | Did steer humanity'; cf. Terence, *Hec.* 311, 'qui eos gubernat animus'. [1968]

285. *fortunes* Odd after 'in', though the plur. itself is common. Daniel's 'in's fortune' is rather bold.

286. S. D. F 'Exeunt'.

1. 2

S.D. *Loc.* (Camb.) *Entry* (F and Camb.) *Alcibiades...Ventidius* F 'the States, the Athenian Lords, Ventigius which Timon redeem'd from prison'; see G. 'state'. Sh. seems to have been reminding himself who Ventidius was. *like himself* i.e. in his ordinary dress, not in his best, like the other guests.

5–6. *bound...free* For play on these words, cf. 1. 1. 106–7.

10–11. *there's...receives* Cf. Luke vi. 34; Acts xx. 35 [Noble].

12. *If...game* if those in high rank expect a return for their so-called gifts.

13. *faults...fair* 'the faults of rich persons... wear a plausible appearance' (Heath).

15. *ceremony* They have evidently assumed formal postures of respect; before this line J. inserted the S.D., 'they all stand ceremoniously looking on Timon'.

17. *Recanting goodness* generosity that takes back its offers; 'Recanting' is intrans., with 'goodness',

rather than with 'ceremony', governing 'goodness', as
Delius supposes.

20. S.D. (Camb. after Rowe); F om.

22. *hanged it* Cf. *Oth.* 4. 1. 38, 'to confess and be
hanged for his labour' [Mal]. The prov. is first quoted
by Tilley, C 587, from Marlowe, *Jew of Malta*,
4. 2. 18–19. 'Hanged' has no obvious force, but the
original point of the prov. itself is uncertain (cf.
O.E.D. 'confess', 10).

26. *ye've* (Camb.) F 'ye'haue', a method of
indicating elision or fusion popular with some 17th-
cent. writers, esp. Jonson.

27. *to* F 'too', cf. *Err.* 4. 1. 47 n.

28–31. *They...indeed* Prose in *Globe*. But the F
verse arrangement, with lines ending 'est', 'angry',
'himself', 'company', 'indeed', may have stood in
Sh.'s draft.

29. *ever* (Rowe) F 'verie'; 'ever' marks the antithesis to 'brevis'.

35. *I...power* App.='I do not want to have the
power to impose silence, as the price of my hospitality'.

37–8. *'twould...thee* The implication appears to
be that, being prepared for flatterers, it would choke
anyone else [Heath].

38–9. *what...Timon* Cf. 1. 1. 205 n.

40. *dip...blood* Tim.'s hospitality is vividly iden-
tified with his life-blood, cf. 3. 4. 93–5, and the more
straightforward figure in 3. 2. 66–7; cf. below, ll.
45–8 n. There may be an allusion, as J. thought, to
'a pack of hounds trained to pursuit by being gratified
with the blood of the animal which they kill'.

41. *too* Shadwell, Warb., 'to 't', which would
give a more pointed expression, and might have been
sp. 'toot'.

43. *without knives* Guests at this period normally
brought their own knives with them.

44. *their meat* (F 2) F 'there meat'.

45–8. *the fellow…kill him* 'the example that will occur almost to everybody will be Judas Iscariot' (Noble). The allusion is led up to by 'dip' in l. 40 (cf. Matt. xxvi. 23, more clearly echoed at 3. 2. 67).

48. *'t has been proved* Prob. an Anglicization of 'probatum est'—'a phrase used in recipes or prescriptions' (O.E.D.). *huge* see G.

50. *notes* 'indications which show where the windpipe is' (J.).

52. *let…round* Cf. *H. VIII*, 1. 4. 97, *Mac.* 3. 4. 11–12. Timon is replying to a toast.

55–6. *healths…ill* Cf. Tilley, H 292, 'To drink health is to drink sickness'.

57–8. *Here's…mire* Pope (+some later edd.) unnecessarily treated this as prose.

57. *too…sinner* i.e. too weak to provoke sin.

65. *harlot…weeping* Cf. Tilley, W 638, 'Trust not a woman when she weeps'.

67. *keeper,* see G.

70. S.D. (J.); F om.

71. *dich* see G., and cf. Buttes, *Dry Dinner*, 1599, sig P 6v (*ap.* Nashe, iv, 280), 'Mytchgoodditchye'.

76. *breakfast of enemies* Cf. *1 H. IV*, 2. 4. 100–1; *3 H. VI*, 5. 5. 85.

78–9. *lord;…'em;* F 'Lord,…'em,'. Most edd. put a stronger stop only after ''em', inappropriately, making 'So…lord' subordinate to 'there's…'em', instead of to the preceding speech. Sisson retains F's commas, which are too light for a modernized text.

82. *kill 'em—* (Sisson) F 'kill 'em:'. Edd. usu. reduce the colon to a comma, or omit it altogether.

85. *use our hearts* 'make trial of our love' (D.).

88–107. *O…you* His attitude here towards the returning of benefits seems to differ from that of ll. 10–11; but 'as a host he pretends to discount all generosity in his hospitality; but to justify his refusal of any return from Ventidius, he sincerely says that to expect favours back is to show oneself lacking in true generosity' (C. B. Young). The speech looks forward ironically to what happens when he does 'have use for' his friends.

91. *have...did* A natural mixture of tenses; cf. *R. III*, 2. 2. 5–7 n. *thousands,* (Theob.) F 'thou-ſands?'.

94. *thus...you* I confirm your professions of good will in so far as I have already credited you with more than your modesty permits you to express.

95–7. *if we should ne'er have need of 'em...should we ne'er have use for 'em* Staunton plausibly suggests that these were alternatives, one of which Sh. intended to cancel. This is supported by the fact that F has a question-mark at the end of each. The sentence, runs more smoothly with the omission of 'should we... 'em?'. (Pope omitted the whole of 'they...'em?'.)

98–9. *resemble...cases* Cf. *R. II*, 1. 3. 163 [Conrad, p. 347].

99. *their* (F 2) F 'there', cf. l. 44.

102. *better or properer* Cf. Franz, §§ 246–8, for comparative adverbs in '-er' in Sh.'s Eng. 'Better' is still poss., but not 'properer'.

103–5. *O...fortunes!* Perh. influenced by Ps. cxxxiii. 1 (B.C.P.), 'Behold, how good and joyful a thing it is: brethren, to dwell together in unity'.

105. *joy,* (Rowe) F 'ioyes,' K. 'joy's', poss. but awkward. *made...born* 'destroyed, turned to tears, before it can be fully possessed' (J.).

106. *cannot...water* are not watertight.

106–7. *methinks....faults,* (Rowe, with colon for full stop). F. 'me thinkes,. .Faults.'.

108. *Thou...drink* Variously explained. J. sees a 'covert sense' of 'what thou losest, they get'; Heath,

'the excess of drinking to which he was now en-
couraging his false friends would prove the source of
tears to him flowing from real regret'; more simply
Rolfe, 'perh. nothing more than a cynical sneer at the
incongruity of making his tears an occasion for their
drinking'.

111. *like...up* Tollet (*ap.* Steev.) seems right in
seeing this as a reference to a movement in the womb,
rather than to birth. Prob. there is a glance at Luke i.
44 (Geneva), 'the babe sprang in my belly for ioye'.

114. S.D. (J.D.W.) F 'Sound Tucket. Enter the
Maskers of Amazons, with Lutes in their hands,
dauncing and playing': evidently a preliminary note,
not finally integrated into the text; cf. W. W. Greg,
The Sh. First Folio, p. 410.

122. S.D. (Cap.) F 'Enter Cupid with the Maske
of Ladies'; cf. *Rom*. 1. 4, notes on opening S.D. and
l. 4.

123-6. *Hail...bosom* Arranged by Theob.; prose
in F.

123. *thee* (F) Han. 'the', to avoid treating 'and...
taste' as parenthetical.

124-8. *The...eyes* On the idea of a banquet of
the senses, as in Chapman, *Ovid's Banquet of Sense,* see
F. Kermode, *R.E.S.* n.s. IV (1953), 324.

126-7. *Th'ear...smell* (Warb. *ap.* Theob), *all*
(Mal.) F 'There...all'. In F 'There' begins a line of
verse, following prose. The addition of 'smell' seems
necessary, and Warb., who first introduced it, deleted
'all'. It seems more likely (Sisson, *Readings*) that 'smell'
dropped out before it than that it was corrupted into it.
The present lineation is that of Rann, who less convincingly read 'and smell', omitting 'all'. Cf. Mas-
singer, *The Duke of Milan*, 1. 3. 3-4, 'All that may
be had | To please the eye, the ear, taste, touch, or
smell'.

130. *Music make* So, without comma, F; i.e. 'let music make'. S.D. (after Cap.).

131. S.D. (after Cap., from F, following ll. 114, 122).

133. *madwomen* (F) Edd. generally print as two words, perh. on grounds of rhythm, but the sense is that of the mod. single word (feminine of 'madman'). Elsewhere in Sh. sp. as two words (as 'madman' sometimes is), but in *M.V.* 4. 1. 441 clearly a single word, and stressed on the first syllable.

134–5. *Like...root* 'the glory of this life [is] just as much madness in the eye of reason, as the pomp appeared to be when compared to the frugal repast of a philosopher' (Mason). The construction comes out more clearly with the omission of F's comma after 'life'.

135. *to* compared to.

136–45. *We...sun* This has a strong appearance of being a rough draft.

137. *drink* Cf. 1. 1. 205 n.

142. *of...gift* 'given by their friends' (D.).

145. *Men...sun* Tilley, S 979, cites various derivatives of Erasmus's *Plures adorant solem orientem quam occidentem* (from Plutarch's *Life of Pompey*); *Son.* 7 is based on this proverb.

147–50. *entertainment...entertained* The repetition suggests a rough draft.

150. *mine own device* Suggests that Tim. had designed the masque [J.]; they have performed it so well that he finds new beauties in it [J.D.W.].

152. 1 Lady (J. conj.) F '1 *Lord*'. The compositor must as J. suggests have misinterpreted 'L.', or else misread 'La' as 'Lo'. *take...best* regard us in the most favourable light; cf. 5. 1. 177.

153–4. *worst...taking* The obscene reference is obvious; there is prob. [Steev.] an allusion to the prov., 'a rotten case abides no handling' (*2 H. IV*, 4. 1. 161).

155. *banquet* see G., and cf. *Rom*. 1. 5. 122,
'a trifling foolish banquet' [Steev.].   *you*, (F, Sisson).
With this punctuation, 'Please...yourselves' is a conditional clause.   Most edd. make it heavier, so that
'Please' is imperative.

157. S.D. (after Cap.) F 'Exeunt'.

158. *Flavius*. The name occurs only in this scene
in F. Subsequently he is always 'Steward'; cf. 2. 2.
192 n.

160. S.D. (J.).

162. *tell him well* i.e. fairly and squarely. Many
read 'tell him—well', with Rowe, making 'well' a
pointless expletive.

163. *crossed* A quibble; see G.; cf. Jonson,
Poetaster, 3. 1. 88–90, 'your mercers booke | Will tell
you with more patience, then I can; | (For I am crost,
and so's not that, I thinke)' [D.].

164. *eyes behind* 'to see the miseries that are following her' (J.).

165. *for his mind* because of what his inclinations
prompt him to.   S.D. F 'Exit'.

168. S.D. (Camb.) F om.

172. *accept it* F 2 'accept'; the pronoun is prob.
elided, as conveyed by the anon. conj. (*ap*. Camb.)
'accept 't'; cf. *Wint*. 2. 2. 53.

174. *gifts*. (F, Delius) Pope substituted a dash for
the full-stop, but the phrase is not really incomplete in
sense.

179. F precedes this line by the S.D. 'Enter
Flauius'. This looks like the work of someone tidying
up the copy for the press, who has noticed that Flav
has not been given an entry, but has failed to see that
he has returned with the casket at l. 168.

181–2. *Near?...thee* So Caes. in *J.C*. 3. 1 7,
'What touches us ourself shall be last served' [D.].

184, 195. Asides (J.).

196–7. *He...coffer* (arr. Steev.) F as a single verse line. Camb., printing as prose, wrongly claims to be following F.

200. *Being* since it (the heart) is.

202–6. *That...out* Arranged by Han. F divides at 'word', 'for't', 'were', 'out', prob. representing the rough draft. The long line 'That...word' suggests that 'he owes...word' may have been Sh.'s second thoughts, intended to take the place of 'is all in debt'.

208. *Than such* Elliptically for 'than he who has such'. *exceed* i.e. 'are worse than'.

209–12. *I...love* (F) Mal., followed by most edd. (not Al.), rearranged as three lines, the first ending with 'yourselves'.

209. S.D. F 'Exit'.

213. *With...it* One line in Pope. Two lines in F, divided after 'thanks'.

218. 3 Lord (Cap. conj.) F '1. *L*.'.

221. *own....true,* F 'owne:...true,'. Most edd. (not Delius or Al.) change the punctuation so as to join 'I'll...true' with what precedes. But it means 'I assure you'. For 'I'll tell you' corr. to mod. 'I tell you', cf. *H. V*, 1. 1. 1, *K.J.* 5. 6. 39 [Steev.], and Franz, § 619 n. 1.

222. *call to* Prob. 'visit', noted by Sandys (*ap*. D.) as 'still common in the West'; cf. E.D.D. 'call', vb. 7 (9). Delius's 'appeal' is also poss.; cf. Webster, *Devil's Law-Case*, 1. 2. 67, 'Till I call to you for a strict account'.

225. *'tis...give* Perh. 'there is not enough for me to give you' [J.D.W., citing *Gent*. 4. 4. 63 for ''tis' = 'there is' in a rather different context]; otherwise, he must mean that mere gifts do not adequately express his feelings.

229. *It...thee* Obscure; prob. 'anything given to you is charity'.

231–2. *pitched...defiled* A far-fetched pun on the prov., 'he that toucheth pitch shall be defiled' (Ecclus. xiii. 1). Cf. *1 H. IV*, 2. 4. 407–8, *Ado*, 3. 3. 56.

236. *All to you* Repeats, and intensifies, l. 234.

239. S.D. (after Camb.) F 'Exeunt Lords'.

239–42. *What...'em* Arranged by Rowe. Prose in F.

240–1. *Serving...becks...legs* see G.

244. *curtsies* F 'Curtsies' Some edd. 'courtesies'. The marking off of this sense by a different sp. is a relatively recent development; J.'s *Dict.* gives 'courtesy' for all senses.

250–1. *give...paper* 'be ruined by his securities entered into' (Warb.). There is a contrast with the genuine valuables he has up to now given away.

253. *an...once*='if ever', or 'as soon as'.

255. S.D. F 'Exit'.

257. *thy heaven* i.e. my advice, which would have saved you [Mason]. Not, as J. thought, 'the pleasure of being flattered'.

259. S.D. F 'Exit'.

2. 1

Loc. (after Cap.) *Entry* (F and Cap.). Sisson gives 'Enter a Senator at his desk', to indicate a 'discovery' of the inner stage (cf. *Readings*)—a possible, but not a necessary, way of staging the scene.

1. *five thousand* Prob. 'crowns' as in 3. 4. 30.

5. *steal but* 'I have only to steal' (D.).

10. *And* As in mod. 'and...at that'; cf. Franz, § 590. *porter* i.e. one to *guard* the gate.

13. *sound* (F+Coll., Al., Sisson). Most edd. read 'found' (Han.); cf. 2. 2. 141. This would have to mean 'find...to have any safe or solid foundation' (J.), and is no easier than F, for which J. suggested the

paraphrase, 'No reason, by sounding, fathoming, or trying his state, can find it safe', though he thought it could in fact only mean 'safely sound', and hence preferred 'found'.

16. *moneys* Plur. as in *M.V.* 1. 3. 105 ff.

17–19. *when...thus* 'when, with words of compliment and courteous gesture, he would bow you out' (D.).

20. *uses* see G.

22. *reliances* The plur. indicates different occasions.

26. *tossed and turned* Metaphor from tennis [D.].

27. *find supply* As if not 'relief' but 'need' had preceded, or as if 'I' had been the subject. Such a change in mid-sentence is common in Sh., and there is no need, with D., to invent the meaning 'demand for restitution' for 'relief'.

28. *aspect* Regularly stressed on the last syllable by Sh.

30–2. *When...phoenix* see G. 'gull'. Sh. has in mind the fable of the crow in other birds' feathers, most familiar, in a Sh. connection, from Greene's attack in the *Groatsworth of Wit* (cf. *Sh. Survey*, IV (1951), 65–6). Cf. T. W. Baldwin, *Sh.'s Small Latine and Lesse Greeke*, 1944, I, 619–20.

30. *sticks...wing* is restored to the bird to which it belongs.

33. Caphis. *I go, sir* (Dyce) F '*Ca.* I go fir. *Sen.* I go fir?', which many retain. But it interrupts the metre, and there seems no point in the hesitation by Caphis which would be necessary to provoke the Senator's ironic and impatient repetition of his words.

34. *in compt* (Theob.) F 'in. Come', which Sisson (*Readings*) defends, interpreting 'Come! (and take the bonds from me)'. But 'compt', which he thinks 'impossible as a misreading of *Come*', could have been spelt 'Comt'. S.D. F 'Exeunt'.

2. 2

Loc. (Al.)　*Entry* (after F, which has 'Steward' for 'Flavius' here and throughout the rest of the play; cf. 1. 2. 158 n.).

4. *resumes* (Rowe)　F 'refume'. Also possible is 'take' for 'takes' in l. 3. The irregularity may go back to Sh.'s MS.

5–6. *never...kind* The exact construction is obscure, and edd. disagree whether 'to be so kind' means 'in order to be' or 'in being'. But the sense is clearly 'there never was a mind created at once so unwise and so kind' (Clarke).

9. *Fie...fie!* He sees the duns approaching. S.D. (J.)　F 'Enter Caphis, Ifidore, and Varro'. Here, and in ll. 10 and 12, Sh. uses the names of the masters for the servants. Cf. Steele, *Spectator*, 88, Garrick, *High Life Below Stairs* (noted by Clarke), Scott, *Redgauntlet*, ch. 2. But it is uncertain whether Sh. would have retained this usage in his final version.

10. *Good even* A greeting used any time after noon; cf. *Rom.* 2. 4. 106–9 [Tyrwhitt *ap.* Steev.].

15. *fear it* i.e. fear that it may not happen; a highly contextual use.

16. S.D. (F; Al.).　Strictly, Alc. need not be specifically mentioned, as he is part of the 'train'.

18. *me?* (Cap.)　F 'me,'; it would also be possible to drop the comma, but for the elliptical 'with me?' = 'do you want to speak to me?' cf. Middleton, *More Dissemblers besides Women*, 2. 3. 36.

23. *To...month* from one day to the next for the past month.

26. *suit* see G.　39. *keep on* proceed.

40. S.D.s (after Cap.; J.).

42. *broken* (Shadwell, Han.)　F 'debt, broken'. Edd. usu. prefer Steev.'s 'date-broke' (cf. 2. 1. 22), for which

the F text could be an auditory error (Kökeritz, p. 175),
but, in view of 'debts' in the next line, 'debt' is perh.
more likely to be an undeleted false start.

43. *detention* Not in sense parallel with 'demands'.
He is 'encount'red' with the *charge* of detaining debts.

49. *See...entertained* I take this to be addressed
to some of Timon's servants. S.D. (after Pope).

50. S.D. F 'Exit'. Though the draft is rough here,
it seems most likely that l. 50 is addressed to the
creditors' men, who, however, prefer to stay and have
sport with the fool and Apemantus.

51. *the fool* As J. notes, it is only in the course of
the scene that we learn that he and the page are the
servants of a courtezan. Sh. might have been less
abrupt if he had finished the play, but there is no reason
to think with J. that a scene has been lost.

58. S.D. (Steev.).

62–3. *thou'rt...yet* 'you stand fool all to yourself,
for you are not yet on his back; if you were, it would
be fool upon fool' (D.).

65. *He* prob.='he who' [D.].

65–6. *Poor...want* This would, as J. noted, be
more happily placed after 'yourselves' in l. 71.

66. *bawds...want* Cf. T. Wilson, *Discourse upon
Usury* (ed. R. H. Tawney, 1925), p. 332, 'Aristotle
saieth that usurers and baudes maye well goe together';
also Jonson, *Epigrams*, LVII (with note).

67. All Servants F 'Al.', subsequently 'All.'. It is
hard to believe that Sh. would have left all these as
speeches to be delivered in chorus.

75. *scald such chickens* J. notes 'that the old name
for the disease got at Corinth was the *brenning*'; cf.
O.E.D. 'burning', *vbl. sb.* 4. *chickens*. They were
scalded to remove feathers; prob. a reference to the loss
of hair in venereal disease; cf. *M.N.D.*, G. 'French
crown'.

76. *Corinth* see G.

77. *Good*, (F) Most edd. read 'Good!', but the meaning is prob 'my good fellow' as in *Tp.* 1. 1. 15, *Rom.* 1. 5. 7, 'Good thou'.

78. *mistress'* (Theob., sp. 'mistress's') F 'Mafters'. Here, and at l. 106, the MS. prob. had 'mastres' (see O.E.D.). Cf. *M.V.* 4. 1. 51, where Q 1 spells 'Maisters'; the reverse error occurs *Shr.* 1. 2. 18, where n. suggests 'Mrs' for 'masters' has been misinterpreted; Jonson, *Underw.* 38. 105 has 'Masters' for 'Mistress'; Middleton, *Phoenix*, 5. 1. 220, 'Master' for 'Mistress'.

79. S.D. (J.).

92. *famish a dog's death* Variation on 'die a dog's death'; Rowe's comma after 'famish', with 'a dog's death' in apposition, is unnecessary. S.D. F. 'Exit'.

92–100. *Answer...thief* Prose throughout in Mal. (1790), following piecemeal changes by earlier 18th-cent. edd.; irregular verse in F.

94. *to Lord Timon's* This scene is really unlocalized, and must here be thought of as merely in the vicinity of Tim.'s house.

96. *If...home* i.e. 'as long as Tim. stays at home, there will be a fool in his house' (D.).

98. *Ay; would* (Cap.) F 'I would'.

104. *My mistress is one* Cf. *Meas.* 3. 2. 6–7 for lechery as 'of two usuries, the merriest' [G.K.H.].

106. *mistress'* (Theob., sp. 'mistress's') F 'Mafters'. Cf. l. 78 n.

116. *with...one* For the quibble, cf. *2 H. IV*, note on 3. 2. 329 (misprinted '326' in Notes), and see G. 'stone'.

117–19. *in all shapes...walks in* For the repetition of 'in', cf. Abbott, § 407, Franz, § 543.

118. *from...thirteen* Cf. *Wint.* 3. 3. 59–60, 'I would there were no age between ten and three-and-twenty'.

125. S.D. (Cap.) F 'Enter Timon and Steward'.

127. *elder brother* 'who, as having more money, would be more extravagant' (D.).

128–9. S.D.s (after Cap.) F 'Exeunt' after l. 129. It is not absolutely necessary that Apem. and the Fool should go first, but at any rate they go separately, and l. 129 is addressed only to the servants.

130–3. *marvel wherefore...means.* (F, Al., Sisson, who inadvertently retains 'means?') Rowe 'marvel; wherefore...means?', evidently offended by the word-order 'had you' in an indirect question. But cf. *Lr.* 2. 1. 69–72, 'dost thou think,...would the reposal... Make thy words faithed?', for a comparable mixture of constructions.

132–3. *rated...means* 'regulated my expenditure as my means would allow' (D.).

133–4. *me....proposed—* (J.C.M.) F 'me:... propoſe. [F 2, propoſ'd.]' Cap. 'me,...propos'd.', which most edd. accept. Al. gives the same sense more clearly by dropping the comma. But 'propose leisure' in the sense of 'propose leisure moments for discussion of a subject' is odd, and the interruption which I suppose is a natural one.

137. *unaptness* see G.

141. *found* (F 2) F 'ſound'. The correction is certain, though no recognized sense of 'find' exactly fits. Perh. Flav.'s honesty is thought of as a book in which the accounts are accurately entered. *honesty.* (Shadwell, Rowe) F 'honeſtie,'.

147. *ebb* A typically Sh. metaphor; cf. *Troil.* 2. 3. 139, *Lr.* 5. 3. 19, *Ant.* 1. 4. 43 [Conrad, p. 351].

148–9. *lord—...now too late,...time—* (J.C.M.) F 'Lord,...now (too late)...time,' Camb. 'lord,— ...now, too late!—...time—'. This attaches the 'though' clause unintelligibly to ll. 150–1, and destroys the balance of 'though...yet'. I treat the whole of l. 149 as parenthetic, and equivalent to 'better late than never'. This is virtually D.'s interpretation (based, as he notes, on Ritson), but he obscures it under the Camb. punctuation. Warb. makes it a little neater than Sh. by glossing 'though it be now too late to retrieve your former fortunes, yet it is not too late to prevent, by the assistance of your friends, your future miseries'. Mal., retaining the F brackets, ingeniously but forcedly glosses, 'though you now *at last* listen to my remonstrances, yet now your affairs are in such a state that the whole of your remaining fortune will scarce pay half your debts. You are therefore wise too late'. A simple correction, favoured by Herford and J.D.W., is Han.'s 'yet now's too late a time'.

151. *present* see G. (so also l. 154).

155. *interim* 'spoken of as a fort which the forces of the future are swiftly approaching to attack' (D.).

155. *at length* in the end.

161. *suspect...falsehood* Zeugma: 'suspect my management, or, in particular, suspect that it has been dishonest'. But the Camb. conj. 'of' for 'or' would be simpler.

164. *offices... oppressed* see G.

165. *feeders* see G.; the literal sense gives the word a special aptness here.

167. *brayed* see G.

168–9. *I...flow* Flav. has wept in unison with the tap that has been left running to waste: a notion that has offended many edd. and led to a number of pointless conjectures.

172. *Timon's* Steev.'s conj. 'Lord Timon's' is attractive, and is accepted by Al.

178. *flies* Cf. Lat. 'musca'='parasite' and Tilley, F 206, citing Robson's *Choice Change* (1585), 'Three guests which are first at a banquet. Flies. Dogs. Flatterers'; so Deloney, *Works*, ed. F. O. Mann (1912), p. 204, 'these trencher flies, these smooth faced

flatterers'; Beaumont and Fletcher, *Four Plays...in One*, Prol. to *The Triumph of Time* [based on Lucian's *Timon*], 'see his false friends like those glutted flyes | That when they've suckt their fill, fall off'.

181. *conscience* see G.

184. *argument* see G. *hearts*, F's comma is rightly retained by Sisson, as 'by borrowing' goes with both 'broach' and 'try'.

186. *Assurance* A metaph. use of the legal sense 'securing of a title to property': see *K.J.*, G. In *K.J.* 2. 1. 471 the noun, and in *Son*. 107. 7 the verb 'assure', are used in proximity to the verb 'crown', as here.

187–9. *And...friends* Reverts to the idea of 1. 2. 94 ff.

187. *are crowned* have a royal dignity.

192. *Flaminius* (Rowe) F 'Flauius', which may be what Sh. wrote, as 'Flaminius' gives an irregular line, but is inconsistent with l. 200 (prefix *Flam.*), and with 3. 1. Moreover, 'Flavius' has been established as the steward's name (cf. 1. 2. 158 n.). The nomenclature of the play did not receive Sh.'s final hand.

S.D. (after Rowe) F. 'Enter three Seruants'. The two names are guaranteed by the prefix to l. 200 and by 3. 1. init. S.D. and 3. 2. 24, S.D.

199. *fifty talents* See Note on the Copy, pp. 93–7.

201. Aside (Cap.).

203. *even...health* i.e. 'he by his generosity had ministered in fullest measure to the state's well-being' (D.).

206. *general* 'compendious, the way to try many at a time' (J.).

209. *in return* sc. 'for my pains'.

211. *fall* see G. *treasure* (F 2) F 'Treature'.

215. *catch a wrench* 'be wrenched away from its natural bent' (D., citing *Lr.* 1. 4. 290–1).

216. *intending* see G.

217. *hard fractions* callous and disjointed remarks (J.D.W.).

218. *half-caps...cold-moving* see G. Both expressions suggest that they are too frozen to be capable of a complete and spontaneous gesture.

221. *hereditary* Always in Sh. (except in *Lr.* 1. 1. 81) used in connection with the inheritance of something evil.

222. *blood is caked* Acc. to Galenic physiology age and sorrow dried up the blood. Cf. *Shr.* Ind. ii. 131–2 n., *K.J.* 3. 3. 42–3, 'if...melancholy, | Had baked thy blood and made it heavy-thick' [J.D.W.]; also J. B. Bamborough, *The Little World of Man* (1952), p. 66.

224. *grows....earth* Prob. simply 'comes nearer to its last home', which is also where it came from (Gen. iii. 19), but perh. with a specific reference to 'crooked age'; cf. *Nice Wanton* (ed. J. M. Manly, *Specimens of the Pre-Sh. Drama*, 1897), 268, 'Croked I crepe to the earth agayne'; Middleton, *Phoenix*, 1. 1. 77, 'he bows unto his grave'; Cowley, 'Dangers of an Honest Man', *Essays* (ed. A. B. Gough, 1915), p. 204, 'gently bending down, | With natural propension to that Earth | Which both preserv'd his Life, and gave him birth'; O.E.D. 'grow', 7 c, citing Palsgrave, 'I growe downwardes, as an aged thing dothe that boweth, or stoupeth downwardes'.

226. *Go to Ventidius* Many edd. since Mal. have treated this, and other instructions concerning Ventid., as addressed to a fourth servant (for whom F gives no entry at l. 192), and not to Flavius. Al. and Sisson rightly revert to F.

232. *five talents* See Note on the Copy, pp. 93–7.

233. *good* Perh. 'bona fide', 'valid' [Clarke], but other senses may also be present, such as 'good as it

may afford Ventid. an opportunity of exercising his bounty...or, some honest necessity, not the consequence of a villainous and ignoble bounty [cf. 2. 2. 180, 3. 2. 41]' (Mal.).

236. *Ne'er* F 'Neu'r'; so in *R. II*, 2. 3. 151, where F's copy (Q 3) has 'ne're'.

239. *That thought* Confused. The thought Flav. wishes he could not think is that Tim.'s fortune *can* sink, but the thought that is bounty's foe is Tim.'s own thought that it *cannot* sink, which leads him into prodigality. The drift is clear, but Sh. would prob. have tidied up both idea and metre.

240. S.D. F 'Exeunt'.

3. 1

Loc. (Camb.) *Entry* (after F, which has 'a Lord' for 'Lucullus').

5. Aside (J.). 8. *respectively* see G.

9. S.D. (after Cap.).

13. *I...well* Pointedly ignores the hint given by Flam.'s stress on 'health'.

24. *keep so good a house* be so hospitable. Laments for the decay of 'housekeeping' are frequent in Sh.'s time; cf. *L.L.L.* 2. 1. 103, *2 H. VI*, 1. 1. 189–90.

26. *of purpose* This form survives in 'of set purpose'. The modernization to 'on' is already found in F 3.

28. *Every...fault* This proverb (Tilley, M 116) is used in a similarly jocular fashion in *Wiv.* 1. 4. 12–13. *honesty* see G.

29. S.D. (Cap. after F, which has 'Enter').

32. *Here's to thee* 'The wine, intended at l. 8 for Flam., is now only drunk to his health' (J.D.W.).

33. *speaks your pleasure* 'is pleased to say so' (D.); an expression of modesty.

37–8. S.D.s (after Theob. and Camb.).

43. *solidares* A purely Sh. unit of coinage, adapting Lat. 'solidus'.

44. *wink at* see G.

46–7. *Is't...lived?* Have we lived to see the world so changed? (J.D.W.).

47. *baseness* Concretely also in *Wiv.* 2. 2. 19 [Conrad, p. 353].

48. S.D. (Cap.).

50. S.D. F 'Exit L.'.

52. *Let...damnation* The pouring of molten gold down the throat, recorded as inflicted by the Parthians on Crassus, is thought of as a punishment in hell for avarice [Mason]. T. Wilson, *Discourse upon Usury* (ed. R. H. Tawney, 1925), p. 258, quotes the story of Crassus in relation to usurers; cf. Kyd., S.T. 1. 1. 67. The notion was evidently traditional: cf. Dunbar, *Dance of the Sevin Deidly Synnis*, ll. 61–6; Nashe, *Pierce Penilesse* (1, 218, l. 14); Beaumont and Fletcher, *The Night-Walker*, Act II (*Works*, ed. Waller, VII, 338). The plunging of the souls of the avaricious in molten gold in Plutarch, *Moralia*, 567, is cited by J. E. Hankins, *PMLA*, LXXI (1956), 493.

53. *disease of a friend* Cf. *Lr.* 2. 4. 224–5, 'my daughter; | Or rather a disease that's in my flesh' [Steev.].

56–7. *I...him* Divided by Pope. F ends the first line at 'Honor': perh. a roughness of the draft, but the change gives two good lines with 'passion' trisyllabic, and with Pope's emendation 'hour'.

57. *Unto this hour* (Pope) F 'vnto his Honor'. Clarke unconvincingly explains 'slave...honour' as ironical: 'this man who claims to be devoted to honour'. Steev., with commas round 'unto his honour', glosses 'to the honour of his character', but what has this to do with having Timon's meat in him? Pope's

correction (accepted by J.) makes all clear. For the converse misreading, cf. *Rom.* 1. 3. 67–8 n. The common corruption 'this' to 'his' would naturally follow.

61. *part of nature* 'part of his animal system' (Steev.). Daniel conj. 'of's'.

63 *prolong his hour* Prob.='its hour' [Steev.], but if 'his'='Luc.'s' the sense is still the same: Flam. wishes a lingering death for him, or 'that his life may be prolonged only for the purpose of his being miserable' (Mal.).

3. 2

Loc. (Cap.) *Entry* Strangers i.e. non-Athenians [Delius].

12. *so many* See Note on the Copy, pp. 93–7.

23. *mistook him* made the mistake (of sending to me instead of to Lucullus); see G. This reflexive use is not elsewhere in Sh., but O.E.D. quotes it from Dekker. On. tentatively accepts D.'s 'misdoubted', which seems less appropriate, and cannot be closely paralleled.

35. *his...occasion* what he urgently needs now.

37. *so many* See Note on the Copy, pp. 93–7.

39–40. *want...wants* Perh. a quibble, Luc. meaning 'he cannot be without' and Ser. 'he needs' [Clarke].

39. *fifty five hundred* See Note on the Copy, pp. 93–7.

41. *virtuous* as he himself is (cf. l. 28).

46. *against* for dealing with.

48. *purchase...part* Text very doubtful. Jackson's transposition of 'and' to follow 'before' is attractive, but leaves 'for...part' obscure. Retaining the F order, Han. deleted 'for' which might be a dittographic error after 'before' (sp. 'befor'). Instead of 'part' a word for what he purchased seems required. The slightest changes are given by 'park' (J.) and 'pearl' (sp. 'parl')

(Kellner), but neither is convincing. Steev. treated 'of honour' as understood after 'part'.

49. *undo* On. glosses 'hinder, be a bar to', but it seems to belong to the general sense 'destroy', here virtually = 'lose'.

61. S.D. (after J.) F 'Exit Seruiḷ.', after l. 60.

63. S.D. F 'Exit'.

64. The F prefixes throughout this dialogue are simply '1', '2' and '3'.

66. *spirit* (Theob.) F, Collier, Delius 'ſport', just poss. as 'the mockery that every flatterer exercises on his victim', but a harsh transition from 'soul'.

67. *dips...dish* Cf. Matt. xxvi. 23 [Steev.].

73. *monstrousness* So ingratitude is 'More hideous ...than the sea-monster' in *Lr.* 1. 4. 282–3 (cf. *Lr.* 1. 5. 43–4) and 'monstrous' in *Cor.* 2. 3. 10.

74. *he* human nature.

75–6. *He...beggars* 'what Luc. denies to Tim. is in proportion to what Luc. possesses, less than [J's slip for 'no more than'] the usual alms given by good men to beggars' (J.).

84. *put...into donation* treated as a gift from Tim. [Steev.].

85. *returned* Either trans. (subject 'I') or intrans. (subject 'the best half'). In either case 'the idea is of something going where it is due, to its proper place' (Evans, citing *Ham.* 1. 1. 91; cf. also 'resume' in 2. 2. 4 above).

88. S.D. F 'Exeunt'.

3. 3

Loc. (Cap.) *Entry* (Cap.) F 'Enter a third ſeruant with Sempronius, another of Timons Friends'.

1. *Must...others?* Arranged by Steev.; two lines in F, divided after 'hum'.

3. *Ventidius* F '*Ventidgius*' (so l. 8). A phonetic spelling; cf. above p. 89 and *Ant.* 2. 3. 32 (F), '*Ventigius*'.

4. *these* Rowe 'three', Pope 'these three', attractively.

5. *Owe* (F 2) F 'Owes'; harsh, though not impossible.

5–7. *My...they denied him* Arranged by Steev. after Cap. Four lines in F, ending 'lord', 'metal', 'him', 'him'. But it is not certain that Sh. intended 'My lord' to form part of l. 5, and perh. two lines, 'My...mettle', 'for...they denied him', would be an improvement.

12. *Thrice* (J. conj.) F 'Thriue', Pope 'Three'. The F reading has been taken to mean 'thrive by his bounty and give him over' or to involve an ellipse of 'who' before 'thrive'. But J.'s conj. solves all difficulties.

14–15. *no...first* no sensible reason why he should not have called on me first in his difficulties.

18. *think...me* think of me as being so backward. Cf. Middleton, *Phoenix*, 1. 1. 147, 'I did not think so unfashionably of you'; O.E.D.'s 'perversely' is less plausible.

21. *I 'mongst lords* (Delius) F ''mong'ft Lords'. F 2 ''mong'ft Lords I'. Delius's version is rhythmically superior, and is supported by *Tp.* 3. 3. 57, 'you 'mongst men'.

23. *but...sake* if only to satisfy my kindly feelings towards him; see G. 'mind'.

24. *courage* see G.   26. S.D. F 'Exit'.

28–30. *The devil...clear* The simplest explanation is that the devil does not want to be 'set clear', i.e. shown as relatively innocent, by man's greater wickedness, but to maintain his supremacy [Mal.].

29. *crossed* see G.

32–3. *those...fire* Various of the recent wars of religion (e.g. in France) may have been in Sh.'s mind. Perh. he was thinking specifically of the Jesuits (rather than, as Warb. thought, the Puritans), whom it was customary a little later to describe as incendiaries: cf. a pamphlet of 1623 quoted in R. C. Bald's ed. of Middleton, *A Game of Chesse* (1929), p. 140.

39. *guard sure* i.e. to save him from being arrested for debt.

41. *keep his house* see G. 'keep' and cf. 3. 4. 73–4; not to be confused with 'keep house' in 3. 1. 24. S.D. F 'Exit'.

3. 4

Loc. (Camb.) *Entry* (Mal.) F 'Enter Varro's man, meeting others. All Timons Creditors to wait for his comming out. Then enter Lucius and Hortensius'.

1. Sp.-pref. (Camb.) F 'Var. man'.

2. *Varro* Cf. 2. 2. 9 n.

2–9. *The like...yet.* It is difficult to arrange these brief exchanges in verse, but they do not seem to be intended as mere prose. F's only clear sign of verse is in l. 7, which is divided after 'brother'. My rearrangement varies in a few details from that of Camb.

5. S.D. Philotus Pope 'Philotas' (and 'Philotas's' in l. 6); this form occurs in North's Plut., and may be what Sh. wrote here.

12–13. *prodigal...sun's* Cf. *3 H. VI*, 2. 1. 21–4 n., though there the sun's daily not its seasonal course is in question.

13–17. *Is...little.* My arrangement. F has 'Is... fear' as one line of verse, and the rest prose. Edd. since Pope usually treat 'That...for that' as two lines divided after 'yet', but 'That is' seems, like 'I fear', to be an isolated phrase in rough draft, and 'One... little' is a good verse line.

13. *like the sun's* 'i.e. showing for a shorter time at one season than at another' (D.). *recoverable* 'capable of being retraced' (O.E.D., as nonce-usage); strictly, it is the former position, rather than the course, that can be recovered.

13–14. *recoverable.* | *I fear* (J.) F 'recouerable, I feare:'. For this use of the colon, cf. *Mac.* 3. 4. 122 n.

25. *And* Awkward; perh. caught up from the following line: if so, one might read '''Tis'.

29. *stealth* see G.

33–4. *Your...equalled* Your master had more confidence in Tim. than mine; otherwise the latter's loan would have equalled the former's [Ritson].

41. *too diligent* Flam. makes the ironic pretence of understanding 'attend' as 'serve, wait upon', whereas Tit. had simply meant 'wait for' [Delius].   S.D. *Exit* (Steev.) *Entry* (F, with 'Steward' for 'Flavius').

43. *cloud* see G.

47 *Ay* Placed here by Camb ; in a separate line Cap.; with l. 48 F.

51. *ate* F 'eate'. Edd. (except Singer and Keightley) have been oddly reluctant to modernize this sp.

57. *reckon* see G.

59. *If* (F 4) F 'If't'.

60. S.D. (Rowe). This exit is not absolutely necessary, but the next speech makes it probable.

64. *broader* see G.; with quibble on the idea of being abroad, i.e. not confined to the house [Delius].

65. *no...in* Cf. *Lr.* 3. 2. 25.

71. *of my soul* from my heart (strengthens the asseveration).

74. *are* who are.

75. *if...health* Odd. Rowe read 'he' for 'it'. Perh. = 'if his situation has changed so much from what it was when he was in good health'.

78. *an answer* (Rowe) F 'anfwer'. The correction

gives a complete line and implies an easy haplographic error, exactly paralleled by F 2 at *Ado*, 1. 2. 20.

79. S.D. (F; Cap.).

81. *free* Cf. Introd., p. xxxv ff.

88. Hortensius (Cap.) F '1. *Var.*'.

89. Both Varro's Servants (Mal. after Cap.) F '2. *Var.*'.

91. *Knock...girdle* see G. 'bill'.

100. S.D. F 'Exit Timon'.

101–2. *throw...money* see G. 'cap', and cf. Nashe, *Four Letters Confuted* (1, 318, ll. 17–18), '*Pierce Pennilesse* may well cast his cappe after it for ever overtaking it', Tilley, C 62, and Lucas on Webster, *Duchess of Malfi*, 4. 2. 111, suggesting that the precise sense is, 'give up in despair, since doing one's utmost is in vain'.

103. S.D. S (i) F 'Exeunt' (ii) (Pope) F 'Enter Timon'; cf. l. 60 S.D.

104–5. *They...devils* Arranged by Rowe; prose in F.

107. *What...so?* The idea of the banquet has evidently come to him.

111. *fitly!* (Rowe) F 'fitly?', but Timon's thoughts have now fixed on his plan.

112. *Sempronius—all* (F 2, with misprint, 'Semprovius') F '*Sempronius Vllorxa:* All'. This *vox nihili* has provoked much speculation not worth recording. Most recently, Sisson takes it to be 'an interlined rewriting of a blotted [*Luc*]*ullus &*, taken by the compositor as an additional name'.

113–16. *O...table* Arr. by Pope; prose in F.

115. *There is* (Cap.) F 'There's'.

117. *Go* Separate line in Camb.; with l. 118 in F.

119. S.D. F 'Exeunt'.

3. 5

For the relation of this scene to the rest of the play, see Introduction, p. xxxviii–xl.

S.D. *Loc.* (Theob.) *Entry* (J.C.M.) F 'Enter three Senators at one doore, Alcibiades meeting them, with Attendants'. As Alc. evidently does not hear ll. 1–4, his entry, roughly jotted down by Sh., is best postponed. On the other hand, 'three senators', evidently a small committee, should be retained rather than altered to 'the Senate' with later edd.

3. *Nothing...mercy.* This is the fourth commonplace of [Cic.] *ad Herennium*, ii. xxx. 48. Cf. *Rom.* 3. 1. 196, *Lucr.* 1687, T. Hughes, *Misfortunes of Arthur* (in *Early Eng. Classical Tragedies*, ed. J. W. Cunliffe), 3. 1. 62–5 [G.K.H.].

4. *him* (Han.) F, Sisson ''em', defensible with difficulty as='such sinners'. It would also be poss., but awkwardly sibilant, to read 'sins' in l. 3.

S.D. (after Dyce).

12–13. *Hath...into't* For the metaphor, cf. *Mac.* 3. 4. 136–8.

12. *past depth* unfathomable.

14. *this* (Warb. conj.) *fault* (Pope). F 'his Fate'. Restoration is uncertain, but Steev.'s paraphrase of F., 'putting this action of his, which was predetermined by fate, out of the question', is forced. The repetition of 'fault' in l. 17 has some, but in a rough draft not much, weight against Pope's emendation; nor 'fact' in l. 16 against Han.'s 'fact' here.

17. *An* (J.) F 'And'. The whole line is in brackets in F, which confirms that it is a parenthesis.

18. *fair* A vague word; S. Walker's 'free' (a recurrent word in *Tim.*) is attractive.

22. *behove* F 'behooue' Rowe 'behave'. 'Behove his anger' seems to be a boldly contextual usage for

'sway his anger to do that which behoved it' (Clarke). Several recent edd. have accepted this reading; Ridley (glossing '? control'), Al., Sisson (glossing 'moderate').

ere 'twas spent The sense seems to be that what began as an outburst of passion became subdued, so that the eventual killing was the outcome of a sense of honour alone.

24. *undergo...strict* see G.

27. *bring...into form* see G. 'form'. Sykes, *N. & Q.* 13 ser. 1 (1923), 189, who attributes this scene to Middleton, quotes *Phoenix*, 4. 1. 6–9, 'I'll strive to bring this act into such form | And credit among men, they shall suppose, | Nay, verily believe, the prince, his son, | To be the plotter of his father's murder'.

27–8. *set...valour* see G. 'head'. Less satisfactorily Schmidt, 'think it the crown, or top of valour'; D., 'make it an adjunct of valour [like a crest]'.

35. *prefer* see G. The heart is thought of as a place of dignity, into which the injuries are ushered; cf. *Cor.* 1. 1. 140, 'the court, the heart'.

37–8. *If...ill* The argument is obscure. Perh. there is a play on two senses of 'evils' and 'ill'. When we kill because of wrongs, we hazard life 'for ill' in the sense of 'because of a preceding evil', but the action can be said to be irrational only in the other sense of 'for ill', viz. 'to gain something evil'. If this seems over-elaborate, 'if' can be taken as 'even if': i.e. 'even if we must kill to avenge wrongs, it is still foolish to risk our own lives for this evil purpose'. The couplet sounds like an attempted epigram that Sh. did not quite get into focus.

49. *bearing* Prob. equivocal: (*a*) bearing children, (*b*) bearing men in sexual intercourse [Danchin]. For the same quibble cf. *Shr.* 2. 1. 201 n., and for (*b*) *Ant.* 1. 5. 21.

51. *felon* (Theob. conj.; see Camb., note XIII)
F 'fellow', but a more specific description is required
to balance 'judge' and to correspond to 'ass' and 'lion'.

55. *sin's extremest gust* Either 'the utmost degree
of appetite for sin' (J.), or a metaphor from gusts of
wind [Steev.], cf. *Shr.* 2. 1. 135, 'extreme gusts'
(literal), and 'gust of sin', cited from G. Daniel (1639)
in O.E.D. 'gust', sb.¹, 2. The second alternative is
supported by 'rashness' in l. 54.

56. *by Mercy* 'I call Mercy herself to witness' (J.)
is simpler than 'by a merciful and clement interpretation of the laws' (Mal.).

61. *Lacedæmon and Byzantium* Sh. could have
found these in Plut.'s *Life of Alcibiades*.

62. *briber* Contemptuous; suggesting that bribes
are the only arguments the senators will listen to
[J.D.W.].

63. *Why, I say* (F 2) F. 'Why fay' Pope 'I say'.
Prob. compositor's omission; the F text would have
to mean 'put it to yourselves'.

67. *'em* (F 2) F 'him'. The whole line is obscure,
seeming to involve a word-play on 'plenteous' and
'plenty' which escapes me. Perh. 'he has revelled too
much on the strength of what he gained by his valour'.

68. *a sin* drunkenness, as appears from what
follows.

73. *inferred* see G.

77. *his own time* App. 'the right of dying when his
time came' (D.). Schmidt lists under 'life', but such
a meaning usu. has more help from the context than
here.

79. *to* see G.

81–3. *security...returns* see G. 'He charges them
obliquely with being usurers' (J.). For the pun on
'security' cf. *Meas.* 3. 2. 220.

82. *honour* F 2's 'honours' seems unnecessary.

86. *For...more* D.'s suggested transposition of 'law' and 'war' would give a more obvious sense.

88. *On...displeasure* Compressed for 'on pain of our highest displeasure'.

89. *another* the blood of another. Awkward and dictated by rhyme.

104. *not...spirit* Obscure. Steev., 'not to put ourselves into any tumour of rage', presumably meaning that his immediate death will allay their anger. Perh. 'not...spirit' is corrupt. The context suggests, as J.D.W. notes, that it contains a threat, but no emendation commends itself.

105. S.D. (after Cap.) F 'Exeunt'.

106–7. *life* | *Only in bone* be mere living skeletons.

110. *interest, I* (Rowe, with semicolon) F 'intereſt. I'.

118. *lands* Suspicious. Mal. 'lords'. Jackson conj. 'bands', which J.D.W. favours, paraphrasing 'most troops think it an honour to be at war'.

119. S.D. F 'Exit'.

3.6

Loc. (Camb.) *Entry* (Camb. after Cap.) F 'Enter diuers Friends at feuerall doores'. The prefixes for the friends and senators throughout this sc. are simply '1', '2', '3', and '4'. Sisson, perh. rightly, identifies them as Lucullus, Lucius, Sempronius and Ventidius.

4. *tiring* see G. 'tire'.

19. *here's* (F 4) F 'heares'.

21. *pieces* i.e. crowns; cf. 3.4.30.

28–31. *The swallow...men* Cf. Tilley, S 1026, citing Taverner's *Proverbes* (1539), 'Kepe no swalowes vnder the same roufe of thy house', with note, 'That is, Brynge not vp, neither kepe thou company with such as in thy prosperitie seke thy frendship, but in aduersitie or when they haue their desyre, forsake the'.

30–1. S.D.s (after J.).

31. *summer birds* Cf. Nashe, *Four Letters Confuted* (1, 291, l. 30), 'fortunes summer folower'; G. Herbert, *The Answer*, ll. 4–5, 'like summer friends, | Flyes of estates and sunne-shine', with Hutchinson's note.

33. *so harshly o'* on such rough fare as. Rowe adds 'as' before 'o'', but cf. 'so...to'='so...as to' (Abbott, § 281).

45. *cumber* Cf. *Tp.* 5. 1. 200, 'burden our remembrance'. *your better remembrance* A vaguely polite turn of phrase, with no clear comparative implication; cf. *Ham.* 1. 2. 15, 'your better wisdoms' [J.D.W.].

46. S.D. Placed here by Dyce; after l. 39 in F. *banquet* F 'Banket', representing the contemp. pronunciation.

56. *upon what?* for what reason?

60. *still* One of the few places in Sh. where the mod. sense 'now as formerly' is more suitable than 'always'.

62. *time will—* Various proverbs would fill the gap, e.g. 'Time reveals all things' (Tilley, T 333), 'Time tries all things' (T 336). *Ado*, 1. 1. 245, 'as time shall try', suggests that 'try' is the word omitted.

65–6. *in all places alike* i.e. not better at one end of the table than at the other [Delius].

78. *as they are* implying 'no better than they should be'. *fees* Perh. 'creatures holding their lives and properties in fee from you' (Clarke); but corruption is possible. Warb.'s 'foes' is simple, and gives tolerable sense.

79. *lag* (Rowe) F 'legge' Anon *ap.* Rann 'tag' (cf. *Cor.* 3. 1. 248). Rowe's reading, taken to mean 'lowest class', is not exactly paralleled, though the plur.='dregs' is recorded. It is poss. that F retains an unrecorded colloquial use of 'leg' in a derogatory sense similar to that of Menenius's 'great toe of this assembly'

(*Cor.* 1. 1. 159); so J. E. Phillips, *The State in Sh.'s Greek and Roman Plays* (1940), p. 128.

80–1. *make...destruction* Unexpectedly instead of 'amend'.

84. S.D. (after J. and Steev., conj.) Steev. added the 'stones', which figure in the anon. *Timon*, painted to resemble artichokes.

88. *smoke* For the sense of 'a "mist" of words, mere talk', On. cites also 4. 3. 143, *L.L.L.* 3. 1. 62, *Lucr.* 1027, *K.J.* 2. 1. 229.

89. *your perfection* 'the highest of your excellence' (J.), or perh. more specifically, 'what you are best at'.

90. *stuck and spangled* Suggests that they are spurious and tinselly. *with your* (Warb.) F 'you with', which looks like a miscorrection of 'with you'. (For the type of error, cf. *Mac.* (F) 2. 1. 57.) It is absurd to defend F by taking 'flatteries' as the 'bounties' which Timon had bestowed on unworthy recipients.

92. S.D. (J.).

95. *fools of fortune* Comes oddly in the midst of vehement insults; D.'s 'empty-headed worshippers of fortune' and Schmidt's 'foolish followers of fortune' are too mild, but I cannot think of a more forcible interpretation. *time's flies* Cf. 2. 2. 178 n.

96. *vapours...minute-jacks* see G. Steev. may be right in seeing an allusion also to the 'Jack of the clock'; cf. *R. II*, 5. 5. 60 (see G.); *R. III*, 4. 2. 111.

97. *Of...malady* 'every kind of disease incident to man and beast' (J.).

100. S.D. (after S. Walker). Edd. from Rowe had him throw the dishes, but l. 119 seems to be meant literally; cf. l. 84 S.D.

103. *Burn...Athens* I follow F in omitting commas after the verbs, which are prob. third person imper.; cf. 1. 2. 130 n.; 4. 1. 7 n.

104. S.D.s (Camb.) F 'Exit | Enter the Senators, with other Lords'. The fact that 'Senators' are here mentioned for the first time suggests the rough state of the draft for this scene.

108. *Push* see G.

119. S.D. F 'Exeunt the Senators'.

4. 1

Loc. (Rowe).

2. *girdles* Cf. Franz, § 152. This second pers. in -*s* is specially common for euphony after *t* (cf. 4. 3. 43, 5. 1. 130), but is found also in other contexts, as in *Ant.* 1. 3. 103, 'thou...goes yet'.

6. *steads. . . .filths* (Shadwell, with 'stead' for 'steads') F 'fteeds,...Filthes.'.

7. *instant,* No comma in F, but l. 8 shows that 'virginity' is addressed. By contrast, I take 'fail' (l. 4) and 'Pluck' (l. 5) to be third pers. imper., and so retain F's absence of commas.

8–9. *fast;...back,* (Anon. conj. *ap.* Theob.) F 'faft...backe;' Shadwell, with commas in both places, may have anticipated the correction.

11. *Large-handed* see G.; ironic use of a word that would more naturally mean 'generous'.

13. *is o'th'brothel* i.e. belongs to it [D.]. Cf. *Lr.* 2. 2. 1, 'Art of this house?'.   *Son* (F 2) F 'Some'.

13–21. *Son...live* The same sort of confusion is described as in *Troil.* 1. 3. 85 ff.

14. *lined* see G.

20. *confounding contraries* contraries (to piety, etc.), which cause general chaos. This fits the context better than Steev.'s 'contraries whose nature is to waste and destroy each other'.

21. *yet* Shadwell (and many edd. since Han.) 'let'; but a paradox is being put forward, to which

'yet' contributes: 'though by such confusion all things seem to hasten to dissolution, yet let not dissolution come, but the miseries of confusion continue' (J.). Less plausibly 'yet' could be taken temporally, = 'still' [D.].

23. *stroke* Perh. specifically Jove's thunder-bolt [J.D.W.]. *cold sciatica* 'cold gout' was a name for sciatica in the 16th century (see O.E.D. 'cold', 19).

25–6. *Lust and liberty...minds and marrows* A chiastic (*abba*) pattern; see G. 'liberty'.

27. *'gainst...strive* Noble notes that 'the identification of striving against the stream with going contrary to the precepts of virtue' is in the Bishops' version of Ecclus. iv. 26. For the prov., cf. Tilley, S 927.

30. *general leprosy* Cf. Dekker, *Satiromastix*, 5. 2. 195–6, 'And turne my *Muse* into a *Timonist*, | Loathing the general Leprozie of Sinne' [Wright, p. 13].

33. *detestable* Regularly stressed 'détestable' by Sh.

34. *Take...too* i.e. when I say I bear nakedness from you, that does not mean I do not also wish it on you along with the other evils. *multiplying* ever increasing; cf. *Mac.* 1. 2. 11.

35. *to the woods* Hankins, p. 178, compares Palingenius's advice (p. 180) to the man 'who naught can bear' to 'lead his life alone in woodes'.

35–6. *where...mankind* Cf. *A.Y.L. passim, R. III*, 1. 2. 71 n.

38. *within and out* Also in *Court of Love* (attributed to Chaucer, but actually a 16th-century poem), 100. Cf. Jonson, *Cat.* 2. 1. 173, 'with, and out' [D.].

41. S.D. F 'Exit'.

4. 2

Loc. (Camb. after Rowe) *Entry* (F, with 'Steward' for 'Flavius'). *two or three* A typical authorial S.D.; cf. *2 H. VI*, p. 119. The servants in F are '1', '2', '3', as is usual with minor group characters in this play.

4. *Let...recorded* let it be recorded of me. *recorded* Best stressed on the first syllable: not elsewhere in Sh., but cf. Marlowe *1 Tamb.* 5. 2. 425, 'I record heaven'.

10. *familiars...fortunes* those who were the familiar friends of his now buried fortunes [Mal.]. The sense 'familiar spirit', i.e. those who haunted his fortunes, may also be present, and would fit in with 'grave' and 'slink away' [J.D.W.].

13. *dedicated beggar to* beggar dedicated to; cf. Abbott, § 419a.

14. *all-shunned* Hyphenated by Pope. This instrumental use of 'all-' in compounds, ='by all', is not common outside Sh. (see O.E.D. 'all', E 8). A late ex. is Byron, *Don Juan*, VII, 6, 'this scene of all-confess'd inanity'.

26–7. *knell...seen better days* Linked also in *A.Y.L.* 2. 7. 113–14, where the attachment of a faithful servant to his master in adversity is again in mind.

28. *all your hands* the hands of all of you; cf. 3. 4. 90, 'All our bills'; Franz, § 324.

29. S.D. (Camb.; F).

33. *to live* For insertion of 'to' in the second of two parallel clauses, cf. Abbott, § 350.

34. *dream of friendship* A typically Sh. figure; cf. *Ham.* 1. 2. 21, 2. 2. 555, *Tw.N.* 2. 5. 196 [Delius; Conrad, p. 361].

35. *all what* all that; cf. *Tit.* 2. 1. 122, 'with all (Q 1: withall) what (Q 2: that) we intend', and Arden (1953) note; Milton, *P.L.* v. 107.

36. *varnished* see G. This precise participial use is rare, but the fig. use of the noun for 'specious gloss or outward show' is recorded from 1565. Cf. Vernish as the name of a false friend in Wycherley's *Plain Dealer* [G.K.H.].

41. *does* (F 4) F 'do'.

48. *it* The means of supplying his livelihood. The draft appears to be very rough at this point.

51. S.D. F 'Exit'.

4.3

Loc. and Entry (Camb.) F 'Enter Timon in the woods'.

2. *Rotten humidity* The accepted notion of the age; cf. *Lucr.* 778, *Ant.* 4. 9. 13, *Tp.* 1. 2. 322–4. *below ...orb* in the sublunary (and therefore corruptible) world.

5. *dividant* Sh. has a liking for words in '-ant', '-ent', with passive meaning; cf. 'credent' (*Wint.* 1. 2. 142), 'intrenchant' (*Mac.* 5. 8. 9) [Hudson].

6–8. *Not...of nature* The multiple senses of 'nature' make this difficult to interpret with confidence. J. paraphrased 'human nature,... besieged as it is by misery... when elevated by fortune, will despise beings of nature like its own'. It seems to me poss. that 'bear' = 'bear without ill effects' and 'but... nature', 'except by despising (and transcending) mere unregenerate nature'. Neilson and Hill gloss 'but... nature' by 'without outraging natural affection'.

6. *Not nature* The metrical harshness prob. belongs to the rough draft, as 'To... siege' seems to call for generalized 'nature', i.e. 'human nature', not for 'a nature' (Fleay) or 'his nature' (Cap.).

9. *deject* (Arrowsmith, *N. & Q.* 2 ser. 1 (1856), 85) F 'deny't', the objection to which is not so much the vague 'it' as the failure in antithesis. The contrast required to 'raise' is not 'deny advancement' but 'cast down'. Arrowsmith cited two places in Middleton where 'raise' and 'deject' are opposed: 'deiect' could easily be misread 'deniet'.

10–11. *The senator...honour* i.e. each will be treated as if born to the position he now occupies.

10. *senator* (Rowe) F 'Senators'.

12. *pasture* (Rowe) F 'Pastour', a phonetic sp. (still rhymed with 'master' by Wordsworth, *Incident ...Dog*, l. 3); cf. Kökeritz, p. 271. *wether's* (Warb. *ap.* Theob.) F 'Brothers' Singer and most edd. 'rother's'. But 'w' could easily be misread as 'br', and for the 'o:e' confusion, cf. *MSH*, 109–10. The reversion to Warb. is due to Sisson (*Readings*), who cites *A.Y.L.* 3. 2. 26, 'good pasture makes fat sheep'.

13. *lean* (F 2) F 'leaue'.

15. *say* (F 2) F 'fay'.

18. *All's obliquy* (Ridley) F 'All's obliquie'. Pope (and most edd.) 'All is oblique'. D. was 'not convinced that Sh. did not here coin "obliquy" for "obliquity"'; I am convinced he did, with an effective play on 'obloquy'. Cf. *Meas.* 1. 3. 30–1, 'quite athwart | Goes all decorum'.

19. *level* see G. The figure is kept up by 'direct'.

23. *fang* seize. The noun 'fangs' is originally just a specialized derivative of this, but its meaning prob. influenced the sense Sh. attached to the obsolescent vb. Cf. the use as a proper name in *2 H. IV*, 2. 1. S.D. (Camb. after Rowe).

26. *Gold...gold* Hankins, pp. 159 ff., sees here and elsewhere in the scene (esp. ll. 383 ff.) indebtedness to Palingenius, pp. 73, 89. Some very interesting comments on this passage in Karl Marx's early work, *Political Economy and Philosophy*, were reprinted and discussed by Kenneth Muir in *Modern Quarterly Miscellany*, 1 [1947], 71–6.

27. *no idle votarist* i.e. I meant what I said in asking for roots.

31. *why this?* Looks like a false start, intended to be replaced by the following 'what this'.

33. *Pluck...heads* Alludes to the custom of drawing away the pillow to allow a dying man to die

more easily. 'Stout' implies that gold will hasten on
their way even those who are not at their last gasp
[Warb.]. Cf. Jonson, *Volp.* 2. 6. 87–8 [D.].

36. *hoar leprosy* Cf. 2 Kings v. 27, 'a leper as white
as snow' [D.].   *place* see G.

39. *wappered* (Mal. conj.) F 'wappen'd'. Mal.'s
form is better authenticated: cf. E.D.D., and *Two
Noble Kinsmen*, 5. 4. 10, 'unwapper'd'. For the sense,
cf. *R. III*, 1. 1. 81, 'The jealous o'erworn widow'.
J. N. Tidwell, *N. & Q.* cxcv (1950), 139–40, suggests that 'wappen' may be a variant of 'wap', for
which the slang sense 'copulate' is recorded.

40–1. *whom...at* 'whom the spital-house, however polluted, would...reject with abhorrence' (Mal.).

41–2. *spices* | *To th' April day* 'restores to her all
the freshness and sweetness of youth' (Tollet *ap.*
Steev.); cf. *Son.* 3. 10, 'Calls back the lovely April of
her prime'.

43. *puts* Cf. 4. 1. 2 n.

45. *Do...nature* The meaning of this depends on
whether Tim. is thinking of the gold he is going to
bury again or the sample he is keeping out. If the
former, 'lie in the earth where nature laid thee' (J.);
if the latter, 'behave like the whore you are' [D.],
which seems more pointed; cf. *Ant.* 5. 2. 261–2, 'the
worm will do his kind', and O.E.D. 'kind', sb., 3 c;
but l. 48 reads like the first intimation that he intends
to keep any out.   *quick* see G., and cf. Lucian,
Timon, 20, describing how wealth is lame on its way
to a man but 'swifter than a dream' [Erasmus's Lat.,
and the anon. *Timon*, 1. 1, have 'than a bird', following
MSS. of Lucian which read ὀρνέων for ὀνείρων] in
leaving him.

46–7. *go...stand* As often, antithetically used; see
G. 'go'.

46. *strong* see G., and cf. *Nice Wanton* (ed. J. M.

Manly, *Specimens of the Pre-Sh. Drama*, 1897), 465–6, 'thy daughter was a strong whore, | And thy sonne a strong thief'. It is a 'thief' because it takes itself away from its owner so promptly.

48. S.D.s (Pope, F).

53. *Misanthropos* Cf. the three marginal notes to the story of Tim. in North's tr. of Plutarch's *Life of Antony* referring to 'Timon Misanthropus'.

64–5. *I...again* 'This alludes to an opinion in former times, generally prevalent, that the venereal infection transmitted to another, left the infecter free (J.). Cf. Beaumont and Fletcher, *Custom of the Country* (Variorum Ed. 1, 1904, 3. 2. 182), '*Hipp.* I'll kiss thee well. *Aen.* I am not sick of that sore'; Donne, *Sat.* IV, 134–5.

74–7. *If...man* Puzzling, as by not promising, or by performing, Alc. will fail to 'maintain' Tim.'s 'opinion'. If the text is sound, he must mean, 'however thou may'st act, since thou art a man, hated man, I wish thee evil' (J.). But there is some temptation to read 'no man...no man', following Shadwell, 'no man... none neither'. Other attempts to achieve a more normal sense are Staunton's conj. 'but promise' for 'not promise', and Cap.'s 'promise and perform' for 'perform'.

84–8. *Be diet* Arranged by Pope; prose in F.

86. *Make use of* profit by (not the mod. weakened sense).   *salt...Season* Perh. alluding to the 'powdering-tub', lit. the tub for salting meat for winter; humorously the sweating-tub for treatment of venereal disease; cf. *H. V*, 2. 1. 75.

88. *tub-fast* (Warb. *ap.* Theob.) F 'Fubfaft'.

106–7. *That...country* Unmetrical; perh. a mere stop-gap in the rough draft.

109–11. *planetary...air* Planets 'in opposition' were supposed to blast objects or persons that fell

beneath their influence, and the plagues that visited
London were often associated with poisonous air and
planetary influence. Cf. *Troil*. 1. 3. 94 ff., *L.L.L.*
5. 2. 394, *Cor*. 2. 2. 117–18, 'struck | Corioli like a
planet'.

117. *window-bars* (J. conj.) F 'window Barne'.
Prob. literal, 'the lattice of her chamber' (J.), though
Staunton and others take as a reference to 'cross-bars
or lattice-work across the breasts'.

119. *But* Pope's omission of this may represent
what would have been Sh.'s final intention.

122. *thy* (Pope) F 'the'; so l. 186. Sisson
(*Readings*) defends F on the ground that the oracle
pronounces only that the babe 'will cut somebody's
throat'; but something more pointed—an Oedipus-
situation—is surely intended.

123. *Swear against objects* 'let not any thing move
you to pity' (Schmidt); cf. *Troil*. 4. 5. 105–6, 'Hector
in his blaze of wrath subscribes | To tender objects'.

130. *yet?* (F 4) F 'yet,'.

130–1. *Hast...counsel* Arranged by Cap.; prose
in F.

135. *to...bawd* Prob. 'to make a bawd leave
making whores' (J.), i.e. retire from business. But
perh. 'to set up as a bawd, making whores instead of
being one'.

137–9. *swear...gods* Cf. *Ant*. 1. 3. 28 [Steev.].

137. *swear* sc., to do all he is about to bid them.

143. *close* And therefore all the stronger: cf. Tilley,
F 265, *Gent*. 1. 2. 30.   *smoke* Cf. 3. 6. 88 n.

144–8. *Yet...still* F lineation, which shows the
roughness of the draft. It seems possible that the odd
appearance of l. 145 in F, 'Be quite contrary, And
Thatch', reproduces what stood in the MS. If so, and
if Sh. broke off and made a fresh start, it is not sur-
prising that the train of thought is obscure. If the

passage is continuous, 'yet...contrary' should prob. be treated as a parenthesis [Mason]. The wish Tim. expresses seems to be that they may for six months (in every year?) suffer pains opposite to their normal ones as whores, viz. 'the severe discipline necessary for the repair of' their diseases [Warb.]. J. conj. 'contraried', explaining 'he wishes that they may do all possible mischief, and yet take pains six months of the year in vain'.

146. *burdens of the dead* false hair from dead bodies. Cf. *M.V.* 3. 2. 92–6, 'those crispéd snaky golden locks...often known | To be the dowry of a second head, | The skull that bred them in the sepulchre'.

149. *mire* see G.

153. *hollow* Cf. *Meas.*, G. Donne, *Sermons*, ed. Potter and Simpson, VI, 18, 262–3, associates Job xx. 11, 'His bones are full of the sin of his youth', with venereal disease. 'Hollow' and 'sharp' are both proleptic [D.].

154. *spurring* Prob. equivocal [Danchin].

157–8. *scolds...himself* inveighs against fleshly desires but does not practise what he preaches; see G. 'quality'.

157. *scolds* (Rowe) F 'fcold'ft'; cf. l. 256, and *R. III*, 1. 2. 39 (F), where the same compositor is responsible.

158–9. *Down...away* An effect of syphilis.

160–1. *his...weal* 'to provide for his private advantage, he leaves the right scent of publick good' (J.); see G. 'foresee', 'particular', 'from'. The figure, suggested by 'nose', is that of a hound which hunts 'counter' (*Ham.* 4. 5. 110).

168–71. *More...again* Verse in Pope; prose in F.

172. *If...well* i.e. if my hopes are realized: a mannered phrase, modelled on the preceding line.

175. *and take* Placed here by Dyce; F at beginning of next line.

176. *beagles* see G.; with implication of smallness also in *Tw.N.* 2. 3. 185, where see n.   S.D. (J.; after Theob.) F 'Exeunt'.

178. S.D. (J., before l. 177; Camb. here).

183. *eyeless venomed worm* blind-worm, falsely believed to be poisonous; cf. *Mac.* 4. 1. 16.

186. *thy* (Shadwell, Pope) F 'the', cf. l. 122. *doth* (Cap.) F 'do' Shadwell 'does' Rowe 'do's'.

188. *Ensear...womb* Cf. *Lr.* 1. 4. 301, 'Dry up in her the organs of increase' [Steev.].

194. *marrows* J. made this correspond specifically to 'morsels unctuous', but that answers 'leas', as 'draughts' answers 'vines'. 'Vines...leas' together is in apposition to 'marrows', explaining the exact nature of what the latter metaphorically refers to [D.]. To make this clearer, I have dropped the comma after 'vines'. Cf. Ps. lxiii. 6 (B.C.P.), 'my soul shall be satisfied, even as it were with marrow and fatness'.

196. *unctuous* F 'Vnctious', a sp. 'common *c.* 1600–1725' (O.E.D.).   *greases* The metaphor turns on 'greasy'=lewd (cf. *L.L.L.* 4. 1. 136).   *pure* Cf. *K.J.* 5. 7. 2 n.; but here the reference seems primarily moral.

203. *infected* Prob. 'caught by infection (from your circumstances)'. On.'s gloss 'affected, factitious' may be right for *Comp.* 323, but is not needed here.

205. *fortune* (Shadwell, Southern MS. in copy of F 4, Rowe) F 'future'.

208. *diseased perfumes* 'diseased perfumed mistresses' (Mal.); cf. *Oth.* 4. 1. 145. Sh. stresses 'perfúme' and 'pérfume' indifferently.

210. *cunning of a carper* Ironical, since any fool can carp [J.D.W.]. The irony recoils on Apem., who has no other 'cunning'.

212. *hinge thy knee* Cf. *Ham*. 3. 2. 59, 'crook the pregnant hinges of the knee' [Steev.].

213. *observe* see G.

216. *bade* F 'bad', F 2 'bid', which some follow. But it is natural for the tense within the comparison to be assimilated to that of the main sentence.

224. *mossed* (Han.) F 'moyſt', which has recently been defended, by Sisson (*Readings*) on the ground that 'Ap. is describing the rigours of nature in hard weather. The brook is cold, and the trees are moist'; by F. P. Wilson (*Proc. Brit. Acad.* xxvii (1941), 180), on the ground that 'the emphasis is not on aged trees', and that 'moist'='full of sap, pithy'—they are trees 'whose strength is such that they have withstood the harshness of nature longer than' the eagle, etc. But the age *is* the point, as something that makes it specially incongruous that they should page Tim.'s heels, just as the bleakness of the air, and the coldness of the brook are incongruous with the task required of them. 'Moist', in either sense suggested, would break the sequence. That 'mossed' as a participial adj. is not elsewhere recorded before Han.'s emendation matters little; it occurs as a participle in *A.Y.L.* 4. 3. 104.

226. *where* (Shadwell, S. Walker) F 'when', but 'point'st out' seems to demand a reference to place; cf. *Err*. 3. 2. 57, *2 H. IV*, Ind. 36, *Ham*. 2. 2. 452 (*MSH*, 107) for the corruption.

227. *morning taste* bad taste in the mouth after the 'o'ernight's surfeit' [Delius].

230. *unhousèd* Cf. 'houseless' twice in the similar passage in *Lr*. 3. 4. 26, 30, and D. G. James cited in New Arden note there, suggesting a play on O.E.D. 'house', sb.², 'covering of textile material'. O.E.D. has one quotation (1560) for 'unhoused' in this sense, and a pun would be in place here.

232. *Answer mere nature* Doubtful; 'cope with

nature in all its stark rigour' (D.), cf. *Lr.* 3. 4. 106;
'have no more than the absolute necessities of nature
requires' (Hudson); J.D.W. prefers 'correspond with
the state of "unaccommodated man" (*Lr.* 3. 4. 111)'.
bid...thee Cf. *A.Y.L.* 2. 1. 6–11.

239. *too* Because he has already called him fool at
l. 233.

240. *sour, cold* Steev. and edd. (not Sisson) hy-
phenate, but the two adjectives are independent.

243–8. *Willing...content* Hankins, pp. 175–6,
thinks this indebted to Palingenius, pp. 18–19. The
theme of contentment in a lowly status is common in
Sh.; cf. *3 H. VI*, 2. 5. 1–54 n., 3. 1. 62–5; *2 H. IV*,
3. 1. 4–31 n.; *H. V*, 4. 1. 226 ff. n.

244. *Outlives incertain* (Rowe; Shadwell 'excel |
Uncertain') F 'Out-liues: incertaine'.   *is crowned
before* 'arrives sooner at the completion of its wishes'
(J.).

245. *filling...complete* Cf. *Cym.* 1. 6. 47–9. In
both places there is prob. a reference to the Danaids,
condemned to attempt perpetually to fill leaky tubs,
who are mentioned in Lucian's *Timon* [D.].

246. *at high wish* at the height of its wishes; perh.
on the model of 'at high tide'.

250. *breath* see G. There may be a quibble on bad
breath, as in *Cor.* 1. 1. 61, 2. 1. 252, *Ado*, 5. 2. 50–1.

253–4. *proceeded...degrees* see G. for word-play.

255. *drugs* F 'drugges' Mason 'drudges'. If
'drugs' is right, it prob. has the general sense of 'all
things in passive subserviency to salutary as well as
pernicious purposes' (Schmidt). As 'poisons' is the
most frequent Sh. sense, a hostile attitude towards
worldly goods is prob. predominant. The conj. (or
interpretation, as 'drug' occurs as a form of 'drudge':
see O.E.D.) 'drudges' is supported by *M.V.* 3. 2.
103–4, where silver is 'pale and common drudge |

'Tween man and man'. This parallel suggests that even if we accept 'drudges', the reference is still a fig. one to inanimate 'drudges'. It is just poss. that a pun depending on the form 'drug'='drudge' is intended.

256. *command*ₗ(Rowe) F 'command'ſt', cf. l. 157 n.

259. *icy* Reason is traditionally cold. *respect* see G.

260. *game* quarry, but 'sug'red' adds suggestion of 'daughters of the game' (*Troil.* 4. 5. 63). *myself* Left hanging, and taken up at l. 267 in 'I to bear this'.

261. *confectionary* see G.; carries on the figure of 'sug'red'.

263. *At duty* 'at my service' (D.). *frame employment* The omission of a postponed preposition (here 'for') is common; cf. *Tit.* 2. 1. 103, 'join for that you jar'.

264–7. *as leaves...blows* Cf. *Son.* 73. 1–3. This comparison to a tree is also in Lucian, *Timon*, 8.

265. *have* This has no grammatical subject, but one is readily understood from 'The mouths...stuck'.

266. *Fell* This pa. pple is also in *Lr.* 4. 6. 54.

266–7. *left...blows* Cf. *Cym.* 3. 3. 64, 'left me bare to weather' [Conrad, p. 367].

267–8. *I to bear this...is some burden* For the construction, cf. *Cym.* 3. 1. 72–3, 'Which he to seek of me again, perforce, | Behoves me keep at utterance'.

276. *worst* sc., in worldly position.

283. *That...this* Perh. based on Caligula's wish that the Roman people had one neck (Suetonius, *Calig.* 30).

284. S.D.s (Rowe; J.).

285. *my* (Shadwell, Rowe) F 'thy'.

287–8. *'Tis...were* Obscure; l. 287 is clear enough: 'no company that consists of yourself can be said to be properly *mended*' [D.]; to add 'if it is not merely botched, I wish it were' is both feeble, and an unlikely concession for Tim. to make. The meaning must be rather, 'I wish my company were mended by the lack of yours'. Perh. the half-line is a mere jotting that Sh. would have deleted.

289. *to Athens* i.e. in Athens; but 'to' (which is necessary for the quibble that follows) can be used because Ap. is going thither; cf. Abbott, § 187.

292–3. *The best...harm* A commonplace since Horace, *Odes* III, iii, 49, 'aurum irrepertum et sic melius situm' [quoted by H. Paul, Introd. to ed. by S. Lee, *University Press Sh.* (1908), p. xxvii].

295. *that's above me* the sky. Cf. *Cor.* 4. 5. 41, 'under the canopy' [Steev.], *Per.* 4. 6. 125, 'under the cope'.

307, 310, 312. *medlar...medlar...meddler* F 'medler...Medler...Medler'.

311. *though...thee* Ironically, 'even one like you'; he really means 'especially one like you'. Perh. the insult is heightened by a glance at the bawdy sense of 'medlar' (cf. *Rom.* 2. 1. 38 n.).

314. *after his means* Usu. taken as 'after his means were spent'. I doubt if this is linguistically possible, and prefer to interpret with D., 'in proportion to his means', i.e. 'no man ever wasted his substance as you have done unless courted and flattered by a herd of parasites whom his means were inadequate to satisfy'.

318–19. *thou...dog* Obscure. J.D.W. takes the 'dog' to be Apem. himself (cf. l. 251–2)—you had enough means to keep alive yourself, the only being who ever loved you. Others take literally. But the difficulty remains that Apem. had claimed to be beloved 'without means', whereas Tim., while appearing to be merely explaining Apem.'s meaning, contradicts him by saying that he had some means.

322. *men—* (K.) F 'men:'.

335. *Wolf* A symbol of greediness also in *Lr.* 3. 4. 96, *Troil.* 1. 3. 121 [G.K.H., comparing Boethius, *Cons. Phil.* IV, Prosa, iii, 13]; Chapman, *Hero and Leander*, IV, 158, 'the wolfie sting of Auarice'; Middleton, *Family of Love*, 2. 4. 275–6, 'his wolf...His avarice'; Donne, *Sermons* (ed. Potter and Simpson), VII, 4, 620, 'an usurious Wolfe'; T. Wilson, *Discourse upon Usury* (ed. R. H. Tawney, 1925), p. 182, of usurers, 'greedie cormoraunte wolfes'.

338. *unicorn* 'a beast of an untamable nature', acc. to Topsell, *Hist. of Four-Footed Beasts* (1607), p. 719. Its 'fury' results in its getting its horn stuck in a tree; cf. *J.C.* 2. 1. 204–6 n.; Spenser, *F.Q.* II. v. 10.

340. *bear...horse* Their hostility is described by Topsell, *Hist. of Four-Footed Beasts*, pp. 42–3 [Evans].

343. *the spots...life* The crimes of your cousin the lion would condemn you to death. There is a quibble on the lion's moral spots and the leopard's physical ones; lions and leopards, with a reference to the latter's spots, are collocated also in *R. II*, 1. 1. 174–5.

348–59. *If...Apemantus* Prose in Pope; irregular verse in F, except in ll. 351–2.

353. *Yonder...painter* Sh. evidently decided on second thoughts to postpone their entry.

361. *to spit upon* For this supreme insult cf. *R. II*, 4. 1. 75, *1 H. IV*, 2. 4. 191, *R. III*, 1. 2. 144.

363. *do stand by thee* are placed by thee for purposes of comparison.

365–6. *If...hands* Arranged by Cap. F divides after 'beat thee'.   *thee*. (Theob.)   *I'ld* (Han.) ...*thee*, F 'thee, Ile...thee;' Most edd. retain 'I'll', and the irregular sequence can easily be paralleled (cf. *Ham.* 2. 2. 157–8, *1 H. VI*, 2. 4. 98–9 n.). But the future seems too impulsive for Tim.'s mood here, and prob. the wrong punctuation (helped by mislineation) came first and the corruption of 'Ide' to 'Ile' was consequential.

370. *swoon* F 'fwoond': other Sh. forms of this verb are 'sound' (*Tit.* 5. 1. 119, Q 1) and 'swound' (*J.C.* 1. 2. 252). Edd. have shown a (rather capricious) attachment to the latter, but it is best to modernize throughout.

371–2. *Would...thee* My arrangement. Edd. usu. follow F in printing 'Away...thee' as prose, but the two blank-verse lines are prob. intentional.

371. *burst* An extremity of passion was supposed to cause the heart literally to burst; cf. *Lr.* 5. 3. 196–9.

372. S.D. (Camb. after Cap.).

378. *the mere necessities* App., what belongs of necessity to life in this world; in this particular case— death.   383. S.D. (Camb. after Pope).

384. *natural* see G.   *son and sire* (Rowe) F 'Sunne and fire' Shadwell (adapting) 'Son | And Father'.

388. *Dian's lap* The reference to Diana as patroness of chastity is appropriate, but the lines also glance at Jupiter's wooing of Danaë in a golden shower (cf. Hankins, p. 166); and Sh. was prob. influenced by the similarity of the names, as also in *Cym.* 2. 3. 72–4, where 'gold' makes 'Diana's rangers false themselves', and *Rom.* 1. 1. 208–13, where an allusion to Danaë (cf. l. 213 n.) closely follows a mention of Dian.

391. *touch* See G.

398. S.D. (after Dyce) F 'Exit Apeman.' after l. 399.

399. *Moe...them* Han. continued to Tim.; F gives to Apem., followed by Fleay and Sisson, Fleay glossing 'I am quit' = 'I am quits with you by this last repartee'. But 'quit' = 'rid of you', 'Moe...men?' echoes l. 198, and 'Eat, Timon' has the ring of a self-address.

399. *them* (Rowe) F 'then', not absolutely impossible in the sense of 'when you have eaten' but
awkward, and perh. a misinterpretation of 'thē'.
S.D. (J.C.M.) F 'Enter the Bandetti', a common
Eliz. sp., cf. *2 H. VI*, 4. 1. 135 for the sing. 'bandetto'.

400. Sp.-pref. F '1'; so '2' and '3' below.   *where
...gold?* i.e., where can he have got it? cf. *Tp.* 5. i.
280–1, 'where should they | Find this grand liquor?';
Oth. 3. 4. 23, 'Where should I lose that handkerchief,
Emilia?'   402. *falling-from* Hyphenated by Cap.

405. *make the assay* The figure of the touchstone,
as in l. 391.

407. *shall's* Conflation of 'shall we' and 'let us';
cf. *Per.* 4. 5. 7 n.

410. 3 Bandit (C. B. Young) F '*All*'. But the
speakers of the preceding and following speeches can
hardly be involved. The compositor prob. caught up
the pref. of l. 413.

416. *two* (Collier) F 'too'. The same error occurs
in *Shr.* 5. 2. 45, 62. Sh. has 'both twain' at *Son.* 42. 11.
See G. 'both two'.

418. *you...meat* J. notes 'an ambiguity between
much want and *want* of *much*. *Timon* takes it on the
wrong side, and tells them that their *greatest want is*,
that, like other men, *they want much of meat*; then
telling them where meat may be had, he asks, *Want?*
why want?'

421. *hips* F 'Heps' (common; see O.E.D.).

423. *mess* see G.   430. *limited* see G.

435. *takes* (Han., J.) F 'take'. It is much more
pointed to have the physician as subject of this clause,
and to leave the injunction to the thieves to kill so that
it can form the climax at l. 447.

436. *villainy* (Rowe) F 'Villaine'.   *do't,* (F 3)
F 'doo't.'.

438–44. *The sun's...thief* Farmer, *Essay on the*

Learning of Sh. (in 18*th C. Essays on Sh.*, ed. D. Nichol Smith (1903), p. 175), noting that Dodd had seen in this an adaptation of the Anacreontic poem which cites the elements as precedents for drinking (T. Bergk, *Poetae Lyrici Graeci* (1843), p. 711), pointed out that it was translated by Ronsard, and that Puttenham, *Arte of Eng. Poesie*, III, xxii (ed. Willcock and Walker, p. 252) mentions Eng. versions of Ronsard. Edd. have followed, omitting Farmer's judicious remark that 'the topicks are obvious, and their application is different'. There is really more resemblance to the praise of debt in Rabelais, III, iii; cf. W. König, *Sh. Jb.* IX (1874), 202–6.

441–2. *The sea's...tears* Douce, II, 72, explains by quoting Bartholomaeus *De Proprietatibus Rerum*, viii. 29 (tr. S. Batman, 1582), 'the Moone gathereth deawe in the aire, for she printeth the vertue of hir moysture in the aire, and chaungeth the ayre in a manner that is vnseene, & breedeth and gendereth deaw in the vtter part thereof'.

442–4. *the earth's...excrement* Cf. *Ant.* I. I. 35 n.
446. *Has* Cf. Abbott, §.333.
450–1. *But...Amen* F lineation. Edd. since Cap., accepting Rowe's 'not less', end lines at 'this' and 'howsoe'er', and make 'Amen' a separate line.

450. *less* Rowe 'not less'. This disrupts the metre (see previous note), but at first sight seems necessary for the sense. But the imper. is, as often, a rhetorical device for stating a condition, 'if you steal less because of this, may gold destroy you whatever happens'.

452–3. *Has...it* This type of 'paradoxical encomium' in Eliz. drama is discussed by A. H. Sackton, *Univ. of Texas Stud. in Eng.* XXVIII (1949), 83–104, with a brief reference to *Tim.* on pp. 101–2; cf. Hamlet's recommendations to Gertrude, *Ham.* 3. 4.181 ff.

455. *us, not* (Rowe) F 'vs not'.

456. *I'll...enemy* i.e. I will assume his advice was that of an enemy, and will therefore do the opposite. Cf. Tilley, T 52, 'Believe no tales from an enemy's tongue' (first in 1659).

458–9. *there is...true* a man 'always has it in his power to become a true, i.e. an honest man' (Mal.). For the philosophy of life involved, cf. Mrs Quickly in *H. V*, 2. 3. 19–21, 'I...bid him a' should not think of God; I hoped there was no need to trouble himself with any such thoughts yet'.

459. S.D.s F 'Exit Theeues. Enter the Steward to Timon.'.

461. *ruinous* see G.; the use of a word more commonly applied to buildings is particularly apt here.

464. *What...made* Mal. unnecessarily divided after 'honour' into two fragmentary lines. *alteration of honour* decline from a state of honour. 'Alter' and 'alteration' normally imply a change for the worse in Sh.'s Eng., as in mod. Fr.; cf. *Son.* 116. 3, *Oth.* 5. 2. 104.

465. *viler* F 'vilder'.

467–8. *How...enemies* how excellently does the injunction once given to man to love his enemies suit the behaviour of these times!

469–70. *rather...do* Perh. 'Let me rather woo or caress those that would mischief, that profess to mean me mischief, than those that really do me mischiefs under false professions of kindness' (J.); cf. Tilley, F 739. But the reference to 'false professions of kindness' is not clear, and the meaning may be 'let those on whom I have to exercise the duty of loving my enemies be only ill-wishers, not actual ill-doers, such as Tim.'s enemies'.

471–4. *Has...master* My lineation. Prose in F. Three lines in Pope, divided after 'present', 'lord'.

477. *Then...thee* One line in Cap.; two in F. *grant'st...man*, (Southern MS. in copy of F 4; Pope

'grantest that thou art', ending line at 'man')
F 'grunt'ft,...man.'.

480. *me, I;* (Steev.) F 'me, I'. Delius's 'me; ay',
is attractive, but the emphatic repetition of the pronoun
is common; cf. *Rom.* 3. 1. 54, 3. 5. 12 [Clarke].

483. *Ne'er* F 'Neu'r'; cf. 2. 2. 236 n.

487. *give* Suggested by 'flinty', 'give' (=sweat,
or exude damp) being commonly used of walls or stone
floors; see O.E.D. 'give', 40d [J.D.W.].

495. *mild* (Thirlby) F 'wilde'.

499. *perpetual-sober* Hyphenated by Han.

509. *Upon...neck* i.e. by treading down their first
lord; cf. *R. II*, 3. 1. 19, *Tw.N.* 2. 5. 191 [J.D.W.].

511. *subtle-covetous* (S. Walker) F 'fubtle, coue-
tous'.

512. *A...as* (Pope) F 'If not a...and as'. 'If
not' may have been caught up from l. 511 [Tyrwhitt],
or may have been a false start Sh. omitted to delete;
'and' may also have stood in the rough draft, but its
omission improves metre and sense.

517. *where* in cases in which; virtually='when',
which Han. read; cf. *J.C.*, G.

522. *For* Both 'for' and 'as for' (see O.E.D. 'as',
33 b) are often used in cent. 16–17 without affecting the
construction of the sentence, so that the following noun
can be direct object, or subject, of a verb. Cf. *H. V*,
2. 2. 155, 'For me, the gold of France did not seduce';
Meas. 5. 1. 396–8, 'For this new-married man...you
must pardon'.

528. *Have* (Rowe) F 'Ha's', which seems unduly
harsh. The anon. conj. (*ap.* Camb.) 'Ha'' may be what
Sh. wrote.

537. *O...master* So in F. Unconvincingly split
after 'stay' by Cap., to complete the half-lines that
precede and follow.

540. S.D. (after Theob.) F 'Exit'.

5. 1

S.D. *Loc.* (Camb. after Cap.) *Entry* (F; J.D.W. after Cap.); cf. l. 30, S.D. n.

3–38. *What's...thee* Prose in Pope; irregular verse in F.

5–6. *Phrynia* (Rowe) *and Timandra* (F 2) F '*Phrinica* and *Timandylo*'.

7–8. *'Tis said...sum.* In a completed version, Sh. would scarcely have let this immediately follow Flavius's exit.

11–12. *palm...flourish* Cf. Psalm xcii. 11 (B.C.P.), 'The righteous shall flourish like a palm-tree' [Steev.]. There may be a reference to the notion that 'Palme growes straight, though handled ne're so rude' (Jonson, *Underwood*, xxv, 26; cf. Herford and Simpson's note).

22. *Good...best* That's excellent!

24. *his* its.

25. *the deed of saying* 'the doing of that which we have said we would do' (Mal., citing *Ham.* 1. 3. 27, 'give his saying deed').

30. S.D. F, before this line, 'Enter Timon from his Caue'; om. Cap. Sh. has not explicitly noted that Tim. overhears the preceding dialogue. He prob. advances a few paces at this point. For 'enter' = 'come forward', cf. Greg, *The Sh. First Folio*, Index, 'enter'. The asides here and at ll. 36, 46 were added by Cap.

43. *serves* A slightly extended use of the common expression with 'time' as subject; cf. *H. V*, 2. 1. 6. *black-cornered* Prob. 'hiding things in dark corners' (Schmidt). Cf. *Meas.* 4. 3. 155–6, 'the old fantastical duke of dark corners [Steev.].

46. *meet...turn* Usu. taken literally: 'when they turn' [Delius], or 'at the turn in the road' [D.], but a fig. use seems more prob. Thus Schmidt, under the sense 'occasion, exigence', suggests 'as soon as it will

seem proper'. Perh. 'play you at your own game';
cf. O.E.D. 'turn', 21 = 'subtle device of any kind'.

50. *admiréd* The context suggests the meaning is
active, 'wondering'; cf. Abbott, § 374, citing *1 H. IV*,
1. 3. 183, 'jeering and disdained contempt'.

51. *worship,...aye* (Rowe) F 'worſhipt,...aye:'.

53. S.D. (Camb. after Mal.).

55. *once* so much as. This intensifying use is
common after a negative. O.E.D. 2 cites Udall,
Erasm. Par. Matt. xviii. 91, 'He shall not once be
receiued into the Kyngdome of heauen'.

65. *size* see G.

66. *Let...better* One line in Pope; two in F.
go naked, (Theob.) F 'go,| Naked'. For the familiar
figure of 'naked truth', cf. *1 H. VI*, 2. 4. 20, Tilley,
T 589.

68. *them* =those ungrateful men you speak of;
understood from 'ingratitude'.

69. *travelled* F 'trauail'd', and some edd. retain
this sp.; 'travel' and 'travail' were not distinguished by
sp. in Sh.'s Eng., and I doubt if there is even a quibble
on the latter sense here.

70. *men* (F 2) F 'man'.

77–8. *therefore...I* that is not why we came. For
word-order, cf. *1 H. IV*, 1. 1. 30, 'therefore we meet
not now'. But perh. unintentionally ambiguous, since
'therefore' might = 'as honest men' [C. B. Young].

81. *lively* see G. Tim.'s hidden meaning, of course,
is that the painter *is* a living counterfeit.

84. *thou...art* i.e. it has become second nature to
you [Delius].

95. The addition of 'let him' would make a complete line, and give 'Keep' a more natural (intrans.)
sense.

105. *You...company* Most simply 'if you go that
way and you this, yet there will still be two together',

as more fully elaborated in the next two lines. Another possibility is to treat 'but...company' as a parenthetical reminder of the conditions at the start of the proposed experiment—'note that there are only two of you together to begin with'. In any event, dashes after 'this' and 'company' are the best equivalents of F's colons.

108. *shall not* are not to.

109. *reside* F 'recide', cf. *Ant.* 1. 3. 103 n., to which add *Troil.* (F) 1. 1. 104, *Oth.* (F) 1. 3. 241.

112, 113. S.D.s (Globe).

113. *alchemist* Cf. *Son.* 114, which likens alchemy and flattery [J.D.W.].

114. S.D.'s (i) (after Staunton) F 'Exeunt'. (ii) F, with 'Steward' for 'Flavius'.

115. *in vain* (F 3) F 'vain', which Al. retains, but 'in vain' is the normal phrase, as well as improving the metre, and the omission of one of three similar short words is a common error.

119. *part and promise* App. a hendiadys, 'the part we have promised to perform'. But S. Walker's 'pact' is poss.; not elsewhere in Sh., but 'compact' several times.

125. *chance* (F 3) F 'chanc'd' F 2 'chanc'e'.

129. S.D. (Camb.) F 'Enter Timon out of his Caue'.

130. *comforts* Cf. 4. 1. 2.   *comforts, burn* cf. *Lr.* 2. 4. 175–6; 'Here eyes are fierce, but thine | Do comfort and not burn' [Steev.].

132. *cantherizing* (F) Rowe, most edd., 'cauterizing'. The form, as Camb. notes, occurs in *The Questionary of Cyryrgiens* (1541), as does 'cantere' for the instrument (='cautery'), and arises from confusion with 'cantharides'='blister-flies'; 'blister' in l. 131 makes it fairly certain that this was also in Sh.'s mind.

134. *Of...Timon* Obscure. Perh. 'my past folly

makes me deserve only such false flatterers as you, and you deserve the reception you are going to receive'.

138. *sorry...in thee* 'to have committed against thee' (Schmidt); cf. *R. II*, 2. 1. 238–9, ''tis shame such wrongs are borne | In him' [i.e. 'in his case'].

143. *general-gross* Hyphenated by S. Walker.

144. *Which* This has no grammatical construction, but the anacoluthon is quite Sh.; cf. 5. 2. 7 [Mal], *Tit*. 3. 2. 9.   *public body* Cf. *Ant*. 1. 4. 44, 'this common body', also in connection with fickleness of judgment.

146. *sense* (Rowe) F 'fince'.

147. *it* its.   *fail* (Cap.) F 'fall', which seems too strong.

148. *render* see G.; part of the run of commercial metaphors, of which 'fail' is prob. one; cf. *Cym*. 2. 4. 7 [J.D.W.].

150. *by the dram* i.e. even when carefully weighed dram by dram.

151. *love and wealth* Regarded by the Athenians as interchangeable commodities.

153–4. *write...thine* A deliberately grotesque figure. Tim. is to be a sort of animate account-book in which he himself can read the amount of love the Athenians bear him.

163. *approaches* Plur. also at *H. V*, 2. 4. 9, *Ant*. 1. 3. 46.

164. *like...savage* Cf. Ps. lxxx. 13 (B.C.P.), 'The wild boar out of the wood doth root it up' [Steev.].

177. *take't at worst* put the worst construction on it; cf. 1. 2. 152.

178. *answer* suffer the consequences.

180. *at my love* An unusual preposition, not easy to distinguish in sense from 'in' (which Han. read); app. extended from 'at' followed by a measure of value.

181. *reverend'st* F 'reuerends', avoiding the awkward collocation 'ndst'; cf. *H. V*, (Q), Camb. IX, 494 (=4. 7. 2), 'the arrants peece of knauery', *Cym.* 3. 3. 103, 'refts' (=reft'st).

182-3. *To...keepers* 'that they may *so* keep and guard you, as jailors do thieves; i.e. for final punishment' (Mal.).

182. *prosperous* see G.; cf. *Wint.* 5. 1. 161.

184. *Why...epitaph* 'It is not easy to supply the suppressed connection here' (D.). It is doubtful if there is one; Tim. seems to be pursuing a private train of thought.

189. *And...enough* Cf. 3. 5. 106-7 [D.].

194. *through* (Rowe) F 'thorow'. This occurs with monosyllabic scansion also in *Lr.* (F) 4. 6. 168. There is no need to retain it in a mod. sp. text.

198. *achës* Cf. 1. 1. 249-50 n.

202. *prevent* see G.

204. *in my close* So in Plut. 'a little yard in my house'. With Tim.'s removal to the woods, this becomes less appropriate in Sh., as W. Maginn noted (*Bentley's Miscellany*, III (1838), 239). In Paynter's version it was 'adioyning to his house in the fields'.

208-9. *that...let him* For the irregular construction cf. *H. V*, 4. 3. 35-6, *Tit.* 3. 1. 151-2; Abbott, § 415. *take his haste* On the analogy of 'take his time' [Clarke]. Cf. 'the haste', where mod. Eng. would omit the article, in *Lr.* 2. 1. 26, *Ant.* 5. 2. 195.

214-18. *Timon...oracle* The one passage, as Hudson noted, which suggests recourse to Paynter's version, 'he ordeined himselfe to be interred vpon the sea shore, that the waues and surges might beate and vexe his dead carcas'.

216. *embossèd* see G. The metaphor is in keeping with the play's animal imagery.

219. *four* Rowe 'sour', an obvious emendation

which all edd. have accepted. Fleay alone defends 'four', rightly. With 'sour' we have an odd use of 'go by' for 'not be spoken', and 'and language end' must be a corrective, 'nay, let words of every kind be silent' (D.). With 'four', 'go by' has the normal sense of 'pass', and the rest means 'and *then* let language end'. For 'four' used of 'an indefinite number, large or small according to circumstances' (On.), cf. *Ham.* 2. 2. 160, and many exx. in K. Elze, *Notes on Eliz. Dramatists* (1880), pp. 86–9; similarly *Rom.* 2. 2. 142, 'three words'. The 'four words' are the three concluding lines of Tim.'s speech. The same phrase is used for a speech of several lines by J. Bale, *Temptation* [*c.* 1548], sig. E 1.

222. S.D. (Dyce) F 'Exit Timon'.

224. *Coupled to nature* 'part and parcel of his nature' (D.).

227. S.D. F 'Exeunt'.

5. 2

S.D. *Loc.* (Camb.)

1. Sp.-pref. (J.D.W.) F '1'; similarly '2', '1' and '3' at ll. 5, 13 and 14 respectively. *painfully* see G.; 'told distressing tidings' (Yale, after Schmidt) is less prob.

7. *Whom* Cf. 5. 1. 144 n.; Mal. paraphrases '*whom*...the force of our old affection wrought so much *upon* as to make *him speak to me* as a friend'. *in general part* prob. 'in public affairs'.

7–8. *general...particular* public...personal; often so opposed in Sh., e.g. *2 H. IV*, 4. 1. 94–6, *Tim.* 4. 3. 160–1, *Ham.* 1. 2. 74–5 ('common', 'particular').

8–9. *made...made* Careless writing. To avoid the repetition Han. read 'had' in l. 8 and Jackson proposed 'bade' in l. 9.

11. *imported* see G. Cf. *Ham.* 1.2.22–3, 'message |
Importing the surrender of those lands'. In both
passages a request is implied, which suggests some
influence of meaning from 'importune'. This is confirmed by the use of 'important' = 'urgent, importunate' (On.) in *Err.* 5.1.138, *Ham.* 3.4.108, *Ado*,
2.1.63–4. Conversely, Spenser has 'importune' =
'import' in *F.Q.* III, i.16.9.

13. S.D. (F; Cap.) Placed here by Cap.; after
'moved' in F.

15. *enemy's* (Delius) F 'enemies' Theob. 'enemies''. The choice is more or less arbitrary.   *scouring*
see G. The first fugitives from the enemy are at hand.

17. *foe's* (J.) F 'foes', which most edd. retain; but
a metaphor by which the foes are described as *being*
the snare is rather violent, and does not give such a
good balance with 'Ours is the fall'. If we read
'enemies'' in l. 15, it would be consistent to read
'foes'' here. For the fig. use of 'snare', cf. *1 H. VI*,
4.2.22, *Ant.* 4.8.18 [Schmidt]. S.D. F 'Exeunt'.

5.3

S.D. *Loc.* (Camb.) *Entry* (F, adding 'in the Woods'
after 'Soldier').

1. *By...place* Cf. *Cym.* 4.1.26, 'this is the very
description of their meeting-place' [P. H. Kocher,
S.A.B. XIV (1939), 238].

2. *Who's here...No answer* So in *Cym.* 3.6.22–4
[Kocher, as above]. *Who's* (F 3) F 'Whofe', cf.
MSH, 117.

3–4. *Timon...man* If this had to be taken as the
soldier's comment, Warb's 'reared; here' for 'read;
there' would be irresistible. Staunton suggested that it
was an inscription composed by Timon, but gave a
far-fetched account of its relation to what follows.

Professor C. Leech has convinced me that we should accept the hint in Camb., Note XVII, that 'the author may have changed his mind and forgotten to obliterate what was inconsistent with the sequel'. This epitaph must then be supposed to have been discarded in order to have Alc. read one of those from Plutarch at the end of the play. Without explicit mention of Timon, 'his' in l. 5 would not have been entirely clear, and Sh. would prob. have revised the scene and not merely deleted this couplet.

3. S.D. (Staunton). *outstretched* 'stretched to its limit' (O.E.D.) does not quite fit. Sh.'s frequent 'out-' compounds usu. convey a sense of going beyond, but here the meaning seems simply 'come to the full extent of'; cf. Spenser, *F.Q.* II. x. 45. 2, 'Till they outraigned had their vtmost date'. *span* see G. This sense was only recently established (O.E.D. 1599), developing from the simile in Ps. xxxix. 6 (B.C.P.), 'thou hast made my days as it were a span long'. The original sense of the distance between the out-stretched fingers of a hand would be vividly present, and would be suggested by 'outstretched'.

4. *there...man* 'nothing worthy of being called a man any longer exists to read it' (Evans).

8. *An...days* A rhetorical commonplace of long standing, discussed by E. R. Curtius, *European Literature and the Latin Middle Ages* [1953], pp. 98–101; cf. Castiglione, *Courtier*, tr. Hoby (Everyman ed., p. 303), 'old in knowledge, though ye be yong in yeares'; Milton, *Sonn. to Vane*, 1, 'Vane, young in yeares, but in sage counsell old', *M.V.* 2. 7. 71, 'Young in limbs, in judgment old', *Gent.* 2. 4. 67 [cited by Kocher, *l.c.* on l. 1, p. 242].

10. S.D. F 'Exit'.

5.4

S.D. *Loc.* (Theob.) *Entry* (F, adding 'before Athens').

4. *With...measure* 'with any measure or degree of licence' (Schmidt). The normal implication of moderation in 'measure' makes the phrase something of an oxymoron.

5. *The scope of justice* 'the space within which justice had free play' (Evans).

6. *stepped* (Danchin conj.) F 'flept', unsatisfactorily explained by D. 'lived our darkened lives'. The corruption 'stept' > 'slept' is easy, and the figure is continued in 'wandered'. Danchin cited 3.5.12, 'stepped into the law'.

7. *traversed* see G.; the normal symbol of resignation; cf. *J.C.* 2.1.240 n., B. L. Joseph, *Eliz. Acting* (1951), p. 39.

9–10. *When...more* i.e. when a strong man's spirits rise in revolt.

10. *breathless wrong* wrongdoers breathless through fear.

18. *their* Reference obscure: either 'griefs' (l. 14) or 'rages' (l. 16), or both.

20. *means* see G., and cf. 5.1.151, but the phrase is odd. Theob.'s ''mends' (i.e. 'amends') is poss.; the form occurs in *Troil.* 1 1.68 (in a different sense), and 'mends' could be misread 'menes'.

24. *griefs* (Theob.) F 'greefe'; cf. l. 14.

24–6. *they...them* Prob. 'those who offended you'. But 'they' may be the 'griefs', though it is awkward to give a different reference from 'them'.

27. *motives* see G.

28. *Shame,...wanted cunning, in excess* (Theob.) F. '(Shame...wanted, cunning in exceſſe)'. The brackets are pointless. For Compositor B's fondness for

them, cf. A. Walker, *Textual Problems of the First Folio* (1953), p. 9. Theob. explains, 'Shame in excess (i.e. extremity of shame) that they wanted cunning (i.e. that they were not wise enough not to banish you)'. Another possibility is to accept J.'s conj. 'coming' for 'cunning', retaining F.'s comma, though not its brackets, and J.'s paraphrase, 'Shame which they had so long wanted, at last coming in its utmost excess'. With the same sense, Dr R. Quirk (privately) conj. 'running'. But it is awkward to interpret 'wanted' as 'had so long wanted'.

30–1. *spread;...death,* (Theob.) F 'ſpred,... death;'.

31. *and...death.* Simply an explanation of 'decimation'.

35. *spotted* guilty; the divinely guided lot is trusted to single them out.

37. *revenges* (Steev.) F 'Reuenge'; cf. l. 32 and, for the error, l. 24. Al. and Sisson retain F, but the metrical irregularity seems quite pointless.

37–8. *like...inherited* i.e. are not inherited like lands. For the word-order (with which mod. Eng. would say 'unlike lands'), cf. *Meas.* 2. 2. 65–6, 'he like you | Would not have been so stern', where F has no commas, and the sense is clearer without them; Milton, *Sonnet...Detraction,* 12–13, 'Thy age, like ours,... Hated not Learning'. Here F has an emphasizing comma (cf. P. Simpson, *Sh.'s Punctuation* (1911), pp. 26–31) after 'crimes', but nothing after 'lands'.

44. *all together* F 'altogether'. The distinction was not regularly made in Sh.'s Eng. (cf. *Err.* 5. 1. 246, *1 H. VI*, 2. 1. 29, *Cor.* 2. 3. 45), but the words were separated by F 2.

45. *enforce...smile* Cf. *A.Y.L.* 2. 7. 102–3, 'Your gentleness shall force | More than your force move us to gentleness'.

46. *hew to't* Prob. 'cut a way to it' (On.); but no parallels are cited, and Daniel's 'hew't out' would be attractive if the stress fell more naturally on 'out'.

55. *Descend* (F 2) F. 'Defend'; at *Cym.* 1. 6. 169, F has 'defended' for 'descended'. *unchargéd* see G.

62. *rendered* (Chedworth) F. 'remedied'.

63. *answer* see G.

64. S.D.s (Mal.; Cap. after Theob.) F 'Enter a Meſſenger', who is obviously the soldier of 5. 3.

69. *Interprets* Perh. quadrisyllabic, unless S. Walker's conj. 'poorer' (withdrawn, but later accepted by Fleay) is right.

70. S.D. (Camb.) F, centred before this line, 'Alcibiades reades the Epitaph'.

70–3. *Here...gait* Both these couplets (*Anth. Pal.* vii. 313; vii. 320) are in North, who, however, has 'wretches' for Sh.'s 'caitiffs'. Sh. had evidently not decided which to use. Plut. attributes the first to Tim. himself, the second (now given to Hegesippus) to Callimachus.

76. *brain's flow* Cf. *Sir Giles Goosecap* (Chapman, *Comedies*, ed. T. M. Parrott, 1914), 2. 1. 156–7, 'I shed not the tears of my brain'; Drayton (ed. J. W. Hebel, 1931–41), *Moses his Birth and Miracles*, III, 583–4, 'But he from rockes that fountaines can command | Cannot yet stay the fountaines of his braine' [Steev.]; Nashe, II, 271, l. 32, 'the teares that issued from his braines'.

82. *use...sword* 'will combine peace with war' (D., who notes a similarly odd use of 'use' at l. 51).

83–4. *Make...leech* For Eliz. ideas of war as a physician, cf. G. R. Waggoner, *Philological Quarterly*, XXXIII (1954), 20–33, citing these lines and *Two Noble Kinsmen* (in *Sh. Apocrypha*, ed. Tucker Brooke), 5. 1. 68–72, a prob. Sh. scene.

85. S.D. F 'Exeunt'.

GLOSSARY

Note. Where a pun or quibble is intended, the meanings are distinguished as (*a*) and (*b*)

ABLE, strong; 2. 1. 10

ABROAD, away from home, out of doors; 3. 5. 48

ADMIRED (see note); 5. 1. 50

ADORING OF, reverential bowing to; 1. 2. 145, S.D.

ADVANCE (metaph.), promote; 1. 2. 172

AFFECT, (i) be fond of; 1. 2. 30, 220; (ii) imitate; 4. 3. 200

AIR, manner, style; 5. 1. 22

ALL (adv.), entirely; 1. 1. 142; 1. 2. 236

ALLOW, invest; 5. 1. 161

AMPLE (adv.), fully; 1. 2. 131

ANON, in a little time; 1. 1. 156; 2. 2. 129; 3. 6. 58

ANSWER (sb.), punishment; 5. 4. 63

ANSWER (vb.) (see note); 4. 3. 232

APPERIL, risk; 1. 2. 32

APPREHEND, understand; 1. 1. 210

APPREHENSION, way of taking (a word); 1. 1. 209

APT, impressionable (cf. *Ven.* 354); 1. 1. 135

ARGUE, be evidence of; 5. 1. 28

ARGUMENT, (i) contents; 2. 2. 184; (ii) subject; 3. 3. 20

ARTIFICIAL, belonging to art or science; 1. 1. 40; 2. 2. 116

ASPECT, look, appearance; 2. 1. 28

ASSAY, trial, test; 4. 3. 405

N.S.T.A.—14

ATONE, appease; 5. 4. 58

ATTEMPT, try to win; 1. 1. 129

ATTEND, (i) await; 1. 2. 155; 3. 4. 39; (ii) expect, 3. 5. 104

AUTHORITY, warrant; 2. 2. 144

BACKWARDLY (see note); 3. 3. 18

BANQUET, dessert; 1. 2. 155

BATE, (i) 'bate of', deduct from; 1. 2. 211; (ii) diminish; 3. 3. 26

BEAGLE, lit., small kind of hound; here, used contemptuously of a woman; 4. 3. 176

BEAR, (i) carry with it; 1. 1. 134; (ii) (abs.), endure something; 1. 1. 180; (iii) carry away; 4. 1. 32

BECK (sb.), bow, curtsy; 1. 2. 240

BEHOVE (see note); 3. 5. 22

BENEATH (adj.), below heaven (only inst. O.E.D.); 1. 1. 47

BILL, (i) note or account of charges or of debts; 2. 2. init. S.D.; 3. 4. 50; (ii) (*a*) as (i); (*b*) long-handled weapon with curved blade; 3. 4. 90

BIND, (*a*) attach by ties of gratitude; (*b*) lit., quibbling on 'free' (l. 106); 1. 1. 107

BLACK-CORNERED (see note); 5. 1. 43

BLEEDING-NEW, newly running with blood; 1. 2. 78

BLOOD, disposition; 4. 2. 38

BLUSH, redness (for gold as red cf. 'gild', *Mac.* 2. 2. 56); 4. 3. 387

BOND, obligation; 1. 1. 147

BOOK, account-book; 1. 2. 204

BOTCH, cobble, patch; 4. 3. 287

BOTH TWO. Common pleonasm (cf. *F.Q.* v. ix. 41. 4); 4. 3. 416

BOUND, indentured, under contract of service; 4. 1. 10

BRAY, emit harsh noises (e.g. like a horse or ass); elsewhere in Sh. of the trumpet; 2. 2. 167

BREAKING, going bankrupt; 5. 1. 9

BREATH, voice; 4. 3. 141, 250

BREATHE, use breath, speak; so, utter, express in speech; 3. 5. 60; 5. 4. 7

BREATHED, lit. long-winded, trained by exercise (cf. O.E.D. 1), hence 'inured' (On.); 1. 1. 10

BRED OUT, exhausted (so as to become), degenerated (into) (cf. *H. V,* 3. 5. 29); 1. 1. 252

BROACH, tap (fig.); 2. 2. 183

BROADER (adv.), with less restraint; 3. 4. 64

BROKE, bankrupt; 4. 2. 5

BRUIT (sb.), rumour; 5. 1. 192

BRUSH (sb.), onset; 4. 3. 265

BUY OUT, redeem; 3. 5. 17

BY, (i) in accordance with; 1. 1. 174; (ii) 'by this', by this time; 5. 3. 9

CALL, (i) 'call to' (see note); 1. 2. 222; (ii) 'call upon,' make a claim for payment of; 2. 2. 25

CANDIED, lit., crystallized by boiling in sugar; hence, 'congealed' (Schmidt); 4. 3. 227

CANKER, spreading sore; 4. 3. 49

CANTHERIZING, cauterizing (see note); 5. 1. 132

CAP, (i) (fig.), chief (cf. *L.L.L.* G., 'corner-cap'); 4. 3. 360; (ii) 'throw one's cap at', give up for lost; 3. 4. 101–2

CAP-AND-KNEE, obsequiously deferential, 'bowing and scraping' (cf. *1 H. IV,* 4. 3. 68); 3. 6. 96

CAPTAINSHIP, leadership; 5. 1. 160

CARRIAGE, moral conduct; 3. 2. 82

CARRY IT, win the day; 3. 5. 49

CAST, 'cast the gorge at', see *gorge;* 4. 3. 41

CAUDLE (vb.), give a warm drink to; 'caudle' a warmed-up drink for sick people, of thin gruel, mixed with wine or ale sweetened or spiced (O.E.D.); 4. 3. 227

CEASE, put off; 2. 1. 16

CHAFE, flow against; 1. 1. 27

CHAMBERLAIN, one who waits on a king or lord in his bed-chamber; 4. 3. 223

CHARACTER, impression of engraved letters; 5. 3. 6

CHARGE, task; 3. 4. 27

CHARITABLE, loving; 1. 2. 91

CHECK (sb.), reproof; 2. 2. 146

CHEER, 'what cheer?', how goes it with you?; 3. 6. 39

CHEER UP, incite; 1. 2. 41

CHEERLY, cheerily; 2. 2. 220

CHERUBIN (adj.), angelic; 4. 3. 63

CHOLER, anger; 4. 3. 369

CLEAR (adj.), (i) innocent; 3. 3. 30; 3. 5. 39; (ii) (a) free of debt, (b) free from obstacles; 3. 4. 77; (iii) morally pure; 4. 3. 28

CLEAR (vb.), free from debt; 2. 2. 232

CLIMB, reach by climbing; 1. 1. 79

CLOSE (sb.), enclosure; 5. 1. 204

CLOSE (adj.), enclosed; 4. 3. 143

CLOSE (adv.), closely; 4. 3. 389

CLOUD, (a) disguise, (b) gloominess; 3. 4. 43

COG, cheat; 5. 1. 94

COIL, fuss; 1. 2. 239

COLD-MOVING, frigid; 2. 2. 218

COME, (i) 'come forth', be published; 1. 1. 28; (ii) 'come off', turn out; 1. 1. 32; (iii) 'come over', light upon; 3. 2. 79

COMFORT, happiness; 1. 1. 102

COMFORTABLE, (i) cheerful; 3. 4. 72; (ii) affording help or comfort; 4. 3. 494

COMMEND, remember kindly; 1. 1. 108; 2. 1. 18; 2. 2. 196; 3. 2. 53

COMPLETE, accomplished; 3. 1. 9–10

COMPOSTURE, compost (use found here only, Sh. coinage); 4. 3. 443

COMPOUND, make up; 4. 2. 35; 4. 3. 274

COMPT (in), reckoned and noted down (cf. *Mac.* 1. 6. 26 and G.); 2. 1. 34

CON THANKS, express or offer thanks; 4. 3. 427

CONCEIT, notion, fancy; 5. 4. 14, 77

CONCEPTIOUS, prolific (O.E.D., only inst.); 4. 3. 188

CONDITION, (i) mental disposition; 1. 1. 55; (ii) (see note); 1. 1. 80; (iii) personal character; 4. 3. 140

CONDITIONED, 'thus conditioned'=on this condition; 4. 3. 529

CONFECTIONARY, place where sweetmeats are kept; 4. 3. 261

CONFOUND, ruin, destroy; 1. 1. 239, 241; 4. 3. 75, 104, 129, etc.

CONFOUNDING, destructive; 4. 1. 20; 4. 3. 393

CONFUSION, ruin, destruction; 4. 1. 21; 4. 3. 128, 326–7

CONJURE, (i) influence by magic; 1. 1. 7; (ii) beseech; 3. 6. 11

CONQUEST, prey; 4. 3. 339

CONSCIENCE, sound judgment; 2. 2. 181

CONSECRATED, sacred; 4. 3. 387

CONSIDERATION, reflection; 4. 3. 197

CONSUMPTION, (any) wasting disease; 4. 3. 152, 202

CONTENTLESS, discontented (earliest inst. O.E.D.); 4. 3. 246

CONTINUATE, uninterrupted; 1. 1. 11

CONVERT (intrans.), change; 4. 1. 7

COPY, pattern; 3. 3. 32

CORINTH, Greek town notorious in ancient times for its prostitutes; 2. 2. 76

COUCHED, lying hidden; 2. 2. 178

COUNTERFEIT (sb.), (a) portrait, (b) spurious imitation; 5. 1. 79

COUNTERFEIT (adj.), sham; 4. 3. 113

COUNTERFEIT (vb.), (a) represent (as an artist), (b) simulate; 5. 1. 81

COUNTERPOISE, give an equivalent for; 1. 1. 148

COURAGE, desire, inclination (O.E.D. 2, citing); 3. 3. 24

CREATURE, 'puppet, instrument, one ready to do another's bidding' (O.E.D. 5, citing); 1. 1. 119

CRISP, 'shining, clear (apparently)' (O.E.D. 4, citing); or 'with curled clouds' (Schmidt); 4. 3. 184

CROSS (vb.), (i) thwart; 1. 2. 161; 3. 3. 29; (ii) (a) as (i), (b) have one's debts cancelled; 1. 2. 163

CUMBER, trouble; 3. 6. 45

CUNNING, (i) skill; 4. 3. 210; (ii) wisdom; 5. 4. 28

CURIOSITY, fastidiousness (in dress, etc.); 4. 3. 306

DEAR, grievous; 4. 3. 383; 5. 1. 227

DECLINE, sink, fall; 1. 1. 91; 4. 1. 20

DEED (OF SAYING), performance (of what is verbally promised) (cf. *All's*, 3. 6. 91; *Ham.* 1. 3. 27); 5. 1. 25

DEGREE, (i) step, successive stage, with quibble on University 'degree' (see also *proceed*); 4. 3. 254; (ii) rank; 5. 1. 207

DENY, refuse; 3. 2. 14, 16, 18, 24, 63; 4. 3. 533

DEPART, take leave of each other; 1. 1. 256

DEPRAVE, vilify; 1. 2. 140

DESPERATE, past hoping for (technical with debts, cf. O.E.D. 3; and with quibble on 'beside oneself'); 3. 4. 103

DETENTION, withholding; 2. 2. 43

DIALOGUE (vb.), hold conversation (with) (cf. *Comp.* 132); 2. 2. 56

DICH, do it ('orig. contraction of "do it you" after "much good"' On.); 1. 2. 71

DIRECT, positive, downright; 4. 3. 20

DISCHARGE, settle with, pay (a creditor); 2. 2. 14

DISCOVER (abs.), reconnoitre; 5. 2. 1

DISCOVERY, disclosure; 5. 1. 34

DISFURNISH, leave unprovided; 3. 2. 45

DISTASTEFUL, showing aversion; 2. 2. 217

DIVIDANT, divided; 4. 3. 5

DO, 'do't', have sexual intercourse, 4. 1. 8

DOIT, Dutch coin, worth half an English farthing; 1. 1. 214

DOUBT (refl.), fear; 1. 2. 154

DOUBTFULLY, in ambiguous language (typical of an oracle); 4. 3. 122

DRAUGHT, privy; 5. 1. 101

DRIFT, aim, what one is driving at; 1. 1. 48

DROP (vb.), come casually; 1. 2. init. S.D.

EARNEST, instalment; 4. 3. 48, 169

EMBOSSED, foaming (usu. of mouth of a hunted animal); 5. 1. 216

ENDEARED, bound by obligation; 1. 2. 235; 3. 2. 33

ENFORCE, compel; 3. 5. 37

ENFORCEDLY, by constraint; 4. 3. 242

ENFRANCHISE, release from imprisonment; 1. 1. 109

ENGAGE, mortgage; 2. 2. 152

ENGLUT, swallow; 2. 2. 172

ENSEAR, dry up (only inst. O.E.D.); 4. 3. 188

ENTERTAIN, (i) receive hospitality; 1. 1. 245; (ii) engage thoughts or attention of; 1. 2. 150; (iii) treat; 1. 2. 189, 2. 2. 49; (iv) retain as one's servant; 4. 3. 492

ENTERTAINMENT, (i) welcome; 1. 1. 48; 1. 2. 182–3; (ii) meal (O.E.D. 11c, citing); 1. 2. 147

ENVY, malice; 1. 2. 139

ESTATE, property, fortune (O.E.D. 2); 1. 1. 122; 2. 2. 147, 230; 3. 2. 7, 70; 3. 3. 5; 5. 1. 40

ESTIMATE, estimated value; 1. 1. 15

EXAMPLE (vb.), furnish (a person) with instances; 4. 3. 437

EXCEPTLESS, making no exception (O.E.D., the only inst.); 4. 3. 498

EXHAUST, elicit; 4. 3. 120

EXPEDITION, haste; 5. 2. 3

FACT, deed, esp. wicked or criminal one; 3. 5. 16

FAIL, fault (of omission); 5. 1. 147

FAINT, lacking zeal, half-hearted; 1. 2. 16; 3. 1. 54; 3. 3. 25

FAIR, (i) excellent; 3. 5. 18, 63; (ii) favourable; 5. 1. 122

FAIRLY, courteously; 1. 2. 178, 188

FALL (sb.), ebb of tide (fig.); 2. 2. 211

FALL (vb.), (i) 'fall to't', begin (to eat); 1. 2. 69; (ii) 'fall off', become estranged; 5. 1. 58

FALLING-FROM, desertion (not elsewhere; cf. 'falling-off', first in *Ham.* 1. 5. 47); 4. 3. 402

FANG (vb.), seize; 4. 3. 23

FAVOUR, 'under favour', by your leave; 3. 5. 41

FEAST-WON, gained by giving feasts; 2. 2. 177

FEE (see note); 3. 6. 78

FEEDER, servant; 2. 2. 165

FELL, fierce, cruel; 4. 3. 61

FELLOW, comrade, equal; 1. 1. 81; 4. 2. 18, 22, 25

FELLOWSHIP, participation; 5. 2. 12

FENCE, protect; 4. 1. 3

FIERCE, wild, excessive; 4. 2. 30

FIGURE, written character; 5. 3. 7

FILE (plur.), ranks (properly the number of men in depth from front to rear of a military formation in lines); 5. 2. 1

FILTH, applied to persons contemptuously; 'general f.'= common drab (cf. *Oth.* 5. 2. 234); 4. 1. 6

FILTHY, contemptible; 1. 1. 200

FIND, (i) (see note); 2. 2. 141; (ii) realize by experience; 4. 3. 175

FITLY, opportunely; 3. 4. 111

FIXED, certain; 1. 1. 9

FLAMEN, priest in ancient Rome; 4. 3. 156

FLOW (sb.), (i) stream (fig.); 2. 2. 3; (ii) of tears, 'set at flow'=cause to weep; 2. 2. 169; 'brain's flow'=tears; 5. 4. 76

FLUSH, full to overflowing (fig.); 5. 4. 8

FOND, foolish; 1. 2. 63; 3. 5. 43

FOR, (i) because of, 1. 2. 165; (ii) as for, as regards; 4. 3. 522

FORESEE, provide for in advance; 4. 3. 160

FORFEITURE, penalty for non-payment on required date; 2. 2. 34

FORM, (i) shape (of a cut jewel); 1. 1. 19; (ii) formal procedure, e.g. at law, legal form; 3. 5. 27

FORTH ON, straight on; 1. 1. 52

FRACTED, broken, unfulfilled; 2. 1. 22

FRACTION, fragment, disjointed remark (cf. fig. use in *Troil.* 5. 2. 158; not pre-Sh.); 2. 2. 217

FRANKLY, freely, without restraint; 2. 2. 185

FREE, generous, liberal; 1. 2. 6; 2. 2. 240

FROM, (i) from among; 1. 2. 91; (ii) contrary to; 4. 3. 161; (iii) at a distance from; 4. 3. 529

GENERAL, (i) (see note); 2. 2. 206; (ii) common, public; 4. 1. 6; 4. 3. 161, 444; 5. 2. 7

GENERAL-GROSS, universally obvious; 5. 1. 143

GENERATION, breed; 1. 1. 202

GERMAN, closely akin (O.E.D. 1; same word as 'germane'); 4. 3. 243

GIVE (see note); 4. 3. 487

GIVE OUT, profess; 1. 1. 163

GLASS-FACED, mirror-faced; 1. 1. 61

GLOSS, speciously fair appearance; 1. 2. 16

GO, (i) (be able to) walk; 4. 3. 46; (ii) 'go to', used to express remonstrance or incredulity, 'nonsense!'; 2. 2. 134

GOOD (see note); 2. 2. 233

GORGE, contents of stomach; hence, 'cast the gorge at', vomit at; 4. 3. 41

GRACE, (i) 'do grace to', embellish; 1. 2. 146; (ii) (theol.) God's saving power; 2. 2. 93; (iii) favour; 3. 5. 97

GRAMERCY, many thanks (<O.F. *grant merci*—God reward you greatly); 2. 2. 73 (plur.); 2. 2. 77 (sing.)

GRATULATE, greet; 1. 2. 126

GRAVE, entomb; 4. 3. 167

GREASE (see note); 4. 3. 196

GREAT, pregnant; 4. 3. 190

GREEN, of tender age; 4. 1. 7

GRIEF, grievance; 5. 4. 14, 24

GRISE, step; 4. 3. 16

GUISE, fashion; 4. 3. 467

GULES, red (heraldic term); 4. 3. 59

GULL, (a) unfledged bird, (b) dupe; 2. 1. 31

GUST (see note); 3. 5. 55

HABIT, (i) dress; 4. 3. 114, 206; (ii) (a) dress, (b) disposition; 4. 3. 240

HALF-CAP, half-courteous salute (O.E.D. 1; only inst.); 2. 2. 218

HALT, limp; 4. 1. 24

·HAPPY, felicitous; 1. 1. 17

HARBOUR, abode; 5. 4. 53

HARNESS, armour; 1. 2. 51

HAUTBOY, oboe; 1. 2. init. S.D., 145 S.D.

HAVING, possessions, wealth; 2. 2. 150; 5. 1. 16

HEAD, 'upon the head', under the category; 3. 5. 28

HEALTH, welfare; 2. 2. 203

HEAP, 'on a heap', in ruins; 4. 3. 102

HEART, 'in heart', heartily; 1. 2. 52

HIGH, 'at high wish', at the height of one's desires; 4. 3. 246

HIGH-VICED, full of great vices (only inst. O.E.D.); 4. 3. 110

HINGE (vb.), bend; 4. 3. 212

HIS, its; 2. 1, 30; 3. 1. 63; 5. 1. 24

HIT, fall in exactly; 3. 1. 6

HOAR (vb.), make white; hence here, smite with leprosy; 4. 3. 156

HOLD, (i) bear; 1. 2. 154; (ii) continue, last; 2. 1. 4, 12; (iii) 'hold for true' be valid; 5. 1. 4

HONEST, chaste; 4. 3. 114

HONESTLY, honourably; 5. 1. 14

HONESTY, generosity; 3. 1. 28

HORSE, horsemen (collect. plur.); 1. 1. 243

HOW, exclam. of surprise= 'what!', 'hallo!'; 3. 2. 15; 3. 4. 61; 3. 5. 92; 3. 6. 55

HOW NOW, hallo!, what is it?; 1. 2. 115, 189; 3. 6. 105

HOWSOE'ER, in any case; 4. 3. 451

HOY-DAY, exclam. of surprise; 1. 2. 132

HUGE, important, mighty; 1. 2. 48

HUMANITY, (i) (see note); 1. 1. 275; (ii) human existence; 4. 3. 303

HUMOUR, disposition; 1. 2. 26

HUNGERLY, hungrily; 1. 1. 255

HUSBANDRY, management of household expenditure; 2. 2. 161

HYMEN, Greek and Roman god of marriage; 4. 3. 385

HYPERION, sun-god; 4. 3. 185

IDLE, trifling, frivolous; 1. 2. 155; 4. 3. 27

IMPLEMENT, instrument; 4. 2. 16

IMPORT (vb.), bear as its import· (see also note); 5. 2. 11

INCERTAIN, insecure, uncertain; 4. 3. 244

INDIFFERENT, tolerably good (cf. Ham. 3. 1. 123, 'indifferent honest'); 1. 1. 33

INDISPOSITION, disinclination; 2. 2. 136

INFECTED (see note); 4. 3. 203

INFER, allege; 3. 5. 73

INFLUENCE, action of the stars on the character of men (astrol. sense, here fig.); 5. 1. 62

INGENIOUSLY, ingenuously (the two forms not yet clearly distinguished); 2. 2. 227

INSCULPTURE, carved inscription; 5. 4. 67

INSTANT (adj.), immediate, or pressing, urgent; 3. 1. 18; 3. 2. 36

INSTANT (adv.), immediately, or urgently; 2. 2. 236

INTEND, pretend; 2. 2. 216

INTENT, project, projected work; 5. 1. 20

INTERPRET, act as interpreter (see note); 1. 1. 37

IRA FUROR BREVIS EST, anger is a passing madness (Hor. *Epist.* 1. 2. 62); 1. 2. 28

IT, its; 5. 1. 147

JUROR (fig.), what decides (life or death); so, decisive evidence; 4. 3. 343

KEEP, (i) dwell; 1. 2. 238; (ii) remain in; 3. 3. 41

KEEPER, gaoler; 1. 2. 67; 5. 1. 183; (with quibble on sense 'owner') 4. 3. 47

KIND, gracious; 1. 2. 148

KINDLY, innate, inherent; 2. 2. 223

KNOT, company (generally implying 'conspiracy' in Sh.); 3. 6. 88

KNOW, (i) ascertain; 2. 2. 2; (ii) 'know me' (pregnant sense), recognize who and what I am; 3. 5. 91; (iii) (a) recognize, (b) acknowledge; 4. 3. 490.

LA LA (interj.), Repeated to express derision; 3. 1. 22

LABOUR, (a) work hard, (b) suffer the pains of childbirth; 3. 5. 26

LABOURING FOR, about to strike (metaph. from childbirth?); 3. 4. 8

LACEDÆMON, Sparta; 2. 2. 157

LAG (see note); 3. 6. 79

LARD (vb.), fatten (cf. *1 H. IV*, 2. 2. 106 n.); 4. 3. 12.

LARGE-HANDED, rapacious (cf. 'large'=free, unrestrained); 4. 1. 11

LATE (adv.), lately; 2. 1. 1

LATEST (abs.), last; 4. 2. 23

LAY FOR, strive to captivate; 3. 5. 117

LEAKED, leaky; 4. 2. 19

LEG, bow (with a quibble); 1. 2. 241

LEVEL (fig.), straightforward (cf. mod. colloq. 'on the level'); 4. 3. 19

LEVELLED, aimed (at any one in particular); 1. 1. 50

LIBERTY, licence; 4. 1. 25

LICENTIOUS, unrestrained by law or morality; 5. 4. 4

LICK UP, destroy (O.E.D. 3 a; but perh. with special ref. to action of a wasting disease); 4. 3. 535

LIMITED, (a) regular, appointed (cf. *Mac.* 2. 3. 51), (b) restricted; 4. 3. 430

LINED, padded; 4. 1. 14

LIQUORISH, sweet; 4. 3. 195

LIVELY (adv.), in a lifelike fashion; 5. 1. 81

LONG, for a long time; 1. 1. 2

LOOK OUT, show oneself; 3. 2. 74

MADE-UP, complete (cf. *R. III*, I. I. 21); 5. I. 97

MAKE, do; 3. 5. 47

MAKE AWAY, destroy; I. 2. 105

MALICE (OF), hatred (for); 4. 3. 454

MARBLED, shining like marble; 'marbled mansion', the sky (cf. *Aen.* VI. 729, 'marmoreo ...aequore'); 4. 3. 192

MARK, goal; 5. 3. 10

MARROW, (i) mod. sense; 4. I. 26; (fig.) 4. 3. 194; (ii) thought of as seat of vitality and strength, hence, fig., strength, courage; 5. 4. 9

MARRY (interj.), indeed, to be sure; 5. I. 87

MAST, fruit of oak, chestnut, etc., esp. as food for swine; here, acorns; 4. 3. 421

MATRON, 'married woman, usually with the accessory idea of (moral or social) rank or dignity' (O.E.D. I); 4. 3. 113

MEAN, of low rank; I. I. 96

MEANING, intention; 5. 4. 59

MEANS, pecuniary resources (not pre-Sh.; cf. *Meas.* 2. 2. 24); 2. 2. 133, etc.; 5. 4. 20

MEASURE (see note); 5. 4. 4

MEDDLER, busybody; 4. 3. 312

MEED, gift (see note); I. I. 280

MEND, (i) raise the value of; I. I. 175; (ii) improve; 4. 3. 284 ff.; (iii) repair; 4. 3. 287

MERE, sheer, downright; I. I. 169; 4. 3. 232, 378

MERELY, nothing but; 4. 3. 518

MESS, dish of food; 4. 3. 423

METTLE, substance; 4. 3. 180

MILKY, timorous; 3. I. 54

MIND, disposition, 'way of thinking and feeling with respect to moral qualities' (On.); I. 2. 165; 3. 3. 23

MINDLESS, unmindful; 4. 3. 94

MINION, favourite, darling; 4. 3. 81

MINISTER (sb.), lit., servant; hence, something serviceable; 2. 2. 137

MINISTER (vb.), officiate; 4. I. 6

MINUTE-JACK, fickle person, changing his mind every moment; 3. 6. 96

MIRE (vb.), sink into the mire, be bogged; 4. 3. 149

MISANTHROPOS, (Greek) man-hater; 4. 3. 53

MISCHIEF (vb.), inflict injury on; 4. 3. 470

MISTAKE (refl. with 'him'), make a mistake; 3. 2. 23

MOCKING, counterfeiting; I. I. 38

MOE, more; I. I. 44; 2. I. 7; 4. 3. 435

MONSTROUS, unnatural; 4. 2. 46; 5. I. 87

MORAL, allegorizing; I. I. 93

MORROW, 'good morrow', good morning; I. I. 181 etc.; 3. 4. I etc.

MOTIVE, instigator; 5. 4. 27

MOUNTANT, rising; 4. 3. 136

MOUTH-FRIEND, pretending friend (cf. 'mouth-honour', *Mac.* 5. 3. 27); 3. 6. 88

MUCH, (i) iron., not at all; I. 2. 114; (ii) very; 3. 4. 32

MYSTERY, profession; 4. I. 18; 4. 3. 455

NATIVE, inborn; 4. 3. 11

NATURAL (son), (son) by birth (the sense, 'illegitimate', is not Sh.); 4. 3. 384

NATURE, (i) human nature; 4. 3. 6, 177; 5. 1. 200, 224; 5. 4. 77; (ii) (see note); 4. 3. 8; (iii) natural feelings; 5. 4. 33

NEAR (adj.), closely affecting one; 3. 6. 10

NEAREST, most closely; 4. 3. 321, 322

NEED, 'what needs?', what is the necessity for?; 1. 2. 251

NEIGHBOURHOOD, neighbourly feelings; 4. 1. 17

NEPTUNE, god of the sea; hence, sea; 5. 4. 78

NOISE (vb.), rumour; 4. 3. 404

OATHABLE, fit to be trusted on oath; 4. 3. 136

OBJECT, pitiable sight; lit., something presented to the eye; 4. 3. 123

OBLIQUY, (moral) crookedness (see note); 4. 3. 18

OBSERVANCE, rule or practice to be observed; 4. 1. 19

OBSERVE, pay court to; 4. 3. 213

OCCASION, emergency, need; 2. 2. 24, 197; 3. 1. 18–19; 3. 2. 24, 35, 41; 3. 6. 10

ODDS, (i) 'no odds', nothing to choose between them; 1. 2. 59; (ii) variance; 4. 3. 43, 393

OF, in (the person of); 4. 3. 233

OFFEND, sin against; 5. 4. 60

OFFICES, kitchen, and servants' quarters generally; 2. 2. 164

OMIT, neglect, let slip (cf. *J.C.* 4. 3. 218); 1. 1. 261

ONCE, (i) 'at once', (to you all) in a body; 3. 4. 6; (ii) (see note) 5. 1. 55

OPEN, generous; 5. 1. 57

OPERANT, potent; 4. 3. 25

OPPOSITE (see note); 1. 1. 275

OPPRESS, (i) crowd; 2. 2. 164; (ii) trouble, harass; 4. 3. 506

ORT, fragment (lit., of food); 4. 3. 401

OUT, exhausted (or perh., lent out); 3. 6. 16

OUTGO, surpass; 1. 1. 277

OUTSTRETCH (see note); 5. 3. 3

PACK, take oneself off; 5. 1. 111

PAGE, follow like a page; 4. 3. 225

PAINFULLY, laboriously, conscientiously; 5. 2. 1

PAINS, trouble (with quibble on pains in childbirth); 3. 5. 26

PAINTED, pretended, unreal (cf. *K.J.* 3. 1. 105; O.E.D. 2 b); 4. 2. 36

PART (sb.), (i) function, duty; 5. 1. 119; (ii) (see note); 5. 2. 7; (iii) (plur.), personal qualities; 2. 2. 26; 3. 1. 37; 3. 5. 76

PART (vb.), (i) share; 1. 2. 46; (ii) separate; 4. 2. 21, 29; (iii) depart; 4. 2. 29, S.D.

PARTICULAR (sb.), personal interest; 4. 3. 160

PARTICULAR (adj.), personal, private; 5. 2. 8

PARTICULARLY, individually, at any individual; 1. 1. 49

PASS, (i) intr., excel; 1. 1. 12; (ii) tr., receive the approval or sanction of; 2. 2. 179; (iii) go outside; 5. 4. 60

PASSION, anger; 3. 1. 56

PATCHERY, roguery; 5. 1. 95

PAWN (vb.), pledge; 1. 1. 150; 3. 5. 82

PELF, possessions; 1. 2. 61

PENCILLED, painted ('pencil'= paint-brush only, 4 times, in Sh.; 'pencilled' again, *Lucr.* 1497); 1. 1. 162

PERFECT, satisfied; 1. 2. 87

PERIOD (vb.), bring to an end; 1. 1. 102

PERSONATE, represent; 1. 1. 72; (verbal noun), 5. 1. 33

PERSUASION, evidence; 3. 6. 7

PHILOSOPHER, person learned in any science (orig. the word 'philosophy' covered science also); 2. 2. 115

PHOENIX (fig.), matchless, unique person; 2. 1. 32

PIECE, (i) work of art; 1. 1. 30, 31, 248; 5. 1. 19; (ii) (gold) coin; 3. 6. 21, 22

PILL (vb.), rob; 4. 1. 12

PITCHED, 'pitched field', field of battle, lit., field prepared by driving stakes into the ground as a defence for the archers against cavalry (see O.E.D. vb. 1; and *1 H. VI*, G.); 1. 2. 231

PLACE, put in office; 4. 3. 36

PLANETARY (astrol. notion), caused by the 'influence' of a planet; 4. 3. 109

PLEASURE (vb.), gratify; 3. 2. 57

PLEDGE, drink a health to; 1. 2. 46

PLUTUS, Greek god of wealth; 1. 1. 279

POLICY, cunning, dissimulation; 3. 2. 88

POLITIC, crafty; 3. 3. 29, 34

POMP, pageant; 1. 2. 251

PORT, gate; 5. 4. 55

POWER, armed force; 5. 4. 52

POX, 'a pox of' (imprecation), curse, 'hang'; 4. 3. 150

PRECEDENT, former; 1. 1. 136

PREDOMINATE, prevail over; 4. 3. 143

PREFER,. present; 3. 4. 50; 3. 5. 35

PRESENT, (i) immediate; 1. 1. 74 (see note); 2. 2. 151, 154; 5. 2. 4; (ii) urgent; 3. 2. 35

PRESENTLY, immediately; 3. 5. 105; 3. 6. 34; 4. 3. 379

PRESENTMENT, presentation; 1. 1. 29

PRETTY, vague epithet of praise, excellent; 3. 1. 14

PREVENT, anticipate; 5. 1. 202

PRIZE, value, estimate; 1. 1. 174

PROCEED, go on or forward to (from the Univ. 'proceed M.A., etc.', of degrees); 4. 3. 253

PRODIGAL (transf. from agent), lavishly expended; 2. 2. 171

PROOF, proved or tested strength, impenetrability; 4. 3. 125

PROPAGATE, augment; 1. 1. 70

PROPER (adv.), appropriately; 1. 2. 102

PROPERTY (vb.), appropriate; 1. 1. 60

PROSPEROUS, auspicious, propitious; 5. 1. 182

PROTEST, make public profession; 4. 3. 436

PROVOKE, call forth, excite;
1. 1. 26

PUFF, inflate; 4. 3. 181

PURCHASE, obtain; 3. 5. 77

PURSY, short-winded; 5. 4. 12

PUSH, tush; 3. 6. 108

PUT, (i) 'put back', repulse;
2. 2. 136; (ii) 'put from',
take away from; 3. 4. 104;
(iii) 'put in' (abs.), make a
claim; 3. 4. 85; (iv) 'put
into', set aside as, treat as,
3. 2. 84; (v) 'put on',
assume, 4. 3. 210

QUALITY, (i) nature, character;
1. 1. 57; 4. 3. 157; (ii) ac-
complishment, attainment;
1. 1. 128; (iii) 'nature with
ref. to origin, (hence) cause'
(O.E.D. 8 b, citing this and
Troil. 4. 1. 44); 3. 6. 106

QUARTER, lodging, billet; 5. 4.
60

QUELL, destroy; 4. 3. 164

QUICK, speedy (with quibble on
'alive', i.e. active); 4. 3. 45

QUICKENING, life-giving; 4. 3.
185

QUILLET, subtle verbal distinction; 4. 3. 156

QUITTANCE, requital; 1. 1. 283

RAG, worthless creature; 4. 3.
272

RAISED, high in rank; 1. 1. 122

RAMPIRED, protected by a
rampart; 5. 4. 47

RANK (WITH), surround with
rows (of); 1. 1. 68

RARELY, excellently; 4. 3. 467

RATE (vb.), (i) price; 1. 1. 171;
(ii) adjust; 2. 2. 132

RECKON, keep accounts of;
3. 4. 57

RECOVERABLE (see note); 3. 4.
13

REGARD (sb.), heed; 1. 2. 254

REGARDFULLY, respectfully; 4.
3. 82

RELIEF, assistance in need;
2. 1. 25

REMAINDER, remnant of one's
fortune; 4. 3. 401

REMORSE, pity; 4. 3. 123

REMOTION, keeping out of the
way; 4. 3. 344

RENDER (sb.), rendering of an
account; hence here, con-
fession; 5. 1. 148

RENDER (vb.), (i) pay; 4. 1. 9;
(ii) surrender; 5. 4. 62

REPAIR (vb.), return; 2. 2. 28;
3. 4. 70

REPUGNANCY, resistance (cf.
Ham. 2. 2. 475, 'repug-
nant'); 3. 5. 46

RESOLVE, dissolve (cf. *Ham.*
1. 2. 130, 'resolve itself');
4. 3. 441

RESPECT, (i) 'in respect of', in
comparison with; 3. 2. 75;
(ii) reflection; 4. 3. 259

RESPECTIVELY, respectfully
(common in 16–17th cent.);
3. 1. 8

RESTRAIN, withhold; 5. 1. 147

RESUME, take (as what is due);
2. 2. 4

RETENTIVE, confining; 3. 4. 82

RETURN, repayment; 1. 1. 282;
3. 5. 83

RIGHT (sb.), due; 2. 2. 27

RIOT, (i) extravagance; 2. 2. 3;
(ii) debauchery; 4. 1. 28;
4. 3. 257

RIOTER, debauchee; 3. 5. 68

RIOTOUS, unbridled, without
restraint (cf. *Lr.* 4. 6. 125);
2. 2. 165

ROTTEN, of air, water etc., foul (used of unwholesome vapours); 4. 3. 2

ROUND, plain-spoken, blunt; 2. 2. 8

ROUT, disorderly crowd; 4. 3. 44

RUINOUS, brought to ruin; 4. 3. 461

SALT, lustful; 4. 3. 86

SANS, without; 4. 3. 123

SAVE, anticipate, and so prevent; 1. 1. 254

SCIATICA, neuralgic pains in the hips, a supposed symptom of venereal disease; 4. 1. 23

SCOPE, 'to scope', to the purpose, fittingly (cf. O.E.D. 'purpose', 5); 1. 1. 75

SCOURING, scurrying about; 5. 2. 15

SEAL, solemnly ratify; 5. 4. 54

SEASON (vb.), (a) make fit; (b) salt (with play on 'salt hours'); 4. 3. 86

SEAT, residence; 4. 2. 45

SECT, party; 3. 5. 30

SECURE, give confidence to; 2. 2. 182

SECURITY, (a) safety, (b) security for debt; 3. 5. 81

SEMBLABLE (sb.), like, fellow; 4. 3. 22

SERVE, (i) be sufficient, 'do'; 1. 1. 260; 3. 4. 58, (with a quibble) 59; (ii) provide, perform; 1. 2. 240; (iii) 'serve in', bring in as a servant; 4. 3. 481; (iv) (see note); 5. 1. 43

SET, (i) '(be) set down before', besiege; 5. 3. 9; (ii) 'set to (himself)' pple, concen-

trated on, wrapped up in (himself); 5. 1. 116; (iii) 'set out', set apart *for* certain treatment (O.E.D. 149, q, citing); 5. 4. 57

SETTLE, cause to be firmly rooted; 5. 1. 50

SEVERAL, separate, different; 1. 2. 224; 3. 6. init. S.D.; 3. 6. 6.; 4. 2. 29, S.D.; 4. 3. 5

SEVERALLY, separately; 2. 2. 194

SHAKE OFF, cast off; 1. 1. 103

SHRINK, fall away (like a deserter; cf. *R. III*, 5. 3. 222); 3. 2. 7

SINGLE, alone; 2. 2. 62

SINGLY, uniquely; 4. 3. 526

SIRRAH. Form of address to men and boys, implying authority over them; 3. 1. 38

SIZE, quantity; 5. 1. 65

SKILL, knowledge; 5. 3. 7

SLIGHT, careless, off-hand; 2. 1. 17

SLIPPERY, fickle, not dependable; 1. 1. 56

SMOOTH (adj.), (i) flattering; 3. 6. 93; (ii) (a) flattering, (b) in smooth-flowing lines; 5. 1. 83

SMOOTH (vb.), (a) make smooth, (b) flatter; 4. 3. 17

So, provided that; 5. 4. 48

So, so. Exclam. of annoyance, 'Well!'; 1. 1. 249

So so (adv.), indifferently well; 5. 1. 81

SOFT, stay!, stop!; 3. 6. 99

SOIL, sully; 3. 5. 16

SOMETHING (adv.), somewhat; 4. 3. 55

SORROWED, sorrowful; 5. 1. 148

SORT, 'in some sort', in a way, to some extent; 2. 2. 187; 4. 3. 77

SPAN, (short) duration of life; 5. 3. 3

SPILTH, spilling; 2. 2. 166

SPITAL-HOUSE, hospital (esp. for lower classes and sufferers from loathsome diseases); 4. 3. 40

SPOTTED, morally stained; 5. 4. 35

SPUR (fig.), speed, eagerness (cf. *J.C.* 5. 3. 29, 'on the spur'); 3. 6. 64

SQUARE, just; 5. 4. 36

STANDING (see note); 1. 1. 34

STARVE, cause to wither (O.E.D. 6b, citing); 1. 1. 250

STATE, (i) fortune; 1. 1. 70; 1. 2. 56, 201; (ii) condition in respect of fortune; 2. 2. 131; (iii) high rank; 4. 2. 35; (iv) member of governing body (here=senator); 1. 2. init. S.D. n.

STEALTH, theft; 3. 4. 29

STEEPY, steep; 1. 1. 78

STICK, (i) be fastened; 2. 1. 30; (ii) adorn; 3. 6. 90

STILL, constantly, always; 1. 1. 260; 4. 3. 140, 473

STINT (vb.), stop; 5. 4. 83

STIR· UP, provoke; 3. 4. 54

STONE, testicle, with quibble on philosopher's 'stone', reputed substance for turning other metals into gold; 2. 2. 116

STOUT, strong; 4. 3. 33

STRAGGLE, stray; 5. 1. 7

STRAIGHT (adv.), immediately; 2. 1. 9

STRAIN (sb.), (i) stock, race; 1. 1. 252; (ii) quality of character; 4. 3. 214

STRAIN (vb.), strain one's resources; 1. 1. 146

STRAIT, exacting; 1. 1. 99

STRANGE, (i) out of the ordinary; 1. 1. 4; (ii) 'strange in', unacquainted with; 4. 3. 56

STRICT, uncompromising; 3. 5. 24

STRONG, (i) (*a*) lit., (*b*) resolute, 'confirmed'; 4. 3. 46; (ii) as (i) (*b*); 4. 3. 142

SUBTLE, (*a*) delicate, (*b*) insidious; 4. 3. 431

SUFFERANCE, suffering; 4. 3. 269; 5. 4. 8

SUIT (vb.), act in conformity; 2. 2. 26

SUPERSCRIPTION, address (of a letter); 2. 2. 83–4

SUPPLY (vb.), (i) fill; 3. 1. 18; (ii) maintain; 4. 2. 47

SURE, safe; 3. 3. 39

SURPRISE, lead unawares; 5. 1. 155

SUSPECT, suspicion; 4. 3. 515, 517

SWATH, swaddling-clothes; 4. 3. 253

SWEEP (sb.), moving along with a continuous, esp. a magnificent, motion; hence here, 'sweep of vanity', vain persons thus moving along; 1. 2. 132

SWORN, inveterate; 3. 5. 68

TAKE, (i) (see note); 1. 2. 152; (ii) 'take't'=let me tell you; 3. 4. 71

TALENT. Orig. a weight in Greece and Rome; then value of this in gold or silver; see Note on the Copy, pp. 93–7; 1. 1. 98, 144; 1. 2. 6, etc.

TEDIOUS, annoying; 4. 3. 371

TELL, (i) count; 3. 5. 109; (ii) 'tell out', count (drop by drop); 3. 4. 95

TENDANCE, (i) care (see note); 1. 1. 60; (ii) (see note); 1. 1. 83

TENDER, lit., pay down (money); here fig., offer; 5. 1. 13; (with 'down') 1. 1. 57

THAT, (i) ellipt., would that; 4. 3. 283; (ii) to think that (expressing surprise or regret); 1. 2. 258; 4. 3. 177; (iii) so that; 2. 2. 188

THIN, scantily covered (with hair) (cf. R. II, 3. 2. 112; M.N.D. 2. 1. 109); 4. 3. 146

THOROUGH, through, because of; 4. 3. 488

THREAT, threaten; 4. 2. 21

THRIFT, money-making; 1. 1. 121

THROUGH, by the favour of; 1. 1. 85

THROW OFF, brush aside; 2. 2. 140

TIDE, (a) tide, (b) time, season; 1. 2. 55

TIME, (i) opportunity; 2. 2. 198; (ii) 'the good time of day', good day; 3. 6. 1

TIRE, lit., a term in falconry= feed ravenously (on); hence, fig., eagerly exercise oneself (on); 3. 6. 4

To, (i) in comparison with; 1. 2. 135; (ii) in addition to, to add to; 3. 5. 79; (iii) as to; 3. 4. 115; 3. 5. 97

TO-NIGHT, last night; 3. 1. 7

TONGUE, language (fig., see note); 1. 1. 177

TOSS AND TURN, bandy to and fro; 2. 1. 26

TOUCH (sb.), touchstone; 4. 3. 391

TOUCH (vb.), (i) reach, go as high as; 1. 1. 15; (ii) try (as with touchstone); 3. 3. 6; 4. 3. 5

TOWARD (adj.), about to take place; 3. 6. 59

TOWARDLY, well disposed; 3. 1. 34

TRACT, traced out path; 1. 1. 53

TRAFFIC (sb.), mercantile trade; 1. 1. 239–41

TRAFFIC (vb.), have dealings (with); 1. 1. 161

TRANSLATE, transform; 1. 1. 75

TRAPPED, adorned with 'trappings', cloth or covering over harness or saddle of horse; 1. 2. 187

TRAVAIL, labour, take pains; 5. 1. 15

TRAVERSED, folded across; 5. 4. 7

TREASURE, money; 2. 2. 211

TRENCHANT, sharp; 4. 3. 116

TRENCHER, (wooden) plate; 1. 1. 123

TRENCHER-FRIEND, toady, parasite; 3. 6. 95

TRIUMPHER, victorious general, celebrating a 'triumph' (as in Rome); 5. 1. 195

TROPHY, monument; 5. 4. 25

TRUE, honest; 4. 3. 459

TRUMP, trumpet; 1. 2. 115

TRUSTER, creditor; 4. 1. 10

TRY (sb.), test (cf. mod. colloq. 'try-on'); 5. 1. 9

TRY (vb.) ,test; 2.2. 184, 189; 3. 6. 3

TUB, treatment for venereal disease by sweating baths; 4. 3. 87

TUB-FAST, abstinence during treatment of venereal disease (see *tub*); 4. 3. 88

TUCKET, signal on a trumpet; 1. 2. 114, S.D.

TURN, (i) see *toss and turn*; 2. 1. 26; (ii) intr., (*a*) turn sour (like milk), (*b*) change (to hostility); 3. 1. 55

TUTOR (vb.), teach; 1. 1. 40

TWINNED, brought forth as twins; hence, twin (cf. *Wint.* 1. 2. 67); 4. 3. 3

UNAPTNESS, disinclination; 2. 2. 137

UNBOLT, explain; 1. 1. 54

UNCHARGED, unassailed; 5. 4. 55

UNCHECKED, unlimited, unrestrained; 4. 3. 446

UNCLEW, lit., unwind ('clew' =ball of thread), undo; hence, ruin; 1. 1. 171

UNCTUOUS, oily; 4. 3. 196

UNDERGO, take on oneself, undertake; 3. 5. 24

UNDO, (i) (see note); 3. 2. 49; (ii) ruin; 4. 3. 212

UNDONE, ruined; 4. 2. 2, 38; 4. 3. 484

UNHOUSED (see note); 4. 3. 230

UNICORN, fabulous one-horned animal; 4. 3. 338

UNNOTED, (?) unobserved, imperceptible; 3. 5. 21

UNPEACEABLE, incapable of being pacified, contentious; 1. 1. 272

UNTHRIFT (sb.), spendthrift, prodigal; 4. 3. 314

USE (sb.), (i) (see note); 1. 1. 283; (ii) need; 1. 2. 97; 2. 1. 20; 3. 2. 37; 5. 1. 205

USE (vb.), make use of; 1. 2. 85; 2. 2. 185, 198; 3. 1. 36; 3. 2. 51; (sexually), 4. 3. 84

VALUE, worth; 1. 1. 82

VANTAGE, opportunity; 2. 2. 135

VAPOUR (fig.), unsubstantial, worthless creature; 3. 6. 96

VARNISHED, pretended; 4.2.36

VILE, worthless; 1. 1. 16; 4. 3. 465

VIRTUE, (i) 'your virtues', your virtuous selves; 3. 5. 7; (ii) characteristic excellence; 3. 5. 8; (iii) efficacy; 4. 3. 392

VIRTUOUSLY, powerfully, strongly (O.E.D. 5, citing as 'used affectedly'); 1. 2. 233

VOICE (sb.), vote (for which it is the normal word in Eng. of Sh.'s time); 3. 5. 1

VOICE (vb.), speak of; 4. 3. 82

VOID (UP), vomit; 1. 2. 138

VOTARIST, votary; 4. 3. 27

VOUCHSAFE, deign to accept; 1. 1. 155

WAFT, signal to come by waving the hand; 1. 1. 73

WAIT, 'wait attendance', remain in attendance; 1. 1. 164

WAPPERED, worn out; 4. 3. 39

WARD, lock (properly, part of lock which prevents any key but the right one fitting); 3. 3. 37

WATER, lustre of jewel; 1. 1. 20

WAX (vb.), become; 3. 4. 11

WEAL, welfare; 4. 3. 161

WEAR, wear out; 1. 1. 3

WEIGH (WITH), lit., be equal in weight (to); here fig., equal in fortune; 1. 1. 149

WHEREOF, wherewith; 4. 3. 181

WHITTLE, clasp-knife; 5. 1. 179

WINK AT, shut one's eyes to, pretend not to see; 3. 1. 44

WIT, intelligence; 1. 1. 236; 2. 2. 122

WITCH, bewitch; 5. 1. 154

WITHAL, in addition; 5. 1. 146

WITHOUT, outside; 5. 4. 39

WREAKFUL, revengeful; 4. 3. 230

YIELD, allow; 1. 2. 198